World Directory of
Modern
Military Vehicles

UNARMORED VEHICLES FROM 1970

Bart Vanderveen

ARCO PUBLISHING, INC.
New York

Published 1984 by Arco Publishing, Inc.
215 Park Avenue South, New York, NY 10003

Library of Congress Cataloging in Publication Data

Vanderveen, Bart H. (Bart Harmannus)
  World directory of modern military vehicles.

  Includes index.
  1. Vehicles, Military.   I. Title.
UG615.V365   1984   623.74   83–17177
ISBN 0–668–06022–0

Printed in Great Britain

Contents

Introduction

Military motor vehicles, particularly the 'soft-skin' high-mobility all-wheel-drive variety, keep attracting the attention of an ever-increasing number of people outside the realms of their manufacturers and users. Today, there is unprecedented activity in this field and many of the heavy-duty vehicles used by armed forces around the world are also available for civil service. On the other hand, many military vehicles are just more or less modified and militarized versions of civilian types.

Covering the period of the 1970s and early 1980s, this Directory continues from *The Observer's Military Vehicles Directory – from 1945* which deals with the post-war period up to around 1970, and which in turn followed two volumes covering the pre-1940 era and the Second World War (*The Observer's Army Vehicles Directory – to 1940* and *The Observer's Fighting Vehicles Directory – World War II* respectively).

In all four books it is apparent that attention has not been focused solely on the well-known mass-produced types of vehicle but that equal consideration has been given to experimental models which never received the nod and therefore remained in the prototype stage. Since such vehicles may still be encountered, either 'in the metal' or in books, films and the like, it is strongly felt that these – often quite advanced – specimens are worthy of mention and that reference works like the present volume would not be complete without them.

This new title differs from the preceding ones in three important respects. First, the shape has changed to a more conventional format (already adopted for several other Warne's Directories). Secondly, a large number of vehicle entries have been given more comprehensive treatment than before, with larger pictures and more details, and, thirdly, the vehicles have been classed by type, rather than by country. This classing by type has proved more practical. Many of today's military vehicles are not even used in their country of origin but only exported, while others were or are sold in their own and to many different foreign nations, sometimes with detail modifications. The world has become 'smaller' and it was considered justified to deal with the vehicles on a worldwide basis.

Quite noticeable, when compared with the previous volumes, is the number of military trucks manufactured or part-manufactured in so-called 'developing' nations and other countries where automotive activities had formerly been confined to importation and small-scale assembly, exemplified by Brazil, Greece, South Korea, the Philippines and South Africa. Some of these countries try vigorously to sell their products to other nations, in addition to supplying their own armed forces. Although the main aim is clearly to be independent from imports, a prominent factor is the possibility of selling these vehicles abroad in order to earn foreign currency and to reduce unit costs.

This Directory has been compiled with the aid of the best available source material, provided largely by the manufacturers – who, with a few exceptions, have been most cooperative – and to some extent by various governments' military authorities, to all of whom a debt is due. Certain gaps have been filled most amicably by friends and other contacts from many countries. Thanks are due particularly to George Avramidis, Günter Buchwald, Colonel Robert J. Icks, Erik van Ingen Schenau, Jean-Gabriël Jeudy and Laurie A. Wright, who have made important contributions. Others who deserve mention include (in alphabetical order): Oliver Barnham, Sven Bengtson, Fred Crismon, H. Denis, Aimé van Ingelgom, Yuichi Ishikawa, William F. Murray, Yasuo Ohtsuka, R. T. P. Peacock, Mark Priestley, J. C. M. Probst, Malcolm J. R. Smith, Ed Storey, Dick Vredeveld, Shin Yoshino and Norman Weeding. To all these contributors, as well as those who are not mentioned by name, gratitude is extended. Yet, in spite of much care, inaccuracies are virtually impossible to eliminate altogether. Moreover, it must be appreciated that many of the vehicles presented in this book were still in the development stage, with specifications subject to change. Other modern vehicles could be adapted to meet specific customers' requirements, there being many options available in terms of alternative engines and transmissions, wheelbase and tyre sizes, different body types, etc.

Contributions for future editions will always be welcome, in the form of additional and updated information, better pictures (in a number of cases) and corrections. After all, as mentioned in the preceding volume, the value of a work of this kind is determined by the degree of accuracy of its contents.

B. H. Vanderveen

Key to Technical Data

Note: for abbreviations see page 6.

Vehicle Nomenclature: Although different countries use different nomenclature, for this international English-language book a uniform system has been used for all vehicles, regardless of nationality. Example: 'Truck, 4-ton, 4 × 4, Cargo', which is a four-wheeled, four-wheel-drive truck for the transport of goods and – usually – personnel, with a rated payload capacity of four tons. '4 × 2' indicates a four-wheeled vehicle with two-wheel drive, etc. For this purpose, dual tyres count as single wheels. The vehicle type is followed by make and model designation in parentheses. The body type, e.g. 'Cargo', is not included in the nomenclature used for those vehicles which are covered by a whole page, since the chassis described is often also used for other types of bodywork, e.g. van, tanker. The load rating for all-wheel-drive trucks applies to off-road conditions. On metalled roads a cross-country vehicle can often carry up to twice the rated payload. 'Rated payload' means the load the vehicle is designed to carry.

Engine: Most but certainly not all of the lighter vehicles have an engine which is made by the same manufacturer as the chassis, whereas most of the heavier types are fitted with a 'proprietary' engine, supplied by specialist engine builders (e.g. Cummins, Deutz, Perkins, etc.). This also applies to gearboxes, axles and other components. The make and model of engine are given where available, 'Own' in the more detailed entries indicating that the engine was made by the vehicle's manufacturer. Engines are generally liquid-cooled and with overhead valves, unless stated otherwise. Power output is given only in the full-page entries; in the others preference has been given to cubic capacity, where known. Conversion from bhp to kW is by multiplication by 0.746. Where cubic capacity (piston displacement) is followed by two figures (e.g. 90 × 100 mm) these are the bore and stroke dimensions.

Transmission: A four-speed-and-reverse gearbox (transmission) is indicated as '4F1R'. '2 × 4F1R' indicates a two-range gearbox. In many instances the drive to the front axle can be disconnected in the transfer box but, as will be seen, an increasing number of vehicles feature a transfer box with a centre differential, providing permanent (full-time) all-wheel drive. Use of differential locks is becoming increasingly widespread, too, both in the central power divider(s) and in the axles themselves. Typical modern terminology includes 'cross-locks' (in the axles), 'inter-axle lock' (between tandem axles on 6 × 6 or 8 × 8 vehicles), 'front-rear lock' (on central/transfer case differential), etc.

Wheelbase: Distance between centres of front and rear wheels (axles) or, in the case of tandem axles (rear and/or front), the centre(s) of the tandem bogie(s). Track is the distance between the centres of the ground contact of the tyres of each axle (centre of each set of two tyres in the case of dual tyre mounting).

Dimensions: All vehicle dimensions are given in mm. Overall width is excluding rear-view mirrors. 'Angle of approach' indicates the angle of the maximum grade that a vehicle can approach on the horizontal and start to climb with no part except tyres coming into contact with the grade. 'Angle of departure' is basically the same but at the rear: the maximum grade from which a vehicle can depart on the horizontal without any parts except tyres coming in contact with the grade. These angles are often approximate, especially on soft-sprung vehicles where they are influenced by any load carried. The ground clearance is the distance between level ground and the lowest point of the vehicle, usually the differential case of the driving axle(s).

In those instances where a vehicle is given full-page coverage, the dimensions and weights given apply to the version shown in the heading picture.

Weights: Vehicle weight is the approximate net kerb weight of the fully-equipped vehicle in operating condition with fuel, lubricants, etc., but without crew or payload, unless indicated otherwise. Gross weight (GVW) is of the vehicle fully equipped and serviced for operation, including crew, plus maximum allowable payload of cargo and passengers. In most instances of cross-country vehicles, the gross weight is for operation on roads; it should be reduced for off-road operation. Gross combination weight (GCW) is the gross weight of the vehicle and any (semi-)-trailers. A ton in this book is 1000 kg, except in the case of some payload ratings of US vehicles, where the 907.2-kg short ton has been retained only for load classification purposes. A US '5-ton' truck is, however, quite capable of carrying a 5000-kg payload.

Conversions:

Length

1 millimetre (mm) = 0.039 in.
1 centimetre (cm) = 10 mm = 0.39 in.
1 metre (m) = 1000 mm = 39.37 in. = 3.28 ft
1 kilometre (km) = 1000 m = 0.62 mile
1 inch (1" or 1 in.) = 25.40 mm
1 foot (1' or 1 ft) = 12 in. = 304.8 mm = 0.30 m
1 mile = 1760 yards = 1609 m

Weights

1 kilogram (kg) = 2.2 lb
1 metric ton = 1000 kg = 0.98 long ton = 1.1 short tons
1 pound (1 lb) = 0.45 kg
1 cwt = 4 quarter = 112 lb = 50.80 kg
1 long ton = 20 cwt = 1.12 short tons = 1016 kg
1 short ton = 2000 lb = 0.89 long ton = 907.2 kg

Capacities

1 cubic centimetre (1 cc or cm^3) = 0.061 cu. in.
1 litre (1 ltr) = 1000 cc = 61.025 cu. in.
1 cubic inch (1 cu. in.) = 16.39 cc
1 Imperial gallon = 1.2 US gallons = 4.55 litres
1 US gallon = 0.833 Imp. gallon = 3.79 litres
1 cubic metre (1 m^3) = 1.308 cu. yd

5

Abbreviations

AA	anti-aircraft		MoD	Ministry of Defence (GB)
AFV	armoured fighting vehicle		NATO	North Atlantic Treaty Organization
APC	armoured personnel carrier		NC	normal control
AT	anti-tank		OD	overdrive
auto.	automatic		OHC	overhead camshaft
bhp	brake horsepower		OHV	overhead valve
cc	cubic centimetre(s)		Pkw	*Personenkraftwagen* (D; car)
CKD	completely knocked down		PTO	power take-off
COE	cab over engine		RAAF	Royal Australian Air Force
diff(s)	differential(s)		RAF	Royal Air Force (GB)
DIN	*Deutsche Industrie Norm*		RAN	Royal Australian Navy
GCW	gross combination weight		RCT	Royal Corps of Transport (GB)
GS	general service		rhd	right-hand drive
GVW	gross vehicle weight		RN	Royal Navy (GB)
hyd.	hydraulic		rpm	revolutions per minute
in	inch		SAE	Society of Automotive Engineers (USA)
kW	kilowatt		swb	short wheelbase
l	litre		trans.	transmission
lhd	left-hand drive		UN	United Nations
lwb	long wheelbase		wb	wheelbase
MG	machine gun			

International Registration Letters
(used in this book to indicate vehicles' country of origin)

A	Austria		IND	India
AUS	Australia		J	Japan
B	Belgium		L	Luxembourg
BR	Brazil		MEX	Mexico
BUR	Burma		NL	Netherlands
CDN	Canada		NZ	New Zealand
CH	Switzerland		P	Portugal
CS	Czechoslovakia		PI	Philippines
D	West Germany (FRG)		PL	Poland
DDR	East Germany (DDR)		PRC	People's Republic of China
DK	Denmark		R	Rumania
DZ	Algeria		RA	Argentina
E	Spain		ROK	South Korea
F	France		S	Sweden
GB	Great Britain		SF	Finland
GR	Greece		SU	Soviet Union (USSR)
H	Hungary		USA	United States of America
I	Italy		YU	Yugoslavia
IL	Israel		ZA	South Africa

Motorcycles and Three-Wheelers

The motorcycle has been used for military service from the earliest days of its existence. Relatively cheap and small, manageable and speedy, it has always been employed for certain types of military work. During the Second World War, it looked as if the two-wheelers were going to be replaced by small four-wheeled machines like the famous 'jeep' and 'Kübel', but it was found that the motorcycle (with the exception of the sidecar-combination) could never really be dispensed with. After the war, motorcycles in the armed forces were used chiefly for police work: traffic control, convoy duties, and occasionally messenger service. Relatively restricted roles. It was not until the 1970s that motorcycles really began to make inroads again, rapidly gaining in use potential. This was largely due to the development in civilian life of the off-road trials bike. Low weight, high ground clearance, tremendous power, the ability to cross streams and exceptionally rough terrain, and low fuel consumption made the military authorities take a fresh look at the two-wheeler.

Several armies bought militarized versions of these civilian off-road machines, as may be seen in the following pages. The Swedish Army, however, went a step further and experimented with a series of special purpose-built military machines which at their request had been designed and developed by Hägglunds, Husqvarna and Monark-Crescent, beginning in the early 1970s. Husqvarna and Monark-Crescent were old-established motorcycle producers, but for Hägglund (manufacturers of a variety of tracked military vehicles) two-wheelers were something entirely new. In 1972 the first prototypes appeared and the Hägglunds was by far the most novel, if not revolutionary.

The Swedish Army had set an impressive list of requirements, including:

(1) Single-cylinder engine of 15–19 kW (20–25 bhp) with automatic transmission.
(2) Easier handling, maintenance and repair than their existing Husqvarna and Jawa machines.
(3) Need for servicing only at 5000-km intervals and a vehicle life span of 25000 km.
(4) Sustained cruising speed of 100 km/h and adequate acceleration, especially in the 40- to 100-km/h speed range.
(5) Ability to negotiate 20 cm of snow, 50 cm of water.
(6) Maximum weight of 150 kg, including over-snow equipment (skids).

The Hägglunds machine (XM72) bristled with unconventional ideas, e.g. a (German) Sachs 293-cc engine with half a DAF Variomatic transmission mounted to the frame in a pivoted fashion so as to have a constant distance between the drive pulleys, shaft drive to the rear wheel, single-tube front and rear suspension with helical springs and hydraulic shock absorbers, disc brakes fore and aft, alloy wheels with six spokes, pressed steel frame with integrated fuel tank and rear mudguard, and several more. After lengthy trials, the machine was modified, becoming the XM74 (1974), with a conventional twin-tube front fork, a Bombardier-Rotax 345-cc engine, drum brakes and other changes. A number of pilot models were produced for further tests, but the Swedish Army requirements were not easy to meet. In addition to having automatic transmission and guaranteed minimum and maximum speeds, the engine had to be capable of running for a while in all positions, including upside down. There were penalties for excess weight and maintenance costs. The noise level had to be kept below 85 decibels.

Husqvarna had also been very active, entering a more orthodox model with a rather unorthodox four-speed automatic gearbox, and in the end came out as the winner, securing the Swedish Army contract and delivering 3000 machines during 1977–81.

Another military off-road motorcycle was developed by Bombardier in Canada, based on their Can-Am 250-cc Enduro model. It was tested by several military authorities and by 1982 was in use with the Canadian, British and Belgian armies and the US Marines. Larger machines were used chiefly by military police forces, BMW being one of the leading suppliers.

Three-wheelers, apart from sidecar-combinations which remained in service only in some Communist countries, were mainly industrial types, used for low-cost transport of light cargo, particularly in confined areas like airfields, workshops, etc. Some of these are shown at the end of this chapter.

The motorcycles are presented in order of engine size (cubic capacity).

MOTORCYCLE, SOLO (HERCULES K125BW)   D

General Data: In the early 1970s the Nuremberg firm of Hercules delivered a large quantity of motorcycles to the West German *Bundeswehr*, where they replaced the Maico M250/B of the 1960s. This Maico, which remained in service for many years, was a 247-cc machine, weighing 165 kg and capable of 95 km/h. The Hercules had the same top speed but only half the engine capacity and about 10% lower weight. Hercules belongs to the Fichtel & Sachs Group and has also supplied 50-cc mopeds to the *Bundeswehr*.

Technical Details: Sachs 1251/5B single-cyl. aircooled 2-stroke petrol engine, 122 cc (54 × 54 mm), 9.2 kW/12.5 bhp (net) at 7000 rpm. Bing carburettor. Multiplate oil-bath clutch. 5F gearbox (ratios 4.6 to 1.153:1). Mechanical drum brakes. Swinging arm front and rear suspension. Tyres 3.25-18 front, 3.50-18 rear. 6-Volt electrics. 15-litre fuel tank.

Dimensions and Weights: Wheelbase 1295 mm. Overall length and width 2035 × 930 mm. Height 1260 mm (mirror). Seat height 830 mm. Ground clearance 230 mm. Weight 140 kg, GVW 300 kg.

above and below: K125BW in service with the *Bundeswehr*.

Motorcycle, Lightweight   **D**
(Hercules Moped 505P)

Single-cyl. 47-cc 2-stroke engine (Sachs 504/1B). Wheelbase 1100 mm. Overall dimensions 1690 × 620 × 970 mm. Weight 42 kg. GVW 150 kg. Max. speed 25 km/h. 4-litre fuel tank. Supplied to the *Bundeswehr*, late 1970s. Originally this was the Zweirad Union's Mofa Prima 2. ZU was absorbed by Fichtel & Sachs.

Motorcycle, Lightweight   **DK**
(SCO Type 3)

Single-cyl. 48-cc 2-stroke engine with 3F gearbox and kickstarter. Manufactured in the early 1970s by Smith & Co. of Odense and used by the Danish Air Force for messenger and light transport service. It featured Bosch flywheel magneto ignition and Dellorto carburettor.

Motorcycle, Solo   **F**
(Peugeot SX8T Armée)

Single-cyl. 79.6-cc 2-stroke engine with 5F gearbox and chain final drive. Wheelbase 1260 mm. Weight 77 kg (dry). GVW 252 kg. Max. speed 80 km/h. Cruising range 300 km. Militarized trials bike, ordered in quantity by the French Army in 1979. Shown is a pilot model of 1978.

Motorcycle, Lightweight   **J**
(Honda C90)

Single-cyl. 89.5-cc 4-stroke ohc engine with centrifugal clutch and 3F gearbox. Fully-enclosed chain final drive. Tyres 2.50-17 front and rear. Wheelbase 1190 mm. Weight 75 kg. Rear luggage rack. Used by Australian Army for local messenger work. Mid-1970s. Also with 72-cc engine (C70).

Motorcycle, Solo   **J**
(Honda 250)

Single-cyl. 248-cc ohc engine with 5F gearbox and chain final drive. Tyres 2.75-21 front, 4.00-18 rear. Drum brakes. Wheelbase 1385 mm. Overall length 2120 mm. Ground clearance 190 mm. Japanese Army machine, derived from civilian Honda XL250 (to which the above details apply).

Motorcycle, Solo   **S**
(Husqvarna Military Automatic)

Single-cyl. 250-cc 2-stroke engine with automatic 4F gearbox. Chain final drive. Mikuni 32 carburettor. Bosch pointless ignition. Overall dimensions 2250 × 860 × 1200 mm. Ground clearance 280 mm. Fording depth 500 mm. Weight 136 kg. 20 produced for Swedish Army trials, 1978.

MOTORCYCLE, SOLO (BOMBARDIER 250)

CDN

General Data: The Bombardier military motorcycle was based on the makers' Enduro trials bike and was also known as the Can-Am. In Britain, 872 machines were ordered in the late 1970s, to be delivered through BSA in Birmingham. The Belgian Army and the US Marine Corps followed in 1981/82. In addition to the 250 model, the company offered 125, 175 and 400 versions. The engines, all of Austrian origin, were of the 2-stroke type with rotary valve, except the 400 which was of the piston port and reed valve design. All models had a tubular double-loop frame with tapered backbone.

Technical Details: Bombardier-Rotax single-cyl. rotary-valve 2-stroke petrol engine, 247 cc (74 × 57.5 mm), 19.3 kW/26 bhp (net) at 7500 rpm. Bosch electronic CDI ignition system. Bing carburettor. Multiplate oil-bath clutch. 5F constant-mesh gearbox (ratios 2.91 to 0.913:1). Mechanical drum brakes. Teledraulic front suspension (with travel up to 250 mm), trailing arm rear. Tyres 3.00-21 front, 4.00-18 rear. 12-Volt electrics. 16-litre fuel tank.

Dimensions and Weights: Overall length and width 2225 × 860 mm. Height 1128 mm. Seat height 840 mm. Ground clearance 230 mm. Weight 132 kg.

above and *below left:* 250 (British); *below right:* 250 (Belgian)

Motorcycle, Solo   **S**
(Husqvarna MC258MT)

Single-cyl. 250-cc 2-stroke engine with automatic 4F transmission. Chain final drive. Weight 130 kg. Max. speed 120 km/h. Following extensive trials with various prototypes made by Hägglunds, Husqvarna and Monark, this machine was chosen by the Swedish Army. By 1981, 3000 units had been delivered.

Motorcycle, Solo   **D**
(Maico 250/Mil.)

Single-cyl. 247-cc 2-stroke engine with 5F gearbox and chain drive. Bing carburettor. Tyres 3.25-18 front, 4.00-18 rear. Weight 130 kg. 17-litre fuel tank. Developed in the late 1970s. 250 units sold to the Sudanese armed forces in 1978. In the 1960s Maico supplied the *Bundeswehr* with their M250/B.

Motorcycle, Solo   **DDR**
(MZ ES250/1A and /2A)

Single-cyl. 243-cc (69 × 65 mm) 2-stroke engine with 4F gearbox and chain final drive. Tyres 3.50-16 front and rear. Overall dimensions 2098 × 862 × 1180 mm (incl. mirror). Weight 156 kg. Max. speed 105 km/h. Made in the DDR for civil and military service, also with sidecar, during the 1960s and 1970s.

Motorcycle, Solo   **DDR**
(MZ TS250/A)

Single-cyl. 243-cc (69 × 65 mm) 2-stroke engine with 4F gearbox and chain final drive. Telescopic front suspension (ES models had rocker arm). Swinging rear fork with telescopic spring struts. Tyres 3.00-16 front, 3.25-16 rear. Wheelbase 1346 mm. Overall length 2050 mm. Weight 130 kg (dry).

Motorcycle, Solo   **J**
(Yamaha DT250MX)

Single-cyl. 246-cc (70 × 64 mm) 2-stroke engine with 5F gearbox and chain final drive. Drum brakes. Tyres 3.00-24 front, 4.00-18 rear. Overall dimensions 2150 × 880 × 1140 mm. Weight 130 kg. 12-litre fuel tank. 1.1-litre oil reservoir. Militarized civilian machine, used by the Danish armed forces from 1980.

Motorcycle, Solo   **S**
(Hägglunds XM72)

Single-cyl. 293-cc 2-stroke engine (Sachs 290R) with centrifugal clutch, automatic transmission (Variomatic) and shaft drive. Tyres 3.00-18 front, 3.50-18 rear. Wheelbase 1360 mm. Overall dimensions 2050 × 820 × 1100 mm. Weight 120 kg. Ground clearance 260 mm. Prototype for Swedish Army, 1972.

MOTORCYCLES AND THREE-WHEELERS

Motorcycle, Solo   **S**
(Monark m/72)

Single-cyl. 292-cc 2-stroke engine (Sachs 290R) with automatic transmission. Chain final drive. Telescopic suspension units, Ceriani front, Girling rear. Tyres 3.25-18 front, 4.00-18 rear. Overall length and width 2150 × 840 mm. Weight 150 kg. Experimental machine, tested by the Swedish Army in the early 1970s.

Motorcycle, Solo   **GB**
(BSA Star B40)

Single-cyl. 343-cc ohv engine with 4F gearbox and chain final drive. Tyres 3.25-18 front, 4.00-18 rear. Wheelbase 1359 mm. Standard machine of British Army and RAF until late 1970s. Army also had BSA Victor Special B44S (441-cc) and Starfire 250, albeit in small numbers. B40 was also used by the Danish Army.

Motorcycle, Solo   **CH**
(Condor A350)

Introduced in 1973, this 340-cc machine was used only by the Swiss Army, along with the same makers' A250 (shaft-drive 248-cc, 1969). A350 measured 2050 × 690 × 1050 mm, weighed 165 kg and had wheelbase length of 1350 mm. Another widely-used Swiss military machine was the famed Condor A580.

Motorcycle, Solo   **S**
(Hägglunds XM74)

Single-cyl. 345-cc 2-stroke engine (Bombardier-Rotax 347) with centrifugal clutch and automatic transmission (Variomatic). Tyres 3.00-21 front, 4.00-18 rear. Wheelbase 1410 mm. Overall dimensions 2210 × 900 × 1110 mm. Weight 139 kg. Ground clearance 237 mm. Developed 1974 for Swedish Army but not adopted.

Motorcycle, Solo   **S**
(Husqvarna 350 Automatic)

Single-cyl. 350-cc 2-stroke engine with fuel injection and automatic hydrostatic transmission. Fully-enclosed final drive chain (design MZ). Tyres 3.00-21 front, 4.00-18 rear. Overall length and width 2200 × 830 mm. Weight 150 kg. Prototype for the Swedish Army, produced in 1972.

Motorcycle, Solo   **GB**
(Triumph 3TA Special)

Twin-cyl. 348-cc ohv engine with 4F gearbox and chain final drive. Rear suspension with Girling coil spring/hydraulic damper units. Tyres 3.25-18 front and rear. Wheelbase 1390 mm. Weight 210 kg. Militarized civilian machine of which the Netherlands Army acquired 1100 units from the late 1960s.

MOTORCYCLE, SOLO (BMW R60)   D

General Data: BMW (Bayerische Motoren Werke, or Bavarian Motor Works) has produced flat-twin motorcycles since the 1920s. The R60/5 '600' shown here was introduced in 1969, along with the R50/5 '500' and R75/5 '750' (498- and 746-cc resp.). These and other BMW machines were and are frequently acquired by the military, including the German, British, French, Dutch and Belgian forces. In the Netherlands Army police force *(Kon. Marechaussee)* the R60 Series (R60/5, /6, /7) was superseded in the early 1980s by the more suitable 798-cc R80/7.

Technical Details: Own R60/5 horizontally-opposed twin-cyl. aircooled ohv petrol engine, 599 cc (73.5 × 70.6 mm), 29.8 kW/

40 bhp (DIN) at 4000 rpm. Bing carburettors. Dry plate clutch. 4F gearbox. Shaft final drive. Mechanical drum brakes. Hydraulic telescopic front suspension, swinging arm rear suspension. Tyres 3.25S19 front, 4.00S18 rear. 12-Volt electrics. 24-litre fuel tank.

Dimensions and Weights: Wheelbase 1385 mm. Overall length and width 2100 × 740 mm. Height 1040 mm (without mirrors and fairing). Seat height 810 mm. Ground clearance 165 mm. Weight 210 kg. GVW 400 kg.

above: R60/5; *below left and right:* Netherlands Military Police machines, without and with cockpit fairing

MOTORCYCLES AND THREE-WHEELERS

Motorcycle, Solo   **D**
(BMW R50/5)

Flat-twin-cyl. 498-cc aircooled ohv engine with 4F gearbox and shaft final drive. Telescopic front suspension, swinging arm rear. Drum brakes front and rear. 24-litre fuel tank. Maximum speed 147 km/h. Acceleration 0–100 km/h in 10.2 seconds. Used by Belgian military police in the early 1970s.

Motorcycle, Solo   **I**
(Moto Guzzi V-50 II)

V-twin-cyl. 490-cc (74 × 57 mm) ohv engine with 5F gearbox and shaft final drive. Telescopic suspension. Disc brakes front and rear. Cast spoke wheels. Tyres 3.50-18 front, 3.50 or 100/90-18 rear. Weight 152 kg. Max. speed 180 km/h. Shown is one of a batch delivered to the Netherlands Royal Marines in 1980/81.

Motorcycle, Solo   **J**
(Kawasaki 650 Police Special)

One of the few in service with the Australian Army's police in the early 1970s. Behind are some standard BSA Star B40 Army machines (later replaced by the Suzuki 400). The detachment shown belonged to 2 Div. MP Coy (a part-time Army Reserve unit). Sydney, August 1974.

Motorcycle, Solo   **GB**
(Triumph Tiger TR7RV)

Twin-cyl. 744-cc ohv engine with 5F gearbox and chain final drive. Disc brakes front and rear. Wheelbase 1420 mm. Tyres 4.10-19 front, 4.10-18 rear. Weight 187 kg. 106 machines ordered by British MoD in 1978, more than 80 of which were for the Army (chiefly Military Police).

Motorcycle, Solo   **D**
(BMW R80/7)

Flat-twin-cyl. 798-cc aircooled ohv engine with 5F gearbox and shaft final drive. Available from the late 1970s in 50- and 55-bhp versions, with max. speeds of approx. 170 and 180 km/h. Disc brake front, drum brake rear. Tyres 3.25-19 front, 4.00-18 rear. Weight 195 kg (dry). 24-litre tank.

Motorcycle, Solo   **USA**
(Harley-Davidson FLH Electra Glide)

The Electra Glide, with its 1207-cc 65-bhp ohv V-2-cyl. engine (good for 170 km/h) and electric starter replaced the Duo-Glide in 1965. Machine shown dated from the early 1970s and was used by the Belgian *Rijkswacht*, one of Europe's last (para-) military customers to buy these luxurious and expensive machines.

Motorcycle, with Sidecar   **SU**
(Dniepr MT9)
Flat-twin-cyl. ohv 649-cc engine with 4F1R gearbox and shaft drive. 4.62:1 gear ratio. Telescopic front suspension. Swinging arm with hydraulic struts at rear. Tyres 3.75-19 front and rear. Commercially available, also as solo machine (Model MT10). Earlier models known as K-650.

Motorcycle, with Sidecar   **PRC**
(Changjiang 750)
Flat-twin-cyl. ohv 746-cc engine with 4F gearbox and shaft final drive. Wheelbase 1420 mm. Overall dimensions 2400 × 1590 × 1000 mm. Weight 633 kg. GVW 933 kg. Maximum speed 85 km/h. Produced by Changjiang Machinery Factory, Zhuzhou, People's Republic of China.

Truck, Lightweight, 3 × 2   **USA**
(Cushman Haulster)
In 1974 the US Army acquired a batch of 19 of these scooter-like vehicles for tests by the 101st Airborne Division (Air Assault) Command at Fort Campbell, Kentucky. A typical registration number was CC9015. Example shown (CC9095) was used at a US Army facility in Europe, 1976.

Truck, Lightweight, 3 × 2   **I**
(Piaggio Ape Car)
Single-cyl. 218-cc 2-stroke engine (AF1M) with 4F1R gearbox. Rear-wheel drive. Wheelbase 2100 mm. Overall dimensions 3275 × 1450 × 1480 mm. Weight 466 kg. GVW 1078 kg. Commercial type, also available as a van, made by Piaggio of Genoa. Example shown in US Army service in Italy, mid-1970s.

Truck, Lightweight, 3 × 1   **NL**
(Spijkstaal Electro)
During the 1960s and 1970s the Dutch Air Force procured several batches of electric-drive platform trucks and tractors for use at airfields, in workshops, stores, etc. Platform truck shown was one of 21 supplied in the early 1970s by Spijkstaal of Hoogeveen, Netherlands. Some had a simple cab enclosure.

Truck, Lightweight, 3 × 2   **USA**
(Westcoaster 060)
Twin-cyl. 820-cc aircooled petrol engine (or electric motor), driving the hypoid-type rear axle. 6-in. wheels. Produced by Westcoaster (a subsidiary of Otis Elevator) in Stockton, Calif., this was one of a batch for the US Army in the early 1970s (example: serial no. 35616, 1972). Production was discontinued in 1975.

Cars and Light Transports

Presented in this chapter is an international selection of vehicles intended chiefly for the conveyance of passengers, as well as typical examples of multipurpose vehicles which carry personnel and/or light cargo, followed by a number of panel vans and pickup trucks, some of which were derived from passenger cars. With one or two exceptions, military passenger cars are civilian types with few if any modifications. They are usually painted glossy green or black, occasionally blue, with only relatively few finished in military livery of a matt green or grey colour. Most of the cars are purchased in quantity – one-off types being rare and usually in the higher price bracket, being used for special purposes like high-grade staff cars. With a few exceptions, staff cars feature four doors.

Military utility cars or station wagons are common in some countries but quite rare in others. Some of these dual-purpose types, also known as 'estate cars' or 'breaks', have four-wheel drive and are covered in a later section (Field Cars/Utility Trucks).

Countries like the USA and Canada who keep considerable forces in far-away places, e.g. West Germany and Japan, have often purchased locally-built cars, chiefly for reasons of cost, maintenance and repair. This also applies to vans and other so-called 'administrative' vehicles (commercial trucks, buses), often operated by civilian drivers. Some countries have procured military-pattern 4 × 2 light multipurpose vehicles, officially designated 'trucks', to replace more expensive 4 × 4 utility trucks for roles where all-wheel drive is an unnecessary and costly luxury. Although these vehicles, exemplified by the DAF 66YA and Volkswagen 181, have a limited off-road capability, they were intended chiefly for operation on metalled roads. With the same idea in mind, the Belgian forces bought a large number of rear-wheel-drive Land-Rovers, the front axle centre part replaced by a simple tube. The American Jeep Dispatcher model is another good example of a utility truck with two-wheel drive only; it is moreover equipped with an automatic transmission, a hardtop body with sliding doors and a rear door and is ideal as a runabout.

The French Citroën Méhari (and its Greek edition, the Pony), basically a civilian utility vehicle, was also offered in optional 4 × 4 configuration. However, all-wheel drive was not essential as owing to its low weight this model could easily be manhandled out of difficulties. An interesting entry in this category was the South African Trax, which had only rear-wheel drive but was fitted with two levers which acted separately on the two rear-wheel brakes, in the same fashion as on pre-war British trials cars. By actuating the brake on the wheel that spins and thus diverting the power to the other wheel, good progress could be made in off-road conditions, especially by an experienced driver. It is believed to have been the only modern production car to have this feature. Another rather unique piece of (optional) equipment on the Trax was a tiny motorcycle, to be used if and when in real trouble.

The West German Kraka was yet another vehicle which was one of a kind. It was originally designed by Nicholas Straussler as another application for his Lypsoid tyres (the first being the three-wheeler which FN of Belgium built in some quantity from 1959). Originally made in the early 1960s by the West German firm Zweirad Union, which was owned by Faun-Werke, the Kraka proved a non-seller in the market segment for which it was thought most suitable: agriculture. In 1966 it became part of Faun's own production programme and the *Bundeswehr* (large-scale customers for Faun heavy-duty trucks) tested some, as a result of which a production order followed which was executed in the mid-1970s. Total production, however, remained well under 1000 units.

Light panel vans of the 'sedan delivery' type have never been popular with the military, unlike the larger forward-control types which, with and without rear side windows, have become quite numerous. The latter are employed in a variety of roles and are invariably off-the-shelf commercial models. Volkswagen vans (and crew-cab pickups) in particular, are used by the armed forces of many countries, also in *Kombi* or minibus configuration. Several ambulances are based on these vans (see 'Personnel Carriers' and 'Medical Vehicles').

Some armed forces, particularly those of the United States and Canada, employ large numbers of commercial pickup trucks, notably Chevrolet, Dodge and Ford. With their wide cabs these vehicles can accommodate up to three people plus a fair amount of small cargo. Some of them have a rear body enclosure or specialist bodywork, including telephone maintenance units and ambulances.

Car, 2-seater, 4 × 2   **GB**
(Enfield 8000)

Produced by Enfield Automotive of Cowes (IOW) this electric car
was acquired in 1974 by the British Army for comparison trials (by
41 Squadron, RCT). It measured 3350 × 1525 mm. Batteries were
located in nose and tail compartments. Range 120 km. Top speed
67 km/h.

Car, 4-seater, 4 × 2   **D/GB**
(Ford Escort)

4-cyl. 1.6-litre petrol engine with 4F1R gearbox. Rear-wheel
drive. 13-in. wheels. Wheelbase 2407 mm. Overall dimensions
3978 × 1596 × 1398 mm. Weight 885 kg. Used by the Netherlands
Army (Military Police) in the early 1980s. The Dutch also used
other Ford cars and station wagons, from Fiesta to Granada.

Car, 4-seater, 4 × 2   **GB**
(Mini 850 Series X/A2S1)

4-cyl. 0.85-litre petrol engine with 4F1R gearbox, mounted
transversely. Front-wheel drive. 10-in. wheels. Wheelbase
2032 mm. Overall dimensions 3050 × 1410 × 1350 mm. Weight
636 kg. Marque name Mini from 1969, prior to which it was either
Austin or Morris. Used in British Army as Grade 5 Staff Car.

Car, 4-seater, 4 × 2   **F**
(Renault 9)

4-cyl. 1.1-litre petrol engine with 4F1R gearbox. Front-wheel drive.
Independent suspension. Wheelbase 2477 mm. Overall dimensions
4063 × 1650 × 1400 mm. Weight 840 kg. GVW 1260 kg. Used
from 1982 by the Netherlands Air Force (which used chiefly
German-made cars).

Car, 4-seater, 4 × 2   **J**
(Toyota Corona Mk II)

4-cyl. 1.7-litre ohc petrol engine with 4F1R gearbox. Rear-wheel
drive. Wheelbase 2510 mm. Overall dimensions 4300 × 1605 ×
1405 mm. Weight 995 kg. Japanese cars were bought by several
armed forces as staff cars. The model shown was in service with
the USAF and USN in Japan in the 1970s.

Car, 4-seater, 4 × 2   **D**
(Volkswagen Golf D)

4-cyl. 1.47-litre diesel engine with 4F1R gearbox. Front-wheel
drive. Wheelbase 2400 mm. Overall dimensions 3815 × 1610 ×
1410 mm. Weight 805 kg. Shown is a 1979/80 2-door model of
the Danish Army. In the early 1980s the 1471-cc diesel engine
was superseded by a longer-stroke 1588-cc unit.

CARS AND LIGHT TRANSPORTS

Car, 4/5-seater, 4 × 2   I
(Alfa-Romeo Giulia TI)

4-cyl. 1.57-litre petrol engine with 5F1R gearbox. Rear-wheel drive. Independent front suspension. Coil springs front and rear. 15-in. wheels. Wheelbase 2510 mm. Overall dimensions 4140 × 1580 × 1430 mm. Weight 1060 kg. Max. speed 165 km/h. Range 440 km. Used by Italian Army and Military Police.

Car, 4/5-seater, 4 × 2   I
(Fiat 131 Mirafiori 1600L)

4-cyl. 1.58-litre petrol engine with 4F1R gearbox. Rear-wheel drive. 13-in. wheels. Wheelbase 2490 mm. Overall dimensions 4264 × 1651 × 1381 mm. Weight 1000 kg. 4-door bodywork. Used by Netherlands Air Force. The Dutch armed forces employed many Fiat cars, including Models 127 and 128.

Car, 4/5-seater, 4 × 2   GB
(Ford Cortina 1.6L)

4-cyl. 1.6-litre petrol engine with 4F1R gearbox. Rear-wheel drive. 13-in. wheels. Wheelbase 2578 mm. Typical example of 'New Cortina' saloon of the British forces. Several variants were in service. The German version (Taunus) was used by several continental governments and also by the US Army in Europe.

Car, 4/5-seater, 4 × 2   D
(Ford Taunus 1.6)

4-cyl. 1.6-litre petrol engine with 4F1R gearbox. Wheelbase 2578 mm. Overall dimensions 4340 × 1706 × 1363 mm. Weight 970 kg. Early 1980s staff car of Netherlands Royal Navy. The Dutch armed forces used a large variety of cars, incl. Citroën, DAF, Fiat, Mercedes-Benz, Morris, Opel, Peugeot, Simca, Volkswagen.

Car, 4/5-seater, 4 × 2   GB
(Hillman Hunter GL)

4-cyl. 1.7-litre petrol engine with 4F1R gearbox. Rear-wheel drive. 13-in. wheels. Wheelbase 2501 mm. Overall dimensions 4267 × 1613 × 1422 mm. Weight 940 kg. Supplied to RAF in 1977 by Chrysler (UK) (previously the Rootes Group but in 1978 taken over by the French Peugeot Group).

Car, 4/5-seater, 4 × 2   AUS
(Holden HQ-Series Belmont)

6-cyl. petrol engine with 3F1R gearbox. Rear-wheel drive. One of several types of Holden cars and derivatives (e.g. station wagons) of many model years (1972 shown) employed by the Australian armed forces. Some of these vehicles were equipped with certain accessories, even with 'bull bars'.

Car, 4/5-seater, 4 × 2   **D**
(Mercedes-Benz 230)

4-cyl. 2.3-litre petrol engine with 4F1R gearbox. Rear-wheel drive. Wheelbase 2795 mm. Overall dimensions 4725 × 1786 × 1438 mm. Weight 1350 kg. Used by the West German *Bundeswehr* in the late 1970s as *Pkw schwer* (heavy car). Also in service was the 220D (as *Pkw Mittelschwer*), with 2.2-litre diesel engine.

Car, 4/5-seater, 4 × 2   **D**
(Mercedes-Benz 240D)

4-cyl. 2.4-litre diesel engine with 4F1R gearbox. Rear-wheel drive. Independent suspension front and rear. Wheelbase 2795 mm. Overall dimensions 4725 × 1786 × 1438 mm. Weight 1385 kg. GVW 1905 kg. Max. speed 143 km/h. Example shown was in service with the Canadian forces in Germany, early 1980s.

Car, 4/5-seater, 4 × 2   **D**
(Opel Rekord)

4-cyl. 1.7-litre petrol engine. 4F1R gearbox. Rear-wheel drive. Wheelbase 2668 mm. Overall dimensions 4568 × 1718 × 1415 mm. Weight 1100 kg. *Bundeswehr* staff car of the mid-1970s. Numerous Opel cars of different types (Kadett, Ascona, Rekord, etc.) were used by the armed forces.

Car, 4/5-seater, 4 × 2   **F**
(Peugeot 305)

4-cyl. 1.3-litre petrol engine with 4F1R gearbox. Front-wheel drive. 14-in. wheels. Wheelbase 2620 mm. Overall dimensions 4237 × 1630 × 1400 mm. Weight 925 kg. Used by the French Army, 1981. Many Peugeot cars, of various types, were and are in military service, including 'breaks'.

Car, 4/5-seater, 4 × 2   **S**
(Volvo 144S)

4-cyl. 2-litre twin-carburettor engine with 4F1R gearbox. Rear-wheel drive. Wheelbase 2600 mm. Overall dimensions 4640 × 1740 × 1460 mm. Weight 1150 kg. Widely used by armed forces in Scandinavia. Also 6-cyl. (164) and station wagon (145S) versions. 1970 model shown (Danish Army, 1982).

Car, 5-seater, 4 × 2   **USA**
(AMC Matador)

Typical of American Motors' cars supplied for military use. During 1969/70 AMC delivered many thousands of Ambassador, Rebel and Hornet sedans and station wagons to the US forces, followed by Matadors (which replaced the Rebel) in 1972/73. This is a 1971 Matador of the Netherlands Army.

Car, 5-seater, 4 × 2   USA
(Ford Custom)

V-8-cyl. 4.9-litre petrol engine with 3F1R automatic transmission. Rear-wheel drive. Wheelbase 3073 mm. Overall dimensions 5491 × 2024 × 1366 mm. Weight 1700 kg. Standard 1971 Ford sedan of the US Army. Station wagons were also supplied, as were smaller Ford Falcon sedans.

Car, 5-seater, 4 × 2   AUS
(Ford Fairlane)

Typical Australian-built Grade 2 staff sedan of Australian Army, RAAF and RAN. Available with 6- or V-8-cyl. engine, this car dates from the early 1970s. Wheelbase 2946 mm. Overall dimensions 4991 × 1867 × 1410 mm. Weight 1500 kg. One of numerous types of Fords used by the Australian forces.

Car, 5-seater, 4 × 2   D/GB
(Ford Granada)

V-6-cyl. 2.8-litre petrol engine with 4F1R gearbox, manual or automatic. Rear-wheel drive. Wheelbase 2769 mm. High-grade staff car of Canadian Army in Germany. Large European Fords (incl. Consul) were employed by several military forces, including the British Royal Navy (3.0 S Saloon).

Car, 5-seater, 4 × 2   AUS
(Leyland P76)

6-cyl. 2.6-litre petrol engine with 4F1R gearbox (4.4-litre V8 and auto. trans. optional). Rear-wheel drive. Wheelbase 2826 mm. Overall dimensions 4890 × 1911 × 1390 mm. Weight 1290 kg. Limited production in Australia in the mid-1970s. This white specimen was operated by the RAAF.

Car, 5-seater, 4 × 2   D
(Opel Admiral)

6-cyl. 2.8-litre petrol engine with 4F1R gearbox (or 3F1R automatic). Rear-wheel drive. Wheelbase 2845 mm. Overall dimensions 4908 × 1835 × 1450 mm. Weight 1480 kg. 1969–72 model shown, in service with the Danish Civil Defence (yellow-on-blue registration number, prefixed CF).

Car, 5-seater, 4 × 2   USA
(Plymouth Valiant)

6-cyl. 3.7-litre (or 5.2-litre V8) engine with manual or automatic transmission. Rear-wheel drive. Wheelbase 2820 mm. Overall dimensions 5050 × 1805 × 1380 mm. Weight 1415 kg. Typical US Army staff car of the 1970s. 1975/76 model shown. From 1976 the Valiant was replaced in production by the Volare.

Car, Utility, 4 × 2   **GB**
(Ford Escort)

4-cyl. 1.1- (or 1.3-)litre petrol engine with 4F1R gearbox. Rear-wheel drive. 13-in. wheels. Wheelbase 2407 mm. During the 1970s the British Army acquired several batches of these virtually standard models, also with the later-style grille. They superseded the 1960s Morris Minor 1000 Traveller.

Car, Utility, 4 × 2   **AUS**
(Holden HK Belmont)

6-cyl. 2.8-litre petrol engine with 4F1R gearbox. Rear-wheel drive. Wheelbase 2819 mm. Overall dimensions 4500 × 1803 × 1435 mm. Known by the makers as a 'Station Sedan' this vehicle was used by the Royal Australian Air Force in the early 1970s. Most of the RAAF's station wagons at the time were Ford Falcons.

Car, Utility, 4 × 2   **F**
(Peugeot 504 Break L)

4-cyl. 1.8-litre petrol engine (diesel optional) with 4F1R gearbox. Rear-wheel drive. Wheelbase 2900 mm. Overall dimensions 4800 × 1690 × 1550 mm. Weight 1275 kg. Example shown was used by the French Navy in 1977/78. From 1980 the 504 Break was available with 4-wheel drive (Peugeot/Dangel, qv).

Car, Utility, 4 × 2   **F**
(Renault 4F4)

4-cyl. 0.84-litre petrol engine with 4F1R gearbox. Front-wheel drive. Wheelbase 2401 mm (left), 2449 mm (right). Overall dimensions 3653 × 1500 × 1710 mm. Weight 690 kg. Break version of 4F4 van, used as general-purpose hack by military administrative services in France, Belgium (shown), Spain, etc.

Car, Utility, 4 × 2   **D**
(Volkswagen Passat Variant)

4-cyl. 1.3-litre petrol engine with 4F1R gearbox. Front-wheel drive. Independent suspension with coil springs. 13-in. wheels. Wheelbase 2456 mm. Overall dimensions 4270 × 1620 × 1360 mm. Weight 920 kg. GVW 1420 kg. Employed by the *Bundeswehr* as *Pkw Kombi*, from 1978. Also available with diesel engine.

Car, Utility, 4 × 2   **S**
(Volvo 245)

4-cyl. 2.1-litre petrol engine with 4F1R gearbox. Rear-wheel drive. Wheelbase 2640 mm. Overall dimensions 4898 × 1707 × 1445 mm. Weight 1335 kg. GVW 1900 kg. Station-wagon version of Volvo 240 Series, delivered to the Swedish Army in the mid-1970s. Registration number of yellow characters on black plate.

TRUCK, 0.25-TON, 4×2 (GURGEL XAVANTE X-12M) BR

General Data: In the mid-1970s, the Brazilian firm Gurgel of Rio Claro introduced a range of VW-powered vehicles for military and civilian use. Utilizing established and proven VW components in conjunction with plastic bodywork (open and closed models) these vehicles were economical to operate and long-lasting. The X-12M was the military version of the civilian X-12. In addition there were the X-15, G-15 and X-20 forward-control models, including an entirely open truck for military applications, e.g. mount for recoilless weapons. Gurgel vehicles were also exported.

Technical Details: Volkswagen 1600 flat-4-cyl. aircooled petrol engine, 1584 cc (85.5 × 69.0 mm), 37 kW/60 bhp (gross) at 4600 rpm. Dry plate clutch. 4F1R gearbox. 4.375:1 axle gear ratio. Hydraulic brakes. Independent suspension with torsion bars at front, coil springs at rear. 5.60-15 tyres. 12-Volt electrics. 57-litre fuel tank.

Dimensions and Weights: Wheelbase 2040 mm. Track, front/rear 1305/1405 mm. Overall length and width 3310 × 1600 mm. Height 1530 mm (canvas top). Ground clearance 280 mm. Weight 790 kg, GVW 1100 kg.

above: X-12M, 1981; *below left:* X-12M, 1976; *below right:* X-12 (civilian version)

TRUCK, 0.25-TON, 4×2 (JEEP DJ5 DISPATCHER 100)   **USA**

General Data: Introduced by American Motors' Jeep Corp., this was a variant of the Jeep CJ5. There was a right-hand-drive version (DJ5G) for postal service. The military version was supplied to the US Army, Navy and Marine Corps as an 'administrative support vehicle'. It was commercially available and sold to civilian customers as an easy-to-operate general purpose vehicle. It had sliding side doors (that could be latched in the open position) and a single rear door. A Jeep Dispatcher had also been available in the late 1950s and early 1960s (Model DJ3A).

Technical Details: AMC 4-121 4-cyl. petrol engine, 1983 cc (86.6 × 84.3 mm), 60 kW/80 bhp (net) at 5000 rpm. Torque con-

verter with 3F1R automatic transmission. No transfer box. 3.73:1 axle gear ratio. Hydraulic brakes. Semi-elliptic leaf springs. E78-15 tyres. 12-Volt electrics. 38-litre fuel tank.
Note: also supplied with 6-cyl. engine.

Dimensions and Weights: Wheelbase 2057 mm. Track, front/rear 1308/1270 mm. Overall length and width 3378 × 1613 mm. Height 1790 mm (roof). Ground clearance 160 mm (rear axle). Angles of approach and departure 43° and 25°. Weight 1000 kg, GVW 1317 kg.

above: USMC; *below left:* US Army; *below right:* USN

TRUCK, 0.25-TON, 4 × 2 (NAMCO/CITROËN PONY)   GR

General Data: The Pony comprised a Greek-built steel body on the French Citroën Méhari chassis. It first appeared in the late 1970s and was ordered by the Greek government for use by the Army, the Navy and the Air Force as a low-cost multipurpose vehicle. The civilian range comprised the basic model and several variants, including an ambulance and a personnel carrier. In 1982 it was reported that several thousand had been sold to 14 countries in the Middle East, Africa and South America. Like the Méhari, the Pony was also offered with 4-wheel drive.

Technical Details: Citroën flat-twin-cyl. aircooled petrol engine, 602 cc (74 × 70 mm), 23.8 kW/32 bhp (net) at 5400 rpm. Dry plate clutch. 4F1R gearbox. Front-wheel drive. 3.875:1 axle gear ratio. Hydraulic brakes (discs front, drums rear). Independent suspension, interconnected front and rear. 135-380 tyres. 12-Volt electrics. 25-litre fuel tank.

Dimensions and Weights: Wheelbase 2320 mm. Track 1260 mm. Overall length and width 3670 × 1470 mm. Height 1630 mm (roll-over bar). Ground clearance 180–210 mm (adjustable). Weight 640 kg, GVW 1115 kg.

above and *below left:* Greek Army version; *below right:* hardtop/ambulance

TRUCK, 0.4-TON, 4×2 (DAF 66YA)   NL

General Data: This limited-mobility vehicle was designed in 1971/72 for the Netherlands Army to replace the 0.25-ton 4 × 4 type vehicle for those roles where off-road capability was not required. It was based on the DAF 66 car. 1200 units were ordered. Quantity production took place during 1973–75. Production models had the 66-type front end and a revised rear-end overhang for improved departure angle.

Technical Details: Renault/DAF BB110E 4-cyl. petrol engine, 1108 cc (72 × 70 mm), 35 kW/47 bhp (DIN) at 5000 rpm. Centrifugal clutch with Variomatic automatic transmission. Overall reduction ratio varying from 14.25:1 maximum to 3.7:1 minimum.

Hydraulic brakes. Independent front suspension with torsion bars. DeDion-type rear axle with semi-elliptic leaf springs. 145 × 14 tyres. 24-Volt electrics. 50-litre fuel tank.

Dimensions and Weights: Wheelbase 2255 mm. Track, front/rear 1310/1240 mm. Overall length and width 3750 × 1500 mm. Height 1580 mm (canvas top). Ground clearance 200 mm (skid plate). Angles of approach and departure 27° and 30° (laden). Weight 870 kg, GVW 1295 kg.

above: military police version; *below left:* standard model; *below right:* prototype with stretcher gear (experimental)

CARS AND LIGHT TRANSPORTS

Truck, 0.25-ton, 4 × 2, Utility   **F**
(Citroën Méhari)

2-cyl. 0.6-litre aircooled petrol engine, 4F1R gearbox. Front-wheel drive. Dyane 6 car chassis with plastic (ABS Cycolac artificial resins) open bodywork with softtop, introduced in 1968. Special 'Armée' model (AY, Series CA) from 1975. 8000 acquired by the French armed forces. 4 × 4 derivative was available also.

Truck, 0.25-ton, 4 × 2, Utility   **AUS**
(Leyland Moke)

4-cyl. 1.1-litre petrol engine with 4F1R gearbox, mounted transversely. Front-wheel drive. 13-in. wheels. Wheelbase 2095 mm. Overall dimensions 3232 × 1448 × 1600 mm. Weight 695 kg (approx.). Produced by British Leyland in Australia for Australian Army, RAAF, RAN and for export, including New Zealand.

Truck, 0.25-ton, 4 × 2, Utility   **DDR**
(Trabant P601/A)

2-cyl. 0.6-litre 2-stroke petrol engine with 4F1R gearbox. Front-wheel drive. Wheelbase 2020 mm. Overall dimensions 3475 × 1500 × 1510 mm. Weight 645 kg. Used by East German border police and therefore known as *Grenz-Trabant* (border Trabant). Derived from Trabant 601 car. 'Tramp' was civilian variant.

Truck, 0.4-ton, 4 × 2, Utility   **D/MEX**
(Volkswagen 181)

4-cyl. 1.58-litre aircooled engine with 4F1R gearbox mounted at rear. Rear axles (swinging type) with stepdown gearing. Diff. lock optional. Wheelbase 2400 mm. Overall dimensions 3780 × 1640 × 1620 mm. Weight 1350 kg. Used by armed forces of e.g. West Germany, Denmark (shown), Netherlands (Air Force) and Belgium.

Truck, 0.5-ton, 4 × 2, Utility   **ZA**
(Chevrolet Nomad)

4-cyl. 2.5-litre petrol engine with 4F1R gearbox. Rear-wheel drive. Limited-slip differential. Independent front suspension with coil springs. 14-in. wheels. Wheelbase 2083 mm. Overall length and width 3466 × 1571 mm. Weight 1027 kg. GVW 1600 kg. Produced by General Motors in Port Elizabeth during the late 1970s.

Truck, 0.5-ton, 4 × 2, Utility   **BR**
(Gurgel X-15)

4-cyl. 1.58-litre aircooled engine (VW) with 4F1R gearbox, mounted at the rear. Wheelbase 2230 mm. Overall dimensions 3700 × 1790 × 1880 mm. Designed and produced in the late 1970s in Brazil with modified VW Transporter chassis components and plasteel' (polyester with steel reinforcements).

CARS AND LIGHT TRANSPORTS

TRUCK, 0.75-TON, 4 × 2 (FAUN KRAKA 640)   D

General Data: Multipurpose motor cart (*Kraftkarren*), first made by Zweirad Union (and MV in Italy), later by Faun Werke who in mid-1974 delivered the first of a batch of 762 of the Type 640 to the German Federal Army's 1st Airborne Division. 5 types were offered (640–644). Type 641 had a Citroën M28/1 engine. The Kraka was extremely versatile and mobile, in spite of its lack of 4-wheel drive. For air transport and storage it could be folded. It never reached large-scale production however.

Technical Details: BMW 427 flat-twin-cyl. aircooled petrol engine, 697 cc (78 × 73 mm), 19.4 kW/26 bhp (net) at 5000 rpm. Dry plate clutch. BMW 959 4F1R gearbox. Rear-wheel drive.

Overall gear ratios 43.76 : 1 to 10.48 : 1. Hydraulic brakes. Transversal leaf springs at front, swinging subframe with rubber springing at rear. Lypsoid 22 × 12 tyres. 12-Volt electrics. 24.5-litre fuel tank.

Dimensions and Weights: Wheelbase 2058 mm. Track, front/rear 1138/1130 mm. Overall length and width 2780 × 1510 mm. Height 1190 mm (steering wheel). Ground clearance 250 mm (front axle). Angles of approach and departure 90° and 85°. Weight 740 kg, GVW 1610 kg.

above and *below left*: 640, basic vehicle; *below right*: with Milan A/T weapon

TRUCK, 0.75-TON, 4×2 (INTERSTATE TRAX 370)   SA

General Data: Launched in the late 1970s the Trax utility vehicle, designed by Interstate Motor Vehicle Co. in Pretoria, was offered for civilian and military use, with a wide range of body styles and component options. The zinc-coated box-section chassis frame is fitted with Chrysler-made front suspension units and rear axle. To improve traction of this 4×2 vehicle, the rear axle has 'fiddle' brakes (2 brake levers acting independently on each rear wheel).

Technical Details: Chrysler 6-cyl. petrol engine, 3687 cc (86 × 105 mm), 106 kW/142 bhp (net) at 4200 rpm. Torqueflite automatic 3F1R gearbox. 4.3:1 axle gear ratio. Hydraulic brakes. Independent front suspension with torsion bars. Rigid rear axle with semi-elliptic leaf springs. 9.00-13 tyres. 12-Volt electrics. 83-litre fuel tank. *Note:* Trax 200 0.5-ton model had Peugeot 4-cyl. 1971-cc engine with manual 4F1R gearbox.

Dimensions and Weights: Wheelbase 2110 mm. Track, front/rear 1465/1396 mm. Overall length and width 3707 × 1570 mm. Height 1600 mm (softtop). Ground clearance 220 mm (rear axle). Angles of approach and departure 52° and 38°. Weight 1324 kg, GVW 2075 kg.

above: military version; *below left:* with trailer and motorcycle; *below right:* civilian version

Van, 0.25-ton, 4 × 2   **GB**
(Mini Series X/KV1)

4-cyl. 0.85-litre petrol engine with 4F1R gearbox. Front-wheel drive. Independent rubber suspension front and rear. 10-in. wheels. Wheelbase 2134 mm. Overall dimensions 3302 × 1410 × 1384 mm. Weight 586 kg Widely used by British forces for messenger work and 'administrative' duties.

Van, 0.25-ton, 4 × 2   **AUS**
(Leyland Moke)

4-cyl. 1.1-litre petrol engine with 4F1R gearbox, mounted transversely. Front-wheel drive. Wheelbase 2095 mm. Example shown used by RAAF to transport guard dogs. Originally a British vehicle, Moke production was transferred to Australia where several improvements were made, incl. larger engine and wheels.

Van, 0.4-ton, 4 × 2   **F**
(Citroën 400)

Flat-2-cyl. aircooled 0.6-litre engine with 4F1R gearbox. Front-wheel drive. Wheelbase 2350 mm. Overall dimensions (unladen) 3805 × 1500 × 1840 mm. Weight 640 kg. Load volume 2.1 m³. Derived from 2CV car and used by several military forces, e.g. in France and the Netherlands (shown).

Van, 0.4-ton, 4 × 2   **F**
(Peugeot 305)

4-cyl. 1.3- or 1.5-litre petrol engine with 4F1R gearbox. Front-wheel drive. Wheelbase 2620 mm. Overall dimensions 4260 × 1630 × 1420 mm. Panel van, retrofitted with rear quarter windows and in service with the CADI (*Cantine Dienst*) of the Netherlands Army from 1981.

Van, 0.9-ton, 4 × 2   **GB**
(Bedford CF220)

4-cyl. 1.7-litre petrol engine with 4F1R gearbox. Rear-wheel drive. Wheelbase 2692 mm. Typical example of 'windowed' panel van supplied to the British forces (Army, RAF, RN) during the 1970s. This was one of 74 recruiting offices for the RAF, converted by Dormobile in 1974.

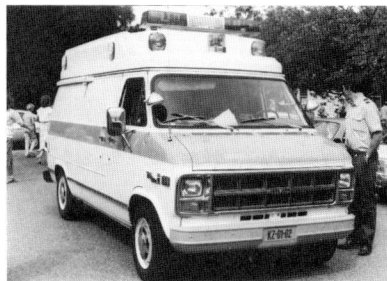

Van, 1-ton, 4 × 2   **USA**
(GMC Vandura)

V-8-cyl. petrol engine with automatic transmission. One of several versions, this van had a raised roof and lights all round, in modern ambulance fashion. Used from 1980/81 by the explosives disposal service of the Netherlands Army, replacing Unimog-based vans for high-speed long-distance work.

Van, 1-ton, 4 × 2   J
(Toyota HI-ACE)

4-cyl. 1.1-litre petrol engine with 4F1R gearbox. Rear-wheel drive. Independent front suspension. 14-in. wheels. Wheelbase 2545 mm. Overall dimensions 4690 × 1690 × 1910 mm. Weight 1470 kg. Commercial panel van, used by several military forces (USAF shown), also as personnel carrier. 1981/82.

Van, 1.5-ton, 4 × 2   D
(Hanomag-Henschel F46)

4-cyl. 3.1-litre diesel engine (D142L1) with 5F1R gearbox. Rear-wheel drive. Wheelbase 3050 mm. Overall dimensions 5140 × 2100 × 2350 mm. Weight 2300 kg (approx.). Panel van body with windows. One of several types used in limited numbers by Welfare Dept (WZZ) of Netherlands Army. 1970s.

Van, 1.5-ton, 4 × 2   D
(Volkswagen LT31D)

4-cyl. 2.7-litre diesel engine with 4F1R gearbox. Rear-wheel drive. Wheelbase 2500 mm. Overall dimensions 4840 × 2020 × 2145 mm. Weight 1720 kg. GVW 3200 kg. From 1975. Used by several armed forces with various body styles. Example shown was employed by the Netherlands Air Force from 1978.

Van, 1.75-ton, 4 × 2   F
(Saviem SG2)

4-cyl. 2.6-litre petrol engine (or 3.3-litre diesel) with 4F1R gearbox. Rear-wheel drive (Model SB2 had front-wheel drive). French Army used several types from the late 1960s. Similar vehicles made under licence in Italy (Alfa-Romeo) and Czechoslovakia (Avia). SG3 had dual rear tyres.

Truck, 0.5-ton, 4 × 2, Pickup   USA
(Chevrolet C10)

Standard commercial Chevrolet Fleetside pickup (Model CC10703) as built from 1973 and widely used by the military. Available with 6- or V-8-cyl. petrol engine, manual or automatic gearbox. Wheelbase 2984 mm, overall length 4858 mm. The pickup box measured 1988 × 1829 mm.

Truck, 0.5-ton, 4 × 2, Pickup   USA
(Chevrolet C10)

Slightly modified commercial C10-Series Fleetside pickup of 1978, employed by the USAF (here by the Flying Supervisor at an overseas air base). Available with 6- or V-8-cyl. petrol or diesel engine and manual or automatic transmission, these trucks were also available with narrow cargo box (Stepside).

Truck, 0.5-ton, 4 × 2, Pickup　　　　　　　**USA**
(Dodge D100)
6-cyl. 3.7-litre 'Slant Six' petrol engine (V8 optional) with 3- or 4-speed gearbox (automatic available). Wheelbase 2896 mm. Lightest in a wide range of Dodge commercial pickup trucks. Styling shown was current (with detail mods, especially to the grille) from 1961 to 1971. Shown is a 1970 model of the USAF.

Truck, 0.5-ton, 4 × 2, Pickup　　　　　　　**USA**
(Dodge D100)
V-8-cyl. 5.2-litre petrol engine with 3F1R automatic transmission (6-cyl., larger V8 and manual gearbox available). Wheelbase 2921 mm. Overall length and width 4917 × 2019 mm. Styling shown current from 1972 to the 1980s with detail changes to grille and trim. 1972/73 model of the USAF shown.

Truck, 0.5-ton, 4 × 2, Pickup　　　　　　　**USA**
(Ford F100)
6-cyl. 3.9- or 4.9-litre petrol engine (V8s optional) with automatic transmission (manual optional). Wheelbase 2921 mm. Overall length 4635 mm. Commercial Ford Custom pickup of 1970 with Flareside body (Styleside was wider) with hoops and tarpaulin. Fords were widely used by all the US armed forces.

Truck, 0.5-ton, 4 × 2, Pickup　　　　　　　**AUS**
(Ford Falcon)
Typical example of Australian-built Ford Falcon 'utility'. Many were in service, of several model years (1971/72 shown) by Army, RAAF and RAN, often with canvas tarpaulin over wire-mesh-covered superstructure. Official nomenclature 'Car, CL, Light Utility'. Holdens were also used.

Truck, 0.75-ton, 4 × 2, Maintenance　　　　**USA**
(International 200)
During the early 1970s the US forces procured several batches of light-duty trucks from International Harvester with various body styles, e.g. panel vans, carryalls, pickups. This is a 1974/75 chassis/cab with telephone maintenance/repair bodywork. They all had V-8-cyl. petrol engines.

Truck, 0.9-ton, 4 × 2, Pickup　　　　　　　**PL**
(ZUK A-13)
4-cyl. 2.12-litre petrol engine (S-21) with 4F1R gearbox. Rear-wheel drive. Independent front suspension, rigid rear axle. 16-in. wheels. Wheelbase 2700 mm. Overall dimensions 4340 × 1820 × 2100 mm. Weight 1400 kg. Made by FSC Lublin, Poland, in the 1970s for civil and (para)military service.

Truck, 1-ton, 4 × 2, Pickup   **CDN**
(Ford F350)

6-cyl. or V-8-cyl. petrol engine with manual or automatic gearbox (several power trains available). Independent front suspension (Twin-I-Beam system). 16-in. wheels. Wheelbase 4229 mm. 1977-type Styleside pickup with 4-door crew cab and 2438-mm (8-ft) box, used by the Canadian Army.

Truck, 1-ton, 4 × 2, Pickup   **J**
(Toyota HI-LUX RN13)

4-cyl. 1.6-litre petrol engine with 4F1R gearbox. Rear-wheel drive. Independent front suspension. 14-in. wheels. Wheelbase 2535 mm. Overall length and width 4215 × 1580 mm. Commercial-type pickup with tilt, used as a utility truck by the Royal Australian Navy (Naval Dockyard Police). 1971.

Truck, 1-ton, 4 × 2, Pickup/Patrol   **J**
(Toyota Stout RK 101-J)

4-cyl. 2-litre petrol engine with 4F1R gearbox. Rear-wheel drive. Independent front suspension. 15-in. wheels. Wheelbase 2800 mm. Overall length and width 4670 × 1695 mm. Commercial pickup truck, modified to shore patrol wagon for use by the Royal Australian Navy in the early 1970s.

Truck, 1-ton, 4 × 2, Pickup   **D**
(Volkswagen Type 26)

4-cyl. 1.58-litre aircooled engine with 4F1R gearbox mounted at rear. Rear-wheel drive. Wheelbase 2400 mm. Overall dimensions 4420 × 1765 × 1955 mm. Weight 1260 kg. GVW 2260 kg. In service with the Swedish Army (and many other military users) with minor changes, including blackout lights.

Truck, 1-ton, 4 × 2, Pickup   **D**
(Volkswagen Transporter)

4-cyl. 1.6-litre aircooled petrol engine with 4F1R gearbox mounted at rear (2-litre engine optional). Wheelbase 2460 mm. Overall dimensions 4570 × 1870 × 1930 mm. Weight 1321 kg. GVW 2360 kg. 3-door cab, seating 5. Dropside rear body, measuring 1880 mm long by about 1850 mm wide. 1980.

Truck, 1.2-ton, 4 × 2, Pickup   **F**
(Peugeot 504 Pickup Armée)

4-cyl. 1.6-litre petrol (or 1.9-litre diesel) engine with 4F1R gearbox. Rear-wheel drive. Limited-slip diff. optional. Wheelbase 2900 mm. Offered especially for military use in developing countries. Carrying capacity was 10–13 men or 1200 kg. 4 × 4 conversion (Dangel) also available. From 1981.

Personnel Carriers and Buses

Most of the world's large motor-vehicle manufacturers offer a range of 'light commercials', usually forward-control models with a choice of engine and transmission options and with a wide variety of body styles, ranging from pickup trucks and panel vans to personnel carriers (vans with rear side windows and seats) and luxurious minibuses. The personnel-carrier type is extensively used by the military services of most if not all nations, for the conveyance of small parties of people and luggage. The rear seats usually being removable, these vehicles can also be employed for carrying light cargo as well as for general purposes.

The concept of these light commercials dates from the 1950s, when Volkswagen, at the instigation of their Dutch distributors, were one of the first manufacturers to offer the familiar and ubiquitous box-like flat-fronted type of vehicle with side and rear doors and the driver's seat right above the front wheels. The Volkswagen had the advantage of a rear-mounted engine, putting some weight on the driven rear wheels even when the vehicle was unladen. Models with the engine at the front were rather problematical when driven without any load, especially on slippery surfaces, and there was much experimenting by various manufacturers to combat this problem, resulting in front-wheel drive on some and placing the seats behind the front wheels on others, or both.

For the movement of larger groups of people, including military music bands, the forces employ medium- and full-size buses and coaches, usually from manufacturers' standard production ranges. Others are custom-bodied, if the buyer has special requirements. Some military buses, for example, have large rear doors and removable seats in the rear so that they can double up as large-capacity ambulances.

The US forces tend to use buses of the 'schoolbus' type with normal control and utility body rather than the more modern forward-control rear-engined type, although the latter are in service in some numbers, German Mercedes-Benz O303s included. As with other so-called 'administrative' vehicles, countries with large forces overseas often buy locally-produced passenger vehicles, rather than shipping out their own with all the problems of servicing, spare parts, and so on. This also applies to other non-tactical vehicles and they are often driven by local personnel.

Buses with all-wheel drive are distinctly rare. After the Second World War, when low-mileage GMC 2.5-ton 6 × 6 chassis were plentiful, many of these were fitted with bus bodies, known examples being those of the US Army in Germany, and the Austrian, French and Taiwanese armed forces. The latter were still using the GMC 6 × 6 bus in the early 1980s. The post-war US Army M-Series 2.5-ton 6 × 6 has occasionally been employed with bus bodywork, e.g. in Greece and, converted to four-wheel configuration, in Japan. The Austrian Army had a few 4 × 4 buses, on Gräf & Stift and ÖAF chassis.

It would appear that ACMAT of France is now the only manufacturer to offer military pattern 4 × 4 buses. Their *Bus, Tous Chemins, 28 Places, Aerotransportable* is based on the makers' normal-control 4 × 4 truck chassis with 12.50-20XL sand tyres and has functional flat-panelled coachwork with double rear doors of such dimensions that when fully open they do not protrude beyond the vehicle's width. Inside, it has two rows of four seats each arranged longitudinally in the rear and three rows placed cross-wise in front; between these seats, down the aisle, there are another three folding seats. All seats are upholstered with non-inflammable material. The body skeleton is strong enough for a load of up to 300 kg to be carried on the roof; for this purpose a luggage rail is fitted, as well as a folding ladder on the rear. Equipment of the ACMAT bus includes a Thomson radio-telephone installation and two large luggage lockers below the floor. With two fuel tanks, holding 185 litres each, and two jerricans (in carriers behind the front bumper), the radius of action of this vehicle is an impressive 1600 km. The ACMAT 4 × 4 bus is just one model in an extensive range of commercially-available military vehicles offered by this manufacturer, from command cars to 6 × 6 wreckers and armoured personnel carriers.

PERSONNEL CARRIERS AND BUSES

Carrier, Personnel, 4 × 2   **GB**
(Austin-Morris 250 JU)
4-cyl. petrol engine with 4F1R gearbox. Rear-wheel drive. Wheelbase 2896 mm. Overall dimensions 4432 × 1880 × 2197 mm. GVW 2540 kg. Earlier models had BMC badge. Fair numbers of utility vans and 7-seater minibuses (shown) were in service with the British Army and RAF throughout the 1970s.

Carrier, Personnel, 4 × 2   **E**
(Avia 1250)
4-cyl. 1.76-litre diesel engine (Perkins 4.108) with 4F1R gearbox. Rear-wheel drive (front-wheel drive on Model 1000). Rigid axles, 15-in. wheels. 8-seat bodywork. 3 side doors, double rear door. Other body options included van, truck and ambulance. They were also marketed as Ebro.

Carrier, Personnel, 4 × 2   **DDR**
(Barkas B1000)
3-cyl. 1-litre 2-stroke engine (312) with 4F1R gearbox. Front-wheel drive. Independent front and rear suspension with torsion bars. 13-in. wheels. Wheelbase 2400 mm. Overall dimensions 4520 × 1860 × 1850 mm. Max. speed 95 km/h. *Kleinbus* version of East German van made by VEB Barkas Werke.

Carrier, Personnel, 4 × 2   **GB**
(Bedford CF220 Series 97170)
4-cyl. 1.7-litre petrol engine (2.2-litre and diesel optional) with 4F1R gearbox. Rear-wheel drive. 13-in. wheels. Wheelbase 2692 mm. Overall dimensions 4262 × 2200 × 1988 mm. 12-seater coach conversion employed by British Army, RAF and RN (shown). Several versions were used, including Model CF250.

Carrier, Personnel, 4 × 2   **USA**
(Dodge Sportsman B100)
V-8-cyl. (6-cyl. optional) engine with manual or automatic transmission. Rear-wheel drive. Wheelbase 2769 mm. Overall length 4470 mm. Introduced in 1971 this type was produced until the 1980s with periodical detail changes. Sportsman was carryall version of Tradesman panel van. 1978 8-seater shown.

Carrier, Personnel, 4 × 2   **CDN/USA**
(Dodge Sportsman B200)
6-cyl. or V-8-cyl. petrol engine with automatic or manual transmission (wide range of power train options available). Rear-wheel drive. Wheelbase 3226 mm. Overall dimensions 5385 × 2030 × 2010 mm. Carryall version of panel van, widely used by the Canadian (shown) and US forces in the 1970s and early 1980s.

Carrier, Personnel, 4 × 2   **USA**
(Ford E150 Club Wagon)

V-8-cyl. 5.7-litre petrol engine with 3F1R gearbox. Rear-wheel drive. Wheelbase 3150 mm. 15-in. wheels. 1975 US pattern, used as 7-seater bus by Colombian Army. One of a range of Ford Econoline vans, which from 1975 had the new bevel-nose styling as shown, as well as disc brakes at front.

Carrier, Personnel, 4 × 2   **D/GB**
(Ford Transit FT100)

V-4-cyl. 1.7-litre petrol engine with 4F1R gearbox. Rear-wheel drive. 14-in. wheels. Wheelbase 2692 mm. This model dated from the mid-1970s and was operated by the Royal Netherlands Marines (or Navy). Transits were manufactured by Ford of Europe in plants in Genk, Belgium and in the UK.

Carrier, Personnel, 4 × 2   **D/GB**
(Ford Transit FT130)

V-4-cyl. 1.7-litre petrol engine with 4F1R gearbox. Rear-wheel drive. 14-in. wheels with 165-14 tyres, dual rear. Wheelbase 2997 mm. 1974 model, operated by the British RAF (44AC79) as 'Motor Coach, Small, 4 × 2, 14-seater'. RAFG (Germany) and Danish Army used left-hand-drive version.

Carrier, Personnel, 4 × 2   **GB**
(Leyland Sherpa 240)

4-cyl. 1.8-litre petrol engine (diesel optional) with 4F1R gearbox. Rear-wheel drive. Used in considerable numbers by British Army (incl. MP), RAF (shown) and RN, as 12-seater personnel carrier or for special purposes. It featured double rear doors and 12-Volt electrics with 16ACR alternator.

Carrier, Personnel, 4 × 2   **D**
(Mercedes-Benz 306D)

4-cyl. 2.2-litre diesel engine (OM615) with 4F1R gearbox. Front-wheel drive. Wheelbase 2940 mm. Overall dimensions 5030 × 1810 × 2080 mm. Originally derived from the Tempo Matador this was a Hanomag-Henschel product until this firm was absorbed by Daimler-Benz. Model shown was made during 1973–77.

Carrier, Personnel, 4 × 2   **PL**
(Nysa T521)

4-cyl. 2.12-litre petrol engine (S21) with 3F1R gearbox. Rear-wheel drive. Wheelbase 2700 mm. Overall dimensions 4500 × 1760 × 2050 mm. Weight 1545 kg. Personnel/cargo carrier (14-seater/800-kg) made by FSD Nysa, Poland, for civil and military service. Also ambulance, minibus and van versions. 1970s.

35

PERSONNEL CARRIERS AND BUSES

Carrier, Personnel, 4 × 2   **F**
(Renault Saviem SG2)
4-cyl. 2.6-litre petrol (or 3.3-litre diesel) engine with 4F1R gearbox. Rear-wheel drive. Independent front suspension. Wheelbase 2680 mm. Overall dimensions 4997 × 1996 × 2540 mm. In service with the French Air Force (shown; colour blue) and Army (light green). Converted 1.4-ton van. Late 1970s.

Carrier, Personnel, 4 × 4   **R**
(TV D12M)
4-cyl. 2.5-litre petrol engine (ARO L25) with 4F1R gearbox and single-speed transfer box. Rigid axles. Wheelbase 2450 mm. Overall dimensions 4700 × 1930 × 2340 mm. 10-seater, also available as 4 × 2. Many other body styles, incl. trucks, vans and ambulances, most in either 4 × 2 or 4 × 4. Made in Romania, 1980.

Carrier, Personnel, 4 × 2   **D**
(Volkswagen Type 22)
4-cyl. 1.58-litre aircooled petrol engine with 4F1R gearbox, mounted at the rear. Rear-wheel drive. Wheelbase 2400 mm. Overall dimensions 4445 × 1815 × 1940 mm. Weight 1375 kg. Early-1970s 9-seater of the Australian Army, which, like many armed forces, employed numerous VW light commercials.

Carrier, Personnel, 4 × 2   **D**
(Volkswagen Type 23)
4-cyl. 1.58-litre aircooled petrol engine with 4F1R gearbox mounted at rear. Rear-wheel drive. Wheelbase 2400 mm. Overall dimensions 4505 × 1720 × 1960 mm. Weight 1260 kg. GVW 2260 kg. Multipurpose vehicle. Example shown was used by the Danish Civil Defence from the mid-1970s.

Carrier, Personnel, 4 × 2   **D**
(Volkswagen Kombi)
4-cyl. 1.58-litre aircooled petrol engine with 4F1R gearbox mounted at rear (1.97-litre and diesel optional). Rear-wheel drive. Wheelbase 2460 mm. Overall dimensions 4570 × 1850 × 1950 mm. New styling as introduced in 1979. Example shown used by Canadian forces in Germany.

Carrier, Personnel, 4 × 2   **F**
(Berliet/Heuliez)
4-cyl. diesel engine with 5F1R gearbox. Rear-wheel drive. Airlam-type rear suspension. Used from the early 1970s by French Constabulary to carry operational intervention units. Featured window protectors, stowage for weapons, helmets, etc. Five doors provided for rapid entry and exit.

Bus, 21-passenger, 4 × 2   **D**
(Mercedes-Benz O309D)

4-cyl. 3.8-litre diesel engine (OM314V) with 5F1R gearbox. Rear-wheel drive. Wheelbase 3500 mm. Overall dimensions 5995 × 2100 × 2655 mm. Weight 3225 kg. GVW 4800 kg. Used by the *Bundeswehr* as *Kraftomnibus, klein*. Many other body styles, from 1973. Also known as the Mercedes 'Düsseldorfer' range.

Bus, 29-passenger, 4 × 2   **F**
(Saviem SG4)

4-cyl. 2.6-litre petrol (or 3.3-litre diesel) engine with 4F1R gearbox. Rear-wheel drive. Wheelbase 3240 mm. Coachwork by Carrosserie Carrier for French Army, 1973. Carrier produced many buses for the French forces and those of several overseas countries, as well as other types of military bodywork.

Bus, 30-passenger, 4 × 2   **USA**
(Chevrolet 60)

Typical American bus of a type traditionally used for transporting pupils to and from schools, hence the common name 'schoolbus'. Several companies mass-produced the bodywork, all to very similar specifications. This example, by Wayne, is on a lwb Chevrolet truck chassis, used by the Greek Navy.

Bus, 32-passenger, 4 × 2   **F**
(Saviem SG5)

4-cyl. 3.3-litre diesel engine with 4F1R gearbox. Wheelbase 3640 mm. Overall length and width 7260 × 2420 mm. Weight 4225 kg (approx). Bodied by Heuliez of Cerizay for the French Army in 1975. Louis Heuliez is a long-established manufacturer of bodywork for civilian and military vehicles.

Bus, 36-passenger, 4 × 2   **USA**
(Dodge S600)

V-8-cyl. 5.2-litre petrol engine (6-cyl. and larger V8 available) with 5F1R gearbox (4-speed and auto. trans. optional). Cast spoke wheels. Wheelbase 6096 mm. Front end styling of 1968–73; grille styling shown was used from 1971. Body by Wayne for USMC for use in Japan.

Bus, 36-passenger, 4 × 2   **GB**
(Ford R1014)

6-cyl. 5.95-litre turbocharged diesel engine with 6F1R gearbox. Wheelbase 4878 mm. British-built chassis with Danish bodywork for use by Danish Army as 'BUS T, VEJ: Ford, R1014, 4 × 2, D'. Ford's R-Series chassis were made from 1965. The Danes also used several types of Bedford buses.

Bus, 36-passenger, 4 × 2   **D**
(Mercedes-Benz O303)

V-8-cyl. 9.6-litre diesel engine (OM401) with 5F1R gearbox. Air suspension. Wheelbase 5083 mm. Overall dimensions 10090 × 2500 × 3050 mm. Weight 9250 kg. GVW 12400 kg. Luxembourg Army, late 1970s. *Bundeswehr* used similar O303-11RHP and -KR. Other O303-Series users included Belgian, Dutch and US forces.

Bus, 37-passenger, 4 × 2   **GB**
(Bedford SB)

Bodied by Marshall of Cambridge (Engineering) this was a typical example of the numerous Bedford-based passenger vehicles used by the British forces at home and abroad. The SB chassis had a wheelbase length of 5486 mm and was available with either petrol or diesel engine. RAF bus shown.

Bus, 39-passenger, 4 × 2   **NL**
(DAF SB1600DT)

6-cyl. 6.17-litre turbocharged diesel engine (DT615), mounted longitudinally behind the rear axle with 5F1R gearbox (ZF, overdrive top). Semi-elliptic leaf springs. Dual-circuit air brakes. Wheelbase 4700 mm. Supplied in 1973 to AFCENT (NATO, central region). RC prefix of reg. number stands for Resource Central.

Bus, 39-passenger, 4 × 2   **S**
(Scania B110)

6-cyl. 11-litre diesel engine (D11) with 5F1R gearbox (G761). Overall dimensions 11095 × 2500 × 3100 mm. Light alloy bodywork by H. Höglund of Säffle. 18 units supplied in 1973 for Swedish Air Force for personnel transport. Could be utilized also for ambulance work.

Bus, 40-passenger, 4 × 2   **USA**
(Ford B600)

V-8-cyl. 5.4-litre petrol engine with 5F1R gearbox. 2-speed rear axle optional. Air brakes with rear-wheel skid-control system. Cast spoke wheels. Bodywork of typical American 'schoolbus' style, made by Superior in the mid-1970s. In service with the Army of Colombia, South America.

Bus, 40-passenger, 4 × 2   **J**
(Hino RC)

6-cyl. 10.2-litre diesel engine, mounted under the floor at the rear. Right-hand drive. Australian bodywork, produced for Royal Australian Air Force in the early 1970s. Colour white, with chrome bumpers. Other military users of Hino buses included the Royal Australian Navy and the US Army in Japan.

**Bus, 40-passenger, 4 × 2
(Volvo F86)** S

6-cyl. 6.7-litre diesel engine (TD70A) with dual-range 4F1R gearbox. Wheelbase 5500 mm. Overall dimensions 10050 × 2500 × 3230 mm. Weight 8630 kg. Bodywork by Hägglunds, 1970/71, for Swedish Army. Convertible for use as ambulance or cargo carrier. GVW 13200 kg. Large doors at rear.

**Bus, 41-passenger, 4 × 2
(Volvo BB57)** S

Employed by the Swedish armed forces from 1976, this was one of a batch of dual-purpose buses built by Van Hool of Belgium on 6000-mm wheelbase Volvo chassis. Overall dimensions 10850 × 2500 × 3200 mm. They featured spacious underfloor luggage lockers and large double loading doors at the rear.

**Bus, 42-passenger, 4 × 2
(Mercedes-Benz O302/11R)** D

6-cyl. 5.67-litre diesel engine (OM352) with 5F1R gearbox mounted at rear. Wheelbase 5050 mm. Overall dimensions 10130 × 2490 × 2900 mm. GVW 12000 kg. Bodywork by Jonckheere for Belgian Army, 1976. Convertible for ambulance use. Jonckheere supplied several types of DAF- and Mercedes-based bus.

**Bus, 45-passenger, 4 × 2
(DAF SB1600DF605)** NL

6-cyl. diesel engine (DF615) mounted at the rear. 2-speed rear axle. Air brakes. Wheelbase 6050 mm. Weight 9200 kg. Coachwork of austere design by Hainje of Heerenveen, Netherlands, for the Dutch Army, Navy (shown) and Air Force. Produced in the early 1970s. Carrying capacity 45 passengers plus 620 kg.

**Bus, 45-passenger, 4 × 2
(GMC DSPA-5019)** USA

V-8-cyl. diesel engine (Cummins). Also built with 6-cyl. diesel. Wheelbase 4420 mm. Overall dimensions 9296 × 2438 × 3110 mm. One of 483 buses built by GMC and Superior for US Army and USN. Example shown was new in 1965, demobbed (in Belgium) in 1982. Could also be used as large ambulance.

**Bus, 53-passenger, 4 × 2
(Saviem E7)** F

6-cyl. 10.7-litre diesel engine (MAN) with 5F1R gearbox plus overdrive. Wheelbase 6230 mm. Overall dimensions 11450 × 2500 × 2920 mm. GVW 15000 kg. Standard production Renault/Saviem bus, operated by the Canadian forces in Germany, 1981/82. French forces were large-scale users of Saviem buses.

PERSONNEL CARRIERS AND BUSES

Bus, 55-passenger, 4 × 2   **GB**
(Leyland Reliance 6U3ZR)

6-cyl. centrally-mounted diesel engine (AEC AH760) with 6F1R gearbox (ZF). Single-reduction rear axle. Air brakes. Bodywork of bolted construction by Marshall of Cambridge. Supplied with rhd or lhd, the latter for BAOR in Germany where by 1978 140 Reliance buses were in service.

Bus, 55-passenger, 4 × 2   **S**
(Volvo B58)

6-cyl. 9.6-litre underfloor diesel engine (THD100D) with semi-automatic 4F1R gearbox. 2-speed rear axle. Wheelbase 6000 mm. Overall length and width 12000 × 2400 mm. GVW 16000 kg. Used by Peruvian Air Force (*Fuerza Aerea del Peru*) from 1976. Peruvian armed forces operated many Volvos at the time.

Bus, 28-passenger, 4 × 4   **F**
(ALM/ACMAT VLRA TPK4.32SB)

6-cyl. 5.8-litre diesel engine (Perkins 6.354.4) with 4F1R gearbox and 2-speed transfer box. Rigid axles with 12.50–20XL tyres. Wheelbase 4300 mm. Overall dimensions 7155 × 2200 × 2800 mm. Weight 5634 kg. GVW 7810 kg. Ground clearance 273 mm. Produced in the early 1980s.

Bus, 29-passenger, 4 × 4   **USA**
(Reo M-Series)

Based on modified M-Series 2.5-ton 6 × 6 chassis (converted to two axles) these buses were produced for military service in Japan, where this photo was taken in 1973. In the early 1950s there had been an experimental 4 × 4 version of the M34 6 × 6 cargo truck, with wheelbase size 3454 mm (XM381).

Bus, 35-passenger, 4 × 4   **A**
(Gräf & Stift OLA210/54)

6-cyl. 10.8-litre diesel engine (Daimler-Benz OM346 I) with 6F1R gearbox and 2-speed transfer box. Hardy Westinghouse air brakes. Wheelbase 5360 mm. Overall dimensions 9400 × 2500 × 3160 mm. Weight 9200 kg. Ground clearance 300 mm. 2 supplied to the Austrian Federal Army (*Bundesheer*) in 1970.

Bus, 35-passenger, 6 × 6   **USA**
(Reo M-Series)

Using the US military M-Series 2.5-ton chassis this bus of the Greek Air Force was bodied by the Greek firm of Tangalakis. This bodybuilder also produced military buses on imported US commercial bus chassis. The Greek forces used a wide range of US military automotive equipment. Photo taken in 1972.

Medical Vehicles

The majority of medical vehicles serving the military forces are ambulances and these exist in two main categories: the commercial type (usually on 4 × 2 chassis, sometimes known as the 'metropolitan' type) and the tactical type (all-wheel-drive field or front-line ambulances). The former are either special-bodied or, increasingly, converted panel vans. Field ambulances are usually based on 4 × 4 and 6 × 6 chassis which are already on the strength of the armed force concerned; they vary from stretcher kits mounted on utility trucks like the 0.25-ton Jeep and Land-Rover to purpose-built enclosures on these and heavier chassis. The commercial-type ambulance is generally equipped with two stretchers ('litters' in American parlance), one above the other, and a wheeled chair, plus seats for medical attendants, lockers for blankets and first-aid material, and a good heating system. Some of these models are fairly large and can carry four or even more stretchers. Field ambulances are either military pattern or based on commercially-available all-wheel-drive chassis, many of the latter being quite acceptable for military service.

Unusual among the six-wheeled types is the US Army's M792, the ambulance version of the controversial M561 'Gama Goat'. The M561 was a high-mobility cargo truck of unique design. Rather complicated and over-engineered it was in theory a first-class cross-country vehicle and the prototypes, built by Ling-Temco-Vought Aerospace Corp. (LTV) of Dallas, Texas, in the early 1960s behaved extremely well during Army evaluation trials. So well, in fact, that after further development it was approved for quantity production in 1966. In the 'open-bid competition' system, the contract for some 15000 units was won by Consolidated Diesel Division of Condec Corporation in Schenectady, New York. The ambulance variant differed from the cargo truck in that the rear compartment, or carrier part of the centre-jointed vehicle, had an insulated canopy assembly with, inside, a fuel-burning heater, three stretchers, an attendant's seat, seat cushions and head pads, lighting, a dispenser bracket assembly and on the tailgate a hinged step. The 'Gama Goat' in the hands of the troops turned out to be unsatisfactory in many respects and plans were soon made to replace all tactical vehicles in the US Army's '1/4- to 5/4-ton' inventory by another new

adventure: the High-Mobility Multipurpose Wheeled Vehicle (HMMWV or 'Humvee'). This vehicle concept was required to incorporate several front-line ambulance kits, namely:

Maxi-ambulance: a four-stretcher glassfibre body with hinge-up rear door; upper stretchers can be lowered to carry sitting patients; transportable in current military aircraft.

Mini-ambulances: glassfibre shelter-type body with two-position top, providing, when raised, the same crew- and patients-carrying capability as the Maxi type; transportable inside CH-47 and CH-53 helicopters.

Softtop ambulance: utilizing the same enclosure as the troop-transport version, this vehicle can transport up to eight patients.

All these versions were designed to be interchangeable and could be installed on the base vehicle at the 'direct support' level. Prototypes for the new 'Humvee' vehicles were developed in the late 1970s and early 1980s by AM General Corporation, General Dynamics, and Teledyne Continental. Several of these are shown and described elsewhere in this book.

Interesting newcomers in the field of front-line ambulances are the products of Keohwa of South Korea. Basing all their models on the proven US Jeep family (0.25- to 1.25-ton 4 × 4), with many added refinements, their line of vehicles makes a lot of sense. The ambulance versions are:

M-7GA6: 0.25-ton utility truck with canvas top, two stretchers to the right of the driver.
M-20G6: 1.25-ton with shelter-type body, two stretchers; described by the makers as 'literally a mobile hospital, capable of transporting and providing emergency medical treatment to a large number of wounded personnel'.

Also in the category of medical vehicles are vans used for the transportation of blood plasma, dental and X-ray vans, etc. These are relatively rare and often constitute one-off models. (For large-capacity ambulances the reader is referred to the chapter entitled 'Personnel Carriers and Buses'.)

MEDICAL VEHICLES

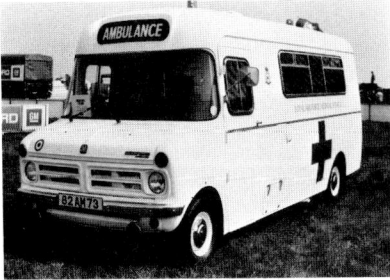

Ambulance, 2/3-stretcher, 4 × 2 **GB**
(Bedford CF280)

4-cyl. 2.3-litre petrol engine with automatic transmission (GM). Rear-wheel drive. Independent front suspension. Rack and pinion steering. Dual-circuit hydraulic brakes with servo assistance. Wheelbase 3200 mm. GVW 2730 kg. Produced in 1977/78 as chassis/cowl, bodied by outside manufacturer for the RAF.

Ambulance, 2-stretcher, 4 × 2 **USA**
(Chevrolet Chevy Van G30)

High-roof ambulance conversion of standard Chevrolet panel van, supplied to the USAF in 1979. Basic vehicle was used for many commercial ambulances and was available with a choice of petrol engines (from 4.1-litre Six to 6.6-litre V8) and manual or automatic transmission. Rear-wheel drive.

Ambulance, 2-stretcher, 4 × 2 **F**
(Citroën H1600)

4-cyl. 1.9-litre petrol engine with 3F1R gearbox. Front-wheel drive. Extended wheelbase. In the mid-1970s the Netherlands Army acquired a batch of these vehicles in green (shown) and white livery. There was a large window on the right-hand side of the rear compartment.

Ambulance, 2-stretcher, 4 × 2 **D**
(Ford Transit FT1100)

V-4-cyl. 2-litre petrol engine with 4F1R gearbox. Rear-wheel drive. Wheelbase 2692 mm. Overall dimensions 4420 × 1960 × 2300 mm. Weight 1600 kg. Christian Miesen conversion of Transit Kombi, 1970 pattern. Used by German *Bundeswehr*, superseding 1965 type and preceding Taunus Transits.

Ambulance, 2-stretcher, 4 × 2 **F**
(Peugeot J7)

4-cyl. petrol engine with 4F1R gearbox. Front-wheel drive. Independent suspension. Wheelbase 2500 mm. Overall dimensions 4750 × 2000 × 2350 mm. Weight 1800 kg. Ambulance conversion of commercial panel van with double rear doors, in service with the Royal Netherlands Navy. 1970s.

Ambulance, 2-stretcher, 4 × 2 **D**
(Volkswagen Type 2)

4-cyl. 1.58-litre aircooled petrol engine with 4F1R gearbox mounted at rear. Wheelbase 2400 mm. Overall dimensions 4505 × 1720 × 2250 mm. Weight 1515 kg. GVW 2100 kg. In service with the Belgian Army from the mid-1970s. Equipment included two stretchers, one wheelchair, oxygen apparatus, etc.

Ambulance, 4-stretcher, 4 × 2   **D**
(Mercedes-Benz L406)

4-cyl. 2-litre petrol engine (diesel optional) with 4F1R gearbox. Rear-wheel drive. Wheelbase 3500 mm. Overall length and width 5990 × 2100 mm. GVW 5190 kg. One of a wide range of Mercedes-Benz light commercials, modified for ambulance work in Denmark, 1972. Colour green, some were red.

Ambulance, 6-stretcher, 4 × 2   **F**
(Saviem SG2)

4-cyl. 2.6-litre petrol engine with 4F1R gearbox. Rear-wheel drive. Wheelbase 2680 mm. Ambulance conversion of standard SG2 panel van by Carrosserie Carrier of Alençon. Capacity 6 stretcher cases and 2 seated or up to 14 sitting patients. Also 4 × 4 version, offered for export in the late 1970s.

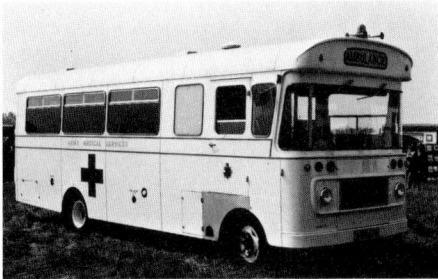

Ambulance, Large, 4 × 2   **GB**
(Bedford VAS/POK)

6-cyl. 5.4-litre diesel or 4.9-litre petrol engine (Bedford 330–98 and 300–114 resp.). Wheelbase 4167 mm. GVW 6577 kg. Chassis designed for 25- to 32-passenger buses. This was a special unit, bodied by Wadham Stringer for the British Army Medical Services in 1977/78. Photographed in mid-1978.

Van, 1-ton, 4 × 2, Medical   **F**
(Peugeot J7F)

4-cyl. 1.8-litre petrol engine with 4F1R gearbox. Front-wheel drive. Wheelbase 2500 mm. Special bodywork, refrigerated for transport of blood plasma. Belgian Army, mid-1970s. Cryogal PS108 cooling system. Loading door on left. Peugeot J7 range succeeded the D4B (from 1955) in 1965.

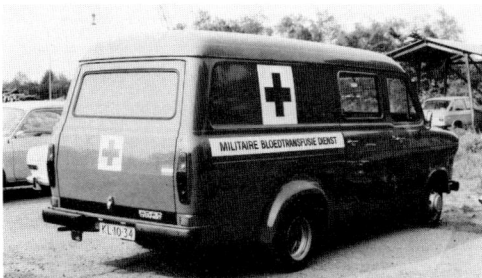

Van, 1.25-ton, 4 × 2, Medical   **D**
(Ford Transit FT130)

4-cyl. 2-litre petrol engine with 4F1R gearbox. Rear-wheel drive. 14-in. wheels with 165R14 tyres, dual rear. Supplied in 1976 to the Netherlands Army's Blood-Transfusion Service (MBTD) and in service until 1981. Note the one-piece rear door and additional side doors.

Truck, 4-ton, 4 × 2, Dental Van   **D**
(Mercedes-Benz LK911B/36)

6-cyl. 5.67-litre diesel engine (OM352) with 5F1R gearbox. Wheelbase 3600 mm. Commercial truck with special bodywork (Christian Miesen) for dental service, used by West German *Bundeswehr*. Picture taken in the mid-1970s. This chassis was used for various military applications, both in 4 × 2 and 4 × 4.

MEDICAL VEHICLES

Truck, 0.25-ton, 4 × 4, Ambulance   **USA**
(AMG M718A1)

4-cyl. 2.3-litre petrol engine with 4F1R gearbox, single-speed transfer box. Wheelbase 2159 mm. Overall dimensions 3632 × 1819 × 1938 mm. Weight 1247 kg. Accommodation for up to 3 stretcher patients. Angle of departure 36°. Derived from M151A2 utility truck by AM General.

Truck, 0.25-ton, 4 × 4, Ambulance   **ROK**
(Asia Motors KM411)

4-cyl. 1.98-litre petrol engine with 4F1R gearbox and 2-speed transfer box. Wheelbase 2032 mm. Overall length and width (without stretcher gear) 3350 × 1475 mm. GVW 1720 kg. Max. speed 96 km/h. Cruising range 340 km. 2 stretchers. Modification of Korean Army standard 0.25-ton 4 × 4. Late 1970s.

Truck, 0.25-ton, 4 × 4, Ambulance   **ROK**
(Keohwa M-7GA6)

6-cyl. 4.2-litre petrol engine (diesel optional) with 4F1R gearbox and 2-speed transfer box. Wheelbase 2390 mm. Overall dimensions 3990 × 1800 × 1935 mm. Weight 1500 kg. GVW 2200 kg. Max. speed 140 km/h. Angles of approach and departure 45° and 30°. Produced by Keohwa of Seoul, South Korea. Early 1980s.

Truck, 0.25-ton, 4 × 4, Ambulance   **AUS**
(Land-Rover 88 Series IIA)

4-cyl. 2.2-litre petrol engine with 4F1R gearbox and 2-speed transfer box. Wheelbase 2235 mm. Basically a standard Australian short-wheelbase Land-Rover GS vehicle, fitted with stretcher conversion kit and extended canvas awning to suit. Assembled in Australia, these featured different front wing cut-outs.

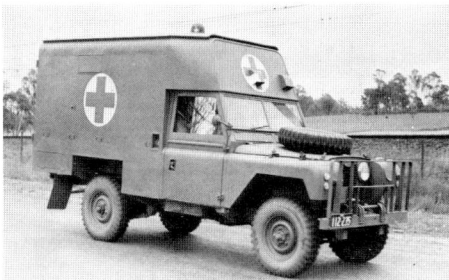

Truck, 0.75-ton, 4 × 4, Ambulance   **AUS**
(Land-Rover 109 Series IIA)

Australian Army 4-stretcher field ambulance on long-wheelbase Land-Rover chassis, assembled and bodied in Australia, used during the 1960s and 1970s. Vehicle shown was rare in being fitted with a capstan winch behind the front bumper. Photo was taken in 1973. Note absence of below-door panels.

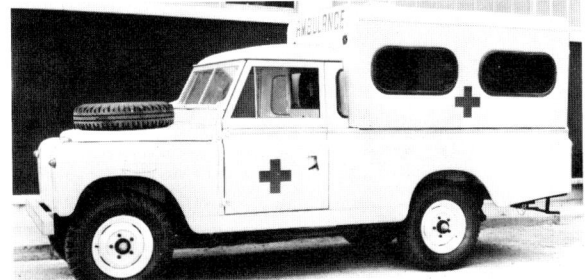

Truck, 0.75-ton, 4 × 4, Ambulance   **GB**
(Land-Rover 109 Series IIA)

This was basically the standard long-wheelbase Land-Rover pickup truck with cab, converted to field ambulance for the South African Army. The bodywork was essentially a tall hardtop enclosure with full-height double doors at the rear, fitted with stretchers, seats, first-aid and other appropriate equipment.

Truck, 0.75-ton, 4 × 4, Ambulance GB
(Land-Rover 109 Series IIA)

Field ambulance modification of long-wheelbase Land-Rover with 'windowed' hardtop, tropical roof, double vertical rear doors, rear step and appropriate interior equipment. This vehicle was in service with the armed forces of Mauretania and may have been supplied by Santana of Spain.

Truck, 0.75-ton, 4 × 4, Ambulance GB
(Land-Rover 109 Series IIA)

4-cyl. petrol engine with 4F1R gearbox and 2-speed transfer box. Wheelbase 2768 mm. Overall dimensions 4830 × 1900 × 2500 mm. Weight 1930 kg GVW 2670 kg. Bodywork by Marshall of Cambridge. Known in British Army as 'FV18067/18073 Ambulance, 2/4-stretcher (Rover 11)'. Also on Series III chassis.

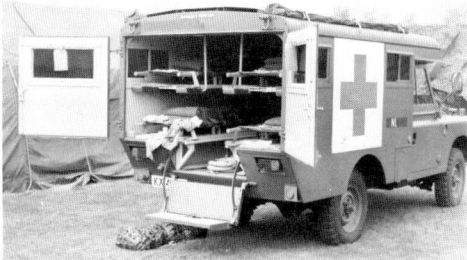

Truck, 0.75-ton, 4 × 4, Ambulance GB
(Land-Rover 109 Series III)

4-cyl. 2.28-litre diesel engine with 4F1R gearbox and 2-speed transfer box. One of 537 supplied to the Netherlands Army in the early 1980s to replace DAF YA126 ambulance and Jeep-mounted stretcher kits. Bodywork by Marshall of Cambridge. Generally similar to the British Army version but diesel-engined.

Truck, 0.8-ton, 4 × 4, Ambulance D
(Mercedes-Benz 230G)

4-cyl. 2.3-litre petrol engine (M115) with 4F1R gearbox and 2-speed transfer box. Rigid axles with coil spring suspension. Wheelbase 2850 mm. GVW 2800 kg. Chassis/cab supplied by Daimler-Benz, ambulance bodywork and equipment by Binz of Lorch, Baden-Württemberg.

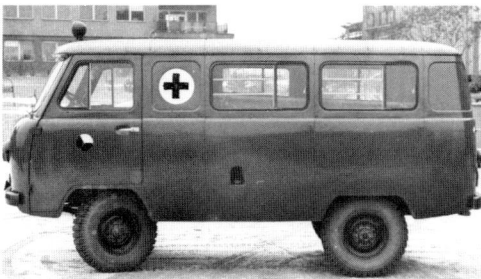

Truck, 0.8-ton, 4 × 4, Ambulance SU
(UAZ-452A)

4-cyl. 2.4-litre petrol engine (ZMZ-451E) with 4F1R gearbox and 2-speed transfer box. Rigid axles with 15-in. wheels. Wheelbase 2300 mm. Overall dimensions 4360 × 1940 × 2090 mm. Weight 1950 kg. Carrying capacity varying from 9 sitting patients to 4 stretchers and 3 sitting cases. Used in civil and military service.

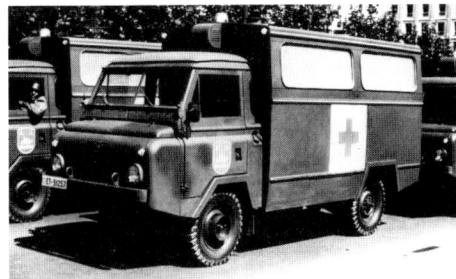

Truck, 1-ton, 4 × 4, Ambulance E
(Land-Rover/Santana 1300)

4-cyl. 2.28-litre petrol (or diesel) engine with 4F1R gearbox and 2-speed transfer box. Wheelbase 2770 mm. Overall length and width 4840 × 1690 mm. Weight 1900 kg (approx.). GVW (with petrol engine) 3060 kg. Produced, also with several other body styles, by the Spanish Land-Rover licencee Santana.

Truck, 1-ton, 4 × 4, Ambulance   **GB**
(Land-Rover 101)
V-8-cyl. petrol engine, 4F1R gearbox with 2-speed transfer box. Full-time 4-wheel drive. Wheelbase 2185. Overall dimensions 4394 × 2130 × 2520 mm. Weight 2800 kg. GVW 3650 kg. 4-stretcher bodywork by Marshall of Cambridge, panelled in aluminium, thermally insulated and fully equipped.

Truck, 1.2-ton, 4 × 4, Ambulance   **F**
(Renault TRM1200/Saviem TP3)
4-cyl. 2.6-litre petrol engine (817-04) with 4F1R gearbox and 2-speed transfer box. Wheelbase 2640 mm. Overall dimensions 4963 × 1996 × 2692 mm. Weight 2975 kg. 6-stretcher ambulance, introduced in the early 1970s on chassis of TRM1200 1.2-ton 4 × 4 truck (qv). Both were in service with the French Army.

Truck, 1.25-ton, 4 × 4, Ambulance   **CDN**
(Chevrolet K20)
V-8-cyl. 5.7-litre (350 CID) petrol engine with automatic transmission. Tyre size 8.75-16.5C. Wheelbase 3340 mm. Produced by General Motors of Canada for Canadian Army. 4-stretcher aluminium-panelled shelter-type body with double rear doors. From 1976.

Truck, 1.25-ton, 4 × 4, Ambulance   **USA**
(Dodge W200/M886)
V-8-cyl. 5.2-litre petrol engine with 3F1R automatic transmission and 2-speed transfer box. Full-time 4-wheel drive. Wheelbase 3327 mm. Overall dimensions 5461 × 2019 × 2565 mm. Weight 2777 kg. GVW 3630 kg. 4-stretcher type based on Dodge W200 of 1976/77. 4 × 2 M893 was 432 kg lighter, 76 mm lower.

Truck, 1.25-ton, 4 × 4, Ambulance   **USA**
(Kaiser Jeep M725)
6-cyl. 3.7-litre ohc petrol engine with 4F1R gearbox and 2-speed transfer box. Wheelbase 3200 mm. Overall dimensions 5328 × 2159 × 2413 mm. Weight 2906 kg. After completion of US military contracts in the early 1970s, vehicle was continued in production as AM715 (AM General) and sold to other armed forces.

Truck, 1.25-ton, 4 × 4, Ambulance   **ROK**
(Keohwa M-20G6)
6-cyl. 4.2-litre petrol engine with 4F1R gearbox and 2-speed transfer box. Wheelbase 3330 mm. Overall dimensions 5360 × 2000 × 2500 mm. Weight 2400 kg. GVW 3650 kg. Max. speed 130 km/h. Accommodation for 2 stretchers and 4 sitting patients. Available with oxygen inhalers and air-conditioning system.

**Truck, 1.25-ton, 4 × 4, Ambulance   USA
(Teledyne HMMWV)**

V-8-cyl. 6.9-litre diesel engine (IHC) with 3F1R auto. trans. (GM). Independent suspension. Wheelbase 3302 mm. Maxi-ambulance configuration of prototype High-Mobility Multipurpose Wheeled Vehicle (HMMWV) for US Army, 1981/82. Also made in mini-ambulance with 2-position roof.

**Truck, 1.5-ton, 4 × 4, Ambulance   GB
(Stonefield P3000)**

V-6-cyl. 3-litre petrol engine (Ford) with 3F1R automatic gearbox and 2-speed transfer box. Full-time 4-wheel drive. Wheelbase 2800 mm. Prototype vehicle, 1978. 4-stretcher bodywork by Pilcher-Greene of Burgess Hill, Sussex. Chassis/cab was produced in Scotland and offered with various power train options.

**Truck, 1.5-ton, 4 × 4, Ambulance   D
(Unimog 404.0)**

6-cyl. 2.7-litre petrol engine (M130) with 6F2R gearbox/transfer box. Rigid portal-type axles with coil springs. Wheelbase 2900 mm. GVW 5000 kg. Standardized van body with double rear doors, fitted out for ambulance role. In service with the Netherlands Royal Marines (shown) and Air Force from the mid-1970s.

**Truck, 1.8-ton, 4 × 4, Ambulance   IL
(AIL M325)**

6-cyl. 3.68-litre petrol engine (Chrysler) with 4F1R gearbox and 2-speed transfer box. Wheelbase 3200 mm. Made in Israel, using Chrysler mechanical components. Full-width double rear doors. Support brackets for maximum of 4 stretchers. Earlier AIL-built ambulances were based on Dodge WM300 Power Wagon chassis.

**Truck, 2-ton, 4 × 4, Ambulance   D
(Magirus-Deutz 130M7FAL)**

6-cyl. 6.1-litre aircooled diesel engine (Deutz F6L 913) with 5F1R gearbox (ZF AK5-35/2) and 2-speed transfer box. Banjo-type axles with leaf springs and 20-in. wheels. Wheelbase 2850 mm. Chassis/cab dimensions 5435 × 2360 × 2783 mm. Weight 3830 kg. GVW 7500 kg. 4-stretcher bodywork. Late 1970s.

**Truck, 2-ton, 4 × 4, Ambulance   J
(Toyota Type 73)**

6-cyl. diesel engine with 5F1R gearbox and 2-speed transfer box. Rigid axles with semi-elliptic leaf-spring suspension and 20-in. wheels. Overall length and width 5300 × 2100 mm (approx.). All-steel cab and integral bodywork with double rear doors on standardized Type 73 medium truck chassis.

Truck, 2-ton, 4 × 4, Ambulance   **D**
(Unimog U1300L)

6-cyl. 5.67-litre diesel engine (OM352) with 8F8R gearbox/transfer box. Rigid portal axles with coil springs. Wheelbase 3250 mm. Bodywork and equipment by Christian Miesen of Bonn. Capacity 4 stretchers and 4 sitting cases. In the early 1980s, 3000 were ordered to replace the *Bundeswehr*'s old Unimog S404.

Truck, 2-ton, 4 × 4, Ambulance   **S**
(Volvo C304/4140 Series)

6-cyl. 2.98-litre twin-carburettor engine (B30) with 4F1R gearbox and 2-speed transfer box. Rigid portal-type axles with stepdown gearing and leaf springs. Wheelbase 2530 mm. GVW 4050 kg. Shelter-type 4-stretcher ambulance bodywork. Fitted with winch and right-hand drive for export to Far East. 1974.

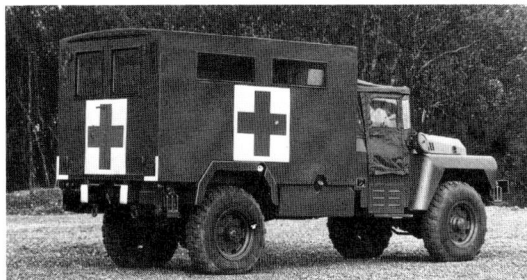

Truck, 2.5-ton, 4 × 4, Ambulance   **F**
(ALM/ACMAT VLRA TPK420SAM)

6-cyl. 5.8-litre diesel engine (Perkins 6.354) with 4F1R gearbox and 2-speed transfer box. Wheelbase 3600 mm. Overall dimensions 5805 × 2036 × 2515 mm. Weight 4500 kg. 4-stretcher bodywork, equipped with 200-litre water reservoir, etc. Commercially-available military vehicle, produced at St. Nazaire, France.

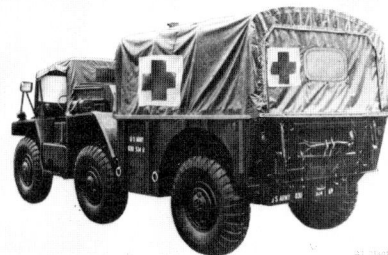

Truck, 1.25-ton, 6 × 6, Ambulance   **USA**
(Consolidated Diesel 2252/M792)

3-cyl. 2.6-litre diesel engine (Detroit Diesel 3-53) with 4F1R gearbox and 2-speed transfer box. Wheelbase 2050 + 2154 mm. Modification of M561 cargo truck (qv) with capacity for 3 stretchers (litters) or 2 stretchers and 3 sitting patients. Rear compartments had insulated canopy, heater, etc. Early 1970s.

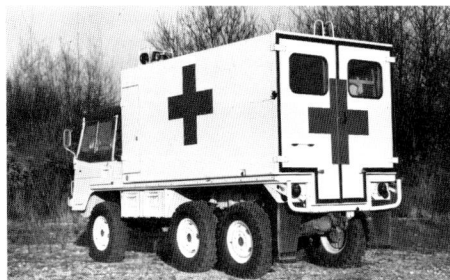

Truck, 1.5-ton, 6 × 6, Ambulance   **A**
(Steyr-Daimler-Puch Pinzgauer 712 Sa. 6 × 6)

2.5-litre 4-cyl. aircooled petrol engine with 5F1R gearbox and 2-speed transfer box. Wheelbase 2490 mm. Overall dimensions 4890 × 1790 × 2800 mm. Weight 2850 mm. Body shell of glass-fibre, made and fitted out by E. Flückiger of Huttwil, Switzerland, for Swiss Army. 4 stretchers. Based on 712M chassis.

Truck, 1.5-ton, 6 × 6, Ambulance   **S**
(Volvo C 03 6 × 6-2-V)

6-cyl. 2.98-litre petrol engine (B30A) with 4F1R gearbox and 2-speed transfer box. Wheelbase 2825 mm. Overall dimensions 5350 × 1900 × 3000 mm. GVW 4500 kg. 5-stretcher body by Specialkarosser of Åtran, Sweden, for Swedish Army. Also 4-stretcher (conveyance) version.

Field Cars/Utility Trucks

The world's military four-wheel-drive light utility truck field has long term been dominated by the US Jeep. During the Second World War, 'jeep' was the universally-accepted nickname for the 'Truck, $\frac{1}{4}$-ton, 4 × 4, Command Reconnaissance' as mass-produced by Willys (MB) and Ford (GPW) and after 1945, when Jeep became an official trademark, Willys continued production of this versatile and ubiquitous vehicle in civilian and military variants. Production of modernized developments also continued when Willys became Kaiser Jeep and, later, Jeep Corporation. By the 1980s, Jeep Corp. and AM General Corp., both as subsidiaries of American Motors, still offered the $\frac{1}{4}$-ton 4 × 4 truck although the name 'Jeep' was applied chiefly to the civilian versions, which also included larger-sized station wagons, trucks, etc.

After 'jeep' had become Jeep, as a registered trademark in the immediate post-war period, the name could no longer be applied officially to the vehicle as a type (a type which had been originated mainly by American Bantam and the US Army in 1940, developed with the aid of Willys and Ford, and produced by numerous manufacturers, with periodic changes, until the present day). However, much to the chagrin of the legal owners of the name, 'jeep' has been used as a generic epithet for this type of vehicle ever since the war and it has proved impossible to persuade the masses, both the public at large and those who know better, to refrain from doing so. Two factors contributed to this habit. First, the name 'jeep' had become so stuck and proved so popular and fitting that a suitable alternative collective international name has never been invented, and secondly, the licencees of Jeep vehicles in many countries around the world could rightfully use the name for their products. Looking at it the other way round, only a very few similar vehicles have managed to establish such an identity of their own, e.g. the Land-Rover and the Toyota Land Cruiser. Indeed, in the media one frequently comes across the name 'landrover' (sic) as a generic name in its own right, and Newsweek (1 March 1982) reported the president of Burundi 'roaming the countryside in a range rover'. It does not look as if this problem is ever going to be solved.

Meanwhile, in the early 1980s, the US Government decided that it was time to terminate the role of the quarter-ton truck in the armed forces and replace it – along with several other light vehicle types in the up to 1.25-ton classes – by a new multipurpose machine with more space, better performance, a diesel engine with automatic transmission and considerably improved 'creature comforts'. Three manufacturers invested a lot of experience and money in prototypes (as will be seen in the following pages) and these were rigorously tested by the military. Whether this decision will also prove correct and ultimately successful in the eyes of the taxpayers remains to be seen. It is thought unlikely to be a wise decision to replace the quarter-ton by a diesel-powered high-performance king-size off-roader, unless another low-cost economical-to-operate replacement is acquired for those 'administrative' jobs for which the quarter-ton in peacetime has traditionally been used most. The Jeep in basically similar form to the original will remain in production for some time to come, particularly in developing countries, e.g. Brazil, India, South Korea.

In this chapter we present a representative number of what could best be called 'utility cars' or 'field cars' and 'utility trucks'. The former are passenger/cargo-carrying vehicles with all-wheel drive, usually with station-wagon-type bodywork and a fixed or detachable roof, and the latter comprising those vehicles which could be considered to have derived from the original 'jeep', including sophisticated state-of-the-art developments which are a far cry from their famous progenitor. 4 × 2 types may be found in an earlier chapter. It is quite noticeable that many, if not most, of the modern field cars and utility trucks are de/facto militarized commercial types (the reverse occasionally also occurs) and that relatively few are built exclusively for military use. A good example of the latter is the US M151A2, which upon demob after its military career is not even allowed to find its way to Civvy Street but, by official order, has to be destroyed beyond repair.

It is interesting to note that more recently the US military have discovered that the simple and relatively cheap civilian 'buggy' might have military potential in a 'hit and run' role. 80 Fast Attack Vehicles (FAV), based on Chenowth off-road racers were ordered in 1983 to be tested with Emerson weapon stations (TOW, grenade launcher, etc.) for possible use in the Rapid Deployment Force.

CAR, UTILITY, 4×4 (LAND-ROVER 109 SERIES III)   GB

General Data: The Land-Rover in the form shown here was introduced in 1958 (Series II) and continued in production for many years with periodic detail modifications and improvements. The Series IIA came in 1961, followed by the Series III 10 years later. A 5-door 12-seater, it was employed worldwide as a command car and for special purposes, occasionally with the top removed. 10-seater and swb models were available, as were diesel and 6-cyl. engines. In 1983 a sophisticated coil-spring version, the One Ten, made its appearance and shared many features with the up-market Range Rover (incl. V8 engine as an option).

Technical Details: Own 2.25-litre 4-cyl. petrol engine, 2286cc

(90.47 × 88.9 mm), 52.2 kW/70.9 bhp (DIN) at 4000 rpm. Dry plate clutch. 4F1R gearbox. 2-speed transfer box with front axle disconnect. 4.7:1 axle gear ratio. Hydraulic brakes. Semi-elliptic leaf springs. 7.50-16 tyres. 12-Volt electrics. 68-litre fuel tank.

Dimensions and Weights: Wheelbase 2768 mm. Track 1330 mm. Overall length and width 4445 × 1690 mm. Height 2010 mm. Ground clearance 209 mm (axles). Angles of approach and departure 45° and 29°. Weight 1732 kg, GVW 2680 kg.

above: British RAF; *below left:* Danish Army; *below right:* Series IIA of Swiss Army (1970)

Car, Utility, 4 × 4   **USA**
(Chevrolet K 10 Suburban)

V-8-cyl. 5.7-litre petrol engine with 3F1R automatic transmission and 2-speed transfer box. Free-wheeling front hubs. Wheelbase 3220 mm. Overall dimensions 5470 × 2021 × 1860 mm. Weight 2300 kg (approx.). Electric Winch. Also available from GMC (Suburban K1500)

Car, Utility, 4 × 4   **USA**
(Kaiser Jeep Wagoneer)

6-cyl. 3.8-litre petrol engine with 3F1R gearbox and 2-speed transfer box. (Other engines and transmissions available.) Wheelbase 2794 mm. Overall dimensions 4665 × 1920 × 1626 mm. Weight 1725 kg (approx.). Originally launched in 1962, early 1970s model shown in Lebanon (UNIFIL).

Car, Utility, 4 × 4   **E**
(Land-Rover/Santana Especial)

6-cyl. 3.4-litre diesel engine with 4F1R gearbox and 2-speed transfer box. Wheelbase 2768 mm. Overall dimensions 4440 × 1676 × 2060 mm. Weight 1820 kg. GVW 3150 kg. 9-seater built in Spain, from 1979, on 1-ton 109 chassis. Bodywork differed from UK version. Santana is 49% owned by Land-Rover.

Car, Utility, 4 × 4   **D**
(Mercedes-Benz 230G)

4-cyl. 2.3-litre petrol engine (M115) with 4F1R gearbox and 2-speed transfer box. Rigid axles, coil spring suspension. Wheelbase 2850 mm. Militarized station wagon with extension (for ambulance use). Available also with 6-cyl. 2.8-litre petrol engine and 4- or 5-cyl. diesel. 1981.

Car, Utility, 4 × 4   **J**
(Mitsubishi Jeep J30/Type 73)

4-cyl. 2.2-litre petrol engine (Hurricane) with 3F1R gearbox and 2-speed transfer box. Wheelbase 2641 mm. Overall dimensions 4290 × 1625 × 1830 mm. Weight 1470 kg. Also available with diesel engine (J30D). 5-door all-steel body. Japanese development on licence-produced CJ3B chassis.

Car, Utility, 4 × 4   **J**
(Toyota Land Cruiser FJ55L)

6-cyl. 4.23-litre petrol engine with 4F1R gearbox and 2-speed transfer box. Rigid axles with 16-in. wheels. Wheelbase 2700 mm. Overall dimensions 4675 × 1735 × 1865 mm. Weight 1930 kg (approx.). Civilian vehicle but also used for military purposes, e.g. in Australia (RAAF, RAN), Libya, etc. Discontinued in 1980.

CAR, UTILITY, 4×4 (PEUGEOT/DANGEL 504 BREAK)   **F**

General Data: From 1978, Henry Dangel of Sentheim, France, converted Peugeot 'breaks' (station wagons) to 4-wheel drive and went into quantity production in 1980. In 1982 a military version was launched, known as the *504 Break Commandement 'Armée' 4 × 4.* It seated 5 with a payload capacity of 500 kg. A front-mounted winch, protection bar and radio equipment were optionally available.

Technical Details: Peugeot XN1 4-cyl. petrol engine, 1971 cc (88 × 91 mm), 69 kW/96 bhp (DIN) at 5200 rpm. Dry plate clutch. 4F1R gearbox. 2-speed transfer box with limited-slip differential. 4.625:1 axle gear ratio. Hydraulic brakes. Independent front suspension with McPherson struts, rigid rear axle with dual coil springs. 185-16 tyres. 12-Volt electrics. 60-litre fuel tank. *Note:* XD2 2.3-litre diesel engine optional.

Dimensions and Weights: Wheelbase 2910 mm. Track, front/rear 1490/1360 mm. Overall length and width 4800 × 1730 mm. Height 1740 mm (unladen). Ground clearance 215 mm (rear axle). Angles of approach and departure 45° and 30°. Weight 1525 kg, GVW 1970 kg.

above: 504 Break; *below left:* 504 GR Break; *below right:* 504 Pickup

CAR, UTILITY, 4×4 (ROVER RANGE ROVER)　　　　　　　　　GB

General Data: The Range Rover was introduced in 1970 as a 3-door high-performance car with V8 engine and full-time 4-wheel drive. It was an ideal high-grade staff car but few were sold for military purposes, far greater quantities going to police forces in several countries. Others were modified for ambulance and fire-fighting use, some being converted to 6-wheelers by specialist firms. In the Netherlands some were used by the Military Police and bomb disposal units. Other military users included the British Royal Military Police in West Berlin and some Middle East countries, e.g. Iraq.

Technical Details: Own V-8-cyl. petrol engine, 3528 cc

(88.9 × 71.1 mm), 98 kW/132 bhp (DIN) at 5000 rpm. Dry plate clutch. 4F1R gearbox. 2-speed transfer box with lockable differential. 3.54:1 axle gear ratio. Hydraulic brakes. Rigid axles with coil springs. 205-16 tyres. 12-Volt electrics. 82-litre fuel tank.

Dimensions and Weights: Wheelbase 2540 mm. Track 1490 mm. Overall length and width 4470 × 1780 mm. Height 1800 mm. Ground clearance 190 mm (axles). Angles of approach and departure 45° and 33°. Weight 1895 kg, GVW 2504 kg.

above: Netherlands Military Police (1978); *below left:* special police version (1979); *below right:* 4-door (1982)

Truck, 0.25-ton, 4 × 4, Utility   **F**
(Citroën A 4 × 4)

Flat-twin-cyl. 0.6-litre aircooled petrol engine with 4F1R gearbox. Lockable rear differential. Inboard disc brakes front and rear. 14-in wheels. Wheelbase 2370 mm. Overall dimensions 3620 × 1550 × 1680 mm. Weight 840 kg. GVW 1135 kg. Derived from Méhari 4 × 4. 5000 ordered by French Army in 1981.

Truck, 0.25-ton, 4 × 4 Utility   **USA**
(Ford Bronco)

6-cyl. 3.3-litre petrol engine with 3F1R gearbox (V8 and automatic optional) and 2-speed transfer box. 15-in. wheels. Wheelbase 2337 mm. Overall dimensions 3863 × 1775 × 1793 mm. Introduced in 1965 and not significantly changed until the 1978 model year. Military use chiefly by US Navy. US Army test vehicle shown.

Truck, 0.25-ton, 4 × 4, Utility   **IND**
(Mahindra Jeep CJ3B)

4-cyl. 2.2-litre engine (Hurricane) with 3F1R gearbox and 2-speed transfer box. Wheelbase 2032 mm. Weight 1077 kg. GVW 1770 kg. Made in India by Mahindra & Mahindra for Indian Army and export. Company also made the exclusive CJ4 and CJ4A, with 2310-mm wheelbase. Both were also offered as 4 × 2.

Truck, 0.25-ton, 4 × 4, Utility   **J**
(Mitsubishi Jeep J54A)

4-cyl. 2.2-litre petrol engine with 4F1R gearbox and 2-speed transfer box. Wheelbase 2020 mm. Overall length and width 3330 × 1595 mm. Weight 1240 kg. Basically the 1950s American Jeep CJ3B. Several variants were offered, also with diesel engine. Vehicle shown carries 2 anti-tank missiles.

Truck, 0.25-ton, 4x4, Utility   **F**
(Renault R1123/Sinpar)

4-cyl. petrol engine with 4F1R gearbox. Front-wheel drive plus Sinpar-designed auxiliary box for optional rear-wheel drive. Converted R4 van, used chiefly by the French Marines. Sinpar (absorbed by Renault in 1974) designed 4 × 4 conversions for several Renault car and van models, available to special order.

Truck, 0.25-ton, 4 × 4, Utility   **F**
(Renault 6 Rodéo/Sinpar)

4-cyl. 1.1-litre petrol engine with 4F1R gearbox driving the front wheels and (if desired) the rear wheels. Commercially available, also on the basis of the Rodéo 4, normally with front-wheel drive only. Conversion to 4-wheel drive by Sinpar. Picture was taken at French Army vehicles' exhibition, Satory, 1973.

TRUCK, 0.25-TON, 4×4 (AMG M151A2 SERIES)   USA

General Data: The M151A2 Series succeeded the M151 and M151A1 in 1970. The original M151, also known as MUTT (Military Utility Tactical Truck) had been developed by Ford and entered production in 1960, gradually replacing the M38 and M38A1 Jeep vehicles in the US armed forces. Derivatives of the M151A2 basic utility truck included the M825 weapon carrier (for mounting the 106-mm recoilless rifle) and the M718A1 front-line ambulance (qv). In addition to all the US forces, more than 100 foreign governments reportedly used the M151A2 Series.

Technical Details: L-142 Military Model 11660425 4-cyl. petrol engine, 2319 cc (98.3 × 76.2 mm), 46.2 kW/62 bhp (net) at 3600 rpm. Dry plate clutch. 4F1R gearbox. Single-speed transfer box with front axle disconnect. 4.86:1 axle gear ratio. Hydraulic brakes. Independent suspension with coil springs, front and rear. 7.00-16 tyres. 24-Volt electrics. 67.3-litre fuel tank.

Dimensions and Weights: Wheelbase 2159 mm. Track 1346 mm. Overall length and width 3371 × 1633 mm. Height 1803 mm (canvas top). Ground clearance 240 mm (chassis). Angles of approach and departure 60° and 37°. Weight 1088 kg, GVW 1632 kg.

above: M151A2; *below left:* optional hardtop; *below right:* M825

TRUCK, 0.25-TON, 4×4 (ASIA MOTORS KM41 SERIES)   ROK

General Data: The KM41 Series, produced by Asia Motors of Seoul, Republic of Korea, was introduced in the late 1970s and was patterned on the American Motors Jeep CJ5. The locally-made bodywork differed from the US original in many details. In addition to the military versions (KM410 utility truck, KM411 ambulance (qv), KM412 TOW missile launcher and KM414 106-mm recoilless rifle carrier) there was a civilian model called Landmaster (with 5 grille slots). The KM410's maximum speed was 96 km/h, gradability 60% and cruising range 340 km. Asia Motors also produced a 1.25-ton 4×4 truck, KM450 (qv).

Technical Details: Model MVA2000 4-cyl. petrol engine,

1985 cc (82×94 mm), 52.2 kW/70 bhp (gross) at 4000 rpm. Dry plate clutch. 4F1R gearbox. 2-speed transfer box with front axle disconnect. 5.375:1 axle gear ratio. Hydraulic brakes. Semi-elliptic leaf springs. 6.00-16 tyres. 12-Volt electrics. 45.5-litre fuel tank.

Dimensions and Weights: Wheelbase 2032 mm. Track 1230 mm. Overall length and width 3350×1475 mm. Height 1705 mm (windscreen). Ground clearance 210 mm (axles). Angles of approach and departure 45° and 30°. Weight 1180 kg, GVW 1720 kg.

above: KM410; *below left:* KM412; *below right:* KM414

TRUCK, 0.25-TON, 4×4 (FORD U-50 CAMPAIGN)

BR

General Data: This Ford/Willys Jeep was a result of the merger in 1969 of Willys Overland do Brasil and Ford Motor do Brasil. The new company, Ford-Willys do Brasil, was later renamed Ford Brasil and the CJ5-patterned Brazilian Jeep remained in production, designated Ford U-50. The Campaign was the short-wheelbase military version, offered in standard general purpose form and as a mount for the 106-mm recoilless rifle. Gradability was in excess of 100%, max. road speed 125 km/h. The company also offered a range of long-wheelbase models (formerly CJ6).

Technical Details: Own 4-cyl. ohc petrol engine, 2300 cc (96.04 × 79.4 mm), 67.9 kW/91 bhp (gross) at 5000 rpm. Dry plate clutch. 4F1R gearbox. 2-speed transfer box with front axle disconnect. 4.89:1 axle gear ratio. Freewheel hubs. Hydraulic brakes. Semi-elliptic leaf springs. 6.00-16 tyres. 12-Volt electrics (24-Volt optional for radio version). 40-litre fuel tank.

Dimensions and Weights (standard model): Wheelbase 2057 mm. Track 1234 mm. Overall length and width 3444 × 1480 mm. Height 1733 mm (canvas top). Ground clearance 204 mm (axles). Angles of approach and departure 45° and 29°. Weight 1100 kg, GVW 1700 kg.

above: recoilless rifle carrier; *below left and right:* standard model

TRUCK, 0.25-TON, 4×4 (INTERNATIONAL SCOUT)   USA

General Data: International Harvester entered the light 4 × 4 vehicle market in the early 1960s with the Scout 800, a rather plain 4-cylinder slab-sided vehicle. Among the military users were the US Army, USN, USMC, Australia and Greece. In 1971 the much-revised Scout II appeared. A long-wheelbase version of the Scout II – named Traveler – superseded the old IHC Travelall station wagon. Production of both the Scout and the Traveler terminated in 1980. The following data apply to a typical Scout II of the mid-1970s. There were many variations.

Technical Details: Own V304 V-8-cyl. petrol engine, 4228 cc (98.4 × 81.7 mm), 106 kW/142 bhp (net) at 3600 rpm. Dry plate clutch. 4F1R gearbox. 2-speed transfer box with front axle disconnect. 3.31:1 axle gear ratio. Hydraulic brakes. Semi-elliptic leaf springs. F78-15 tyres. 12-Volt electrics. 72-litre fuel tank.

Dimensions and Weights: Wheelbase 2540 mm. Track 1450 mm. Overall length and width 4210 × 1770 mm. Height 1680 mm (hardtop). Ground clearance 160 mm (axles). Angles of approach and departure 44° and 22°. Weight 1900 kg, GVW 2450 kg.

above and *below left:* Scout II 1974/75 (US Army); *below right:* Scout 800 (RAAF, Australia)

TRUCK, 0.25-TON, 4×4 (JEEP EBRO CJ3M)

E

General Data: The US Jeep CJ3B has been licence-produced in Spain for many years by the VIASA division of MMC, later CAF of Zaragoza. More recently, VIASA merged with Motor Iberica and for the home market the civilian vehicles were renamed Jeep Ebro and Jeep Avia. There was also a long-wheelbase CJ6, which, unlike the US CJ6, had CJ3B sheet metal. The military versions were CJ3M and CJ6M, sometimes prefixed HU (Hurricane petrol engine) and PE (Perkins diesel engine). They were also known as the Jeep Ebro Military and Military L.

Technical Details: Perkins 4.108 4-cyl. diesel engine, 1760 cc (79.4 × 88.9 mm), 45.5 kW/61 bhp (gross) at 4000 rpm. Dry plate clutch. 4F1R gearbox. 2-speed transfer box with front axle disconnect. 5.38:1 axle gear ratio. Hydraulic brakes. Semi-elliptic leaf springs. 7.00-16 tyres. 12- or 24-Volt electrics. 39-litre tank.

Dimensions and Weights: Wheelbase 2032 mm. Track 1244 mm. Overall length and width 3400 × 1450 mm. Height 1840 mm (canvas top). Ground clearance 230 mm (axles). Angles of approach and departure 46° and 35°. Weight 1250 kg, GVW 1790 kg.

above: standard version; *below left and right:* with 106-mm recoilless rifle

TRUCK, 0.25-TON, 4×4 (JEEP CJ5 8305)

USA

General Data: The CJ5 was originally introduced in the early 1950s as a civilian version of the M38A1. The latter was in due course superseded by the M151 Series and a militarized version of the CJ5 was made available as M606A2 and A3. Many CJ5s were bought by the US armed forces (and other countries). The following data apply to the 1975 standard vehicle.

Technical Details: Own 232CID 6-cyl. petrol engine, 3803 cc (95.2 × 88.9 mm), 75 kW/100 bhp (net) at 3600 rpm. Dry plate clutch. 3F1R gearbox. 2-speed transfer box with front axle disconnect. Axle gear ratio 4.27:1 front, 3.73:1 rear. Hydraulic brakes. Semi-elliptic leaf springs. E78-15 tyres. 12-Volt electrics.

59-litre fuel tank. *Note:* 4.2-litre Six and 5-litre V8 engine, 4F1R and auto. trans. optional.

Dimensions and Weights: Wheelbase 2134 mm. Track, front/rear 1308/1270 mm. Overall length and width (incl. side-mounted spare wheel and steps) 3530 × 1820 mm. Height 1770 mm (windscreen). Ground clearance 203 mm (axles). Angles of approach and departure 45° and 30°. Weight 1105 kg, GVW 1700 kg.

above: metal full cab (USAF, 1978); *below left:* military top (Colombia); *below right:* convertible top (US Army)

TRUCK, 0.25-TON, 4×4 (KEOHWA M-5, M-7) ROK

General Data: Keohwa of Seoul recently introduced a range of military vehicles, the lightest in the M-5 and M-7 Series, with wheelbase sizes 2134 mm and 2390 mm. Of the former, there is only one version, the M-5GA2 recoilless rifle carrier. The M-7 Series comprises: M-7GA1 basic utility truck, M-7GA3 with machine gun, M-7GA5 with searchlight, M-7GA6 ambulance (qv), M-7GA7 with TOW missile system, M-7GA8 TOW missile carrier and M-7GA1H hardtop version of M-7GA1. Following applies to the M-7GA1.

Technical Details: AMC 6-cyl. petrol engine, 4229 cc (95.25 × 99.06 mm), 85 kW/114 bhp (gross) at 3200 rpm. Dry plate clutch. 4F1R gearbox. 2-speed transfer box with front axle disconnect. 3.73 : 1 axle gear ratio. Hydraulic brakes. Semi-elliptic leaf springs. 7.00-15 or 9.00-15 Wide Track (shown) tyres. 12-Volt electrics. 70- and 20-litre fuel tanks. 4-cyl. 2.8-litre diesel optional.

Dimensions and Weights: Wheelbase 2390 mm. Track (standard), front/rear 1308/1270 mm. Overall length and width 3800 × 1700 mm. Height 1815 mm (canvas top). Ground clearance 240 mm (axles). Angles of approach and departure 45° and 30°. Weight 1400 kg, GVW 2200 kg.

above: M-7GA1; *below left:* M-5GA2; *below right:* M-7GA7/A8

TRUCK, 0.25-TON, 4×4 (LAND-ROVER 88 SERIES IIA)   AUS

General Data: The Australian Army, RAAF and RAN have for many years been using the short- and long-wheelbase Land-Rover for a variety of roles, in many instances with special-purpose bodywork. The vehicles were assembled and, where necessary, adapted for their role, in Australia. By far the majority were easily recognizable as 'Australian Pattern' by the unusual shape of the front mudguard cutouts and the large brushguard. Series IIA vehicles were later superseded by Series III or other makes.

Technical Details: Own 4-cyl. petrol engine, 2286 cc (90.47 × 88.9 mm), 53 kW/71 bhp (net) at 4500 rpm. Dry plate clutch. 4F1R gearbox. 2-speed transfer box with front axle disconnect. 4.7:1 axle gear ratio. Hydraulic brakes. Semi-elliptic leaf springs. 6.00 or 6.50-16 tyres. 12-Volt electrics. 2 × 45-litre fuel tanks.

Dimensions and Weights: Wheelbase 2230 mm. Track 1308 mm. Overall length and width 3620 × 1690 mm. Height 1960 mm (canvas top). Ground clearance 178 mm (axles). Angles of approach and departure 46° and 30°. Weight 1560 kg, GVW 2020 kg.

above: GS vehicle of RAAF; *below left:* Army 'Ceremonial'; *below right:* fitted for US M40 rifle, 106-mm.

TRUCK, 0.25-TON, 4×4 (LAND-ROVER 88 SERIES III)   GB

General Data: The short-wheelbase Land-Rover was originally introduced as a civilian vehicle in 1948 (80-in wb) and was soon being bought for military purposes. The current model first appeared in 1958 (Series II) and developed through Series IIA (1961) and Series III (from 1971), with detail modifications. For military use, the regular Series III 88-in wb model has been largely replaced by the military pattern 0.5-ton type (qv).

Technical Details: Own 4-cyl. petrol engine, 2286 cc (90.47 × 88.9 mm), 53 kW/71bhp (DIN) at 4000 rpm. Dry plate clutch. 4F1R gearbox. 2-speed transfer box with front axle disconnect. 4.7:1 axle gear ratio. Hydraulic brakes. Semi-elliptic leaf springs. 6.50-16 tyres. 12-Volt electrics. 45-litre fuel tank.
Note: also available with diesel engine and many other options in regard of electrical equipment, tyres, fuel tanks, etc.

Dimensions and Weights: Wheelbase 2230 mm. Track 1308 mm. Overall length and width 3620 × 1690 mm. Height 1960 mm (canvas top). Ground clearance 178 mm (axles). Angles of approach and departure 46° and 30°. Weight 1330 kg, GVW 2020 kg.

above: Series III, 1978, GS; *below left:* with hardtop (Series IIA shown); *below right:* Belgian Army Series III (4 × 2 modification).

TRUCK, 0.25-TON, 4×4 (LAND-ROVER/SANTANA MIL. 88) E

General Data: Metalurgica de Santa Ana have produced Land-Rover models under licence for many years. In the mid-1970s they followed the UK parent company in introducing a special military-pattern version of the short-wheelbase Land-Rover 88, known as the Military 88 or 88 Ligero, 3500 of which were made. Although it was similar in configuration to the British 0.5-ton 'Lightweight' model, it differed in many details. From 1980 a civilian edition was offered.

Technical Details: Own 4-cyl. petrol engine, 2286 cc (90.47 × 88.9 mm), 53 kW/71 bhp (net) at 4000 rpm. Dry plate clutch. 4F1R gearbox. 2-speed transfer box with front axle disconnect. 4.7:1

axle gear ratio. Hydraulic brakes. Semi-elliptic leaf springs. 6.50-16 tyres. 24-Volt electrics. 2 × 45-litre fuel tanks.
Note: also with 2286-cc 62-bhp diesel engine.

Dimensions and Weights: Wheelbase 2230 mm. Track 1310 mm. Overall length and width 3720 × 1650 mm. Height 2060 mm (canvas top). Ground clearance 210 mm (axles). Angles of approach and departure 50° and 40°. Weight 1352 kg, GVW 2200 kg.

above: general purpose vehicle; *below left:* radar (RASURA); *below right:* recoilless rifle

Truck, 0.25-ton, 4 × 4, Utility   **BR**
(Volkswagen QT)

Flat-4-cyl. 1.6-litre aircooled engine with torque converter (replacing conventional clutch) and 4F1R gearbox at rear driving the rear wheels and, if required, the front wheels via VW Passat front-drive components. Experimental military vehicle, designed and produced in 1976/77 by Volkswagen do Brasil.

Truck, 0.4-ton, 4 × 4, Utility   **SU**
(GAZ-69AM)

4-cyl. 2.43-litre petrol engine (UAZ-69B) with 3F1R gearbox and 2-speed transfer box. Rigid axles with 16-in. wheels. Wheelbase 2300 mm. Overall dimensions 3850 × 1750 × 1950 mm. Weight 1500 kg. GVW 1960 kg. Introduced in the early 1950s and continued in production (from 1956 by UAZ) for many years.

Truck, 0.4-ton, 4 × 4, Utility   **SU**
(LUAZ-969M)

V-4-cyl. aircooled 1.2-litre petrol engine with 5F1R gearbox. 4-wheel drive. Diff. lock at rear. 13-in. wheels. Wheelbase 1800 mm. Overall dimensions 3385 × 1560 × 1770 mm. Weight 960 kg. GVW 1360 kg. Modernized edition of LUAZ-969A, which had been derived from the ZAZ-969 car. In production from 1979.

Truck, 0.4-ton, 4 × 4, Utility   **J/BUR**
(Mazda X2000)

4-cyl. 2-litre petrol engine with 4F1R gearbox and 2-speed transfer box. Rigid axles with 5.286:1 ratio. Wheelbase 2250 mm. Track 1400 mm. Overall dimensions 3835 × 1695 × 1810 mm. Produced by Tokyo Kogyo, Japan, 1968-73, for use in Burma. Later, full-scale production in Burma for military/government service.

Truck, 0.4-ton, 4 × 4, Utility   **F**
(Panhard M7/Heuliez)

Flat-4-cyl. aircooled 1.2-litre petrol engine (Citroën G103) with torque converter transmission (Verto). Wheelbase 2283 mm. Overall dimensions 3360 × 1580 × 1725 mm. Angles of approach and departure 45° and 66°. Weight 850 kg. GVW 1270 kg. Bodywork by Heuliez. Prototype 1973. No quantity production.

Truck, 0.4-ton, 4 × 4, Utility   **PRC**
(Tientsin/T'ien-chin TJ210C)

4-cyl. 2.4-litre petrol engine (492) with 3F1R gearbox and 2-speed transfer box. Axle gear ratio 4.55:1. Rigid axles with leaf springs. 16-in. wheels. Wheelbase 2050 mm. Overall dimensions 3427 × 1500 × 1850 mm. Weight 1300 kg. Produced by T'ien-chin Motor Vehicle Plant in the People's Republic of China.

TRUCK, 0.4-TON, 4×4 (NISSAN PATROL)   J

General Data: The Nissan Patrol went into quantity production in the early 1950s and continued in the form shown, with periodical improvements, until 1980. Many variants have been made, including swb, lwb, lhd, rhd, open and closed bodywork, 2- and 4-door station wagons, ambulances, pickups, fire trucks, etc. Some were available as 4 × 2, with rear-wheel drive only. Patrols were used for military purposes by Japan and several foreign countries, including Jordan. In India, the Patrol was licence-produced with the marque name Jonga.

Technical Details: Own P40 6-cyl. petrol engine, 3956 cc (85.7 × 114.3 mm), 97 kW/130 bhp (net) at 3600 rpm. Dry plate clutch. 3F1R gearbox. 2-speed transfer box with front axle disconnect. 4.1:1 axle gear ratio. Hydraulic brakes. Semi-elliptic leaf springs. 6.50-16 tyres. 12-Volt electrics. 72-litre fuel tank.

Dimensions and Weights: Wheelbase 2200 mm. Track, front/rear 1386/1404 mm. Overall length and width 3770 × 1714 mm. Height 1980 mm (canvas top). Ground clearance 222 mm (axles). Angles of approach and departure not specified. Weight 1590 kg, GVW 2100 kg.

above: 60U; *below left:* L60 6-seater; *below right:* LG60H lwb pickup

TRUCK, 0.4-TON, 4×4 (PEKING BJ-212)   PRC

General Data: Introduced in the late 1960s, this 4/5-seater field car/utility vehicle was produced by several factories in the People's Republic of China, with minor detail differences. It was destined for both military and civil service and became one of the most numerous vehicles to be encountered in its home country. It was also exported to several nations, albeit in relatively small numbers. The seating capacity was 5 persons (incl. driver) plus 50 kg of luggage. The vehicle could tow a trailer load of 800 kg. A 2-door model with tailgate, canvas top and removable longitudinal seats (Model BJ-212A) was also produced (qv).

Technical Details: Own 4-cyl. petrol engine, 2445 cc (92 × 92 mm), 56 kW/75 bhp (net) at 3500–4000 rpm. Dry plate clutch. 3F1R gearbox. 2-speed transfer box with front axle disconnect. 4.55:1 axle gear ratio. Hydraulic brakes. Semi-elliptic leaf springs. 6.50-16 tyres. 12-Volt electrics. 85-litre fuel tank.

Dimensions and Weights: Wheelbase 2300 mm. Track 1440 mm. Overall length and width 3860 × 1750 mm. Height 1870 mm (canvas top). Ground clearance 220 mm (axles). Angles of approach and departure 45° and 35°. Weight 1530 kg, GVW 1955 kg.

above and below: BJ-212 standard version

Truck, 0.5-ton, 4 × 4, Utility   **USA**
(Chevrolet Blazer K 10)

Militarized commercial model of the mid-1970s. Wheelbase 2705 mm. Overall dimensions 4686 × 2019 × 1803 mm. Several power train options: 6- or V-8-cyl., manual 3- or 4-speed or Turbo Hydramatic auto. trans. V8-engined models had full-time 4-wheel drive. 4 × 2 was available also. Few supplied for military service.

Truck, 0.5-ton, 4 × 4, Utility   **D/F**
(Citroën C44)

4-cyl. 1.8-litre petrol engine (Citroën CX) with 5F1R gearbox. 16-in. wheels. Wheelbase 2017 mm. Overall dimensions 3972 × 1520 × 1837 mm. Weight 1370 kg. GVW 2000 kg. Modified Volkswagen Iltis, with adapted Citroën power unit (as in CX Athena car). 10 produced for French Army trials but not accepted.

Truck, 0.5-ton, 4 × 4, Utility   **PI**
(Delta Explorer RJ2B)

4-cyl. 1.6-litre petrol engine (Toyota 12RM) with 4F1R gearbox (GM) and 2-speed transfer box. Wheelbase 2185 mm. Overall dimensions 3575 × 1595 × 1925 mm. Weight 1070 kg. GVW 1740 kg. Made in Metro Manila, Philippines. Isuzu diesel engine optional. Also civilian version (RJ2F), incl. 4 × 2.

Truck, 0.5-ton, 4 × 4, Utility   **USA**
(Dodge Ramcharger AW100)

V-8-cyl. or 6-cyl. petrol engine with manual or auto. trans. and 2-speed transfer box with lockable diff. Wheelbase 2692 mm. Overall length and width 4689 × 2019 mm. GVW 2224 kg. Introduced in 1974. Some were tested by the US Army in 1975/6 (standard Six and high-performance V8 models).

Truck, 0.5-ton, 4 × 4, Utility   **USA**
(Jeep AM7)

6-cyl. 4.2-litre petrol engine with 4F1R gearbox and 2-speed transfer box. Wheelbase 2375 mm. Overall dimensions 3890 × 1520 × 1720 mm. Weight 1275 kg. GVW 1880 kg. Militarized Jeep CJ7 model, commercially available in lhd or rhd, with various 'severe use features'. Auto. trans. optional. 1982.

Truck, 0.5-ton, 4 × 4, Utility   **E**
(Jeep CJ6M)

4-cyl. petrol (Hurricane) or diesel (Perkins) engine with 4F1R gearbox and 2-speed transfer box. Wheelbase 2565 mm. Overall length and width 3967 × 1450 mm. Weight 1300 kg. Made in Spain and also known as Jeep Viasa or Jeep Ebro Military L. Shown with 106-mm recoilless rifle.

TRUCK, 0.5-TON, 4×4 (ARO 240 SERIES)   **R**

General Data: Produced by Uzina Mecanica Muscel of Romania, this range of field cars/utility vehicles gradually replaced the Soviet-pattern M461 type in production. The ARO 240 Series was entirely new in 1970, with full-width bodywork and independent front suspension. The following variants were made: 240 (2-door, softtop), 241 (4-door 5-seater, softtop), 242 (2-door, pickup), 243 (3-door, hardtop), 244 (5-door, station wagon). There was also a truck version (ARO 320) and a range of smaller models (ARO 10).

Technical Details: Own L-25 4-cyl. petrol engine, 2495 cc (97 × 84.4 mm), 59.7 kW/80 bhp (DIN) at 4200 rpm. Dry plate clutch. 4F1R gearbox. 2-speed transfer box with front axle disconnect. 4.71:1 axle gear ratio. Hydraulic brakes. Independent suspension with coil springs at front, rigid axle with leaf springs at rear. 6.50-16 tyres. 12-Volt electrics. 95-litre fuel tank. *Note:* 7.50-16 or 8.20-15 tyres optional.

Dimensions and Weights: Wheelbase 2350 mm. Track 1445 mm. Overall length and width 4033 mm × 1775 mm. Height 1888 mm (canvas top). Ground clearance 220 mm (rear axle). Angles of approach and departure 47° and 31°. Weight 1590 kg, GVW 2130 kg.

above: 241; *below left:* 240; *below right:* 244

TRUCK, 0.5-TON, 4×4 (FIAT 1107AD)

General Data: Introduced in the early 1970s, the Fiat Nuova Campagnola was designed to replace the older Campagnola vehicles which had been in production since the early 1950s. The Italian armed forces soon ordered 3000 of the new model. It was available with canvas or hardtop and with short or long body, seating 7 and 9 people respectively. In Yugoslavia the vehicle was produced under licence by Zastava from c. 1975.

Technical Details: Own 4-cyl. petrol engine, 1995 cc (84 × 90 mm), 59.7 kW/80 bhp (DIN) at 4600 rpm. Dry plate clutch. 5F1R gearbox. 2-speed transfer box with front axle disconnect. Limited-slip differentials. 5.375:1 axle gear ratio. Hydraulic brakes.

Independent suspension with torsion bars. 7.00-16 tyres. 24-Volt electrics. 57-litre fuel tank. *Note:* low-grade petrol engine, diesel engine, power steering and 7.50-16 tyres optional.

Dimensions and Weights: Wheelbase 2300 mm. Track, front/rear 1365/1404 mm. Overall length and width 3775 × 1580 mm. Height 1355 mm (canvas top). Ground clearance 275 mm (belly). Angles of approach and departure 44° and 45°. Weight 1740 kg, GVW 2490 kg.

above and *below left:* 1107AD standard military model; *below right:* diesel with long body and hardtop

TRUCK, 0.5-TON, 4×4 (LAND-ROVER 88 SERIES III)   GB

General Data: The 0.5-ton Land-Rover (Rover I in British Army parlance) was developed in the late 1960s and went into quantity production for the British forces in 1968. It was a militarized version of the Land-Rover 88 Regular, with completely redesigned bodywork, made largely of flat panels so that windscreen assembly, doors, upper body and tailgate panels could be easily detached, reducing weight and size for airportable role. The vehicle is also known as the 'Lightweight'. A diesel engine was optional.

Technical Details: Own 4-cyl. petrol engine, 2286 cc (90.47 × 88.9 mm), 51.5 kW/69 bhp (DIN) at 4000 rpm. Dry plate clutch. 4F1R gearbox. 2-speed transfer box with front axle disconnect. 4.7:1 axle gear ratio. Hydraulic brakes. Semi-elliptic springs. 6.00 or 7.00-16 tyres. 12-or 24-Volt electrics. 2 × 45-litre fuel tanks.

Dimensions and Weights: Wheelbase 2230 mm. Track 1308 mm. Overall length and width 3650 × 1520 mm. Height 1950 mm (canvas top). Ground clearance 220 mm (axles). Angles of approach and departure 49° and 36° (58° and 38° in stripped-down condition). Weight 1510 kg, GVW 2162 kg.

above: GS FFR (24-Volt); *below left:* with 120-mm WOMBAT (Royal Marines); *below right:* Netherlands Marines

Truck, 0.5-ton, 4 × 4, AT Gun   **GB**
(Land-Rover 88 Series III)

Basically similar to standard 0.5-ton 'Lightweight' but modified by Marshall of Cambridge to mount the US 106-mm recoilless rifle. Equipment included Michelin 7.50-16XS tyres, blast shield over spare wheel, stowage for 4 rounds of ammunition, twin folding windscreens, etc. Produced for export in the mid-1970s.

Truck, 0.5-ton, 4 × 4, AT Gun   **GB**
(Land-Rover 88 Series III)

Improved edition of the earlier 'Gunship', supplied to some Middle East countries. Relocated spare wheel, improved windscreens and barrel clamp, capacity for 6 rounds and 4 (instead of 2) men in the rear compartment, with hinged backrests. Made for export in 1977/78.

Truck, 0.5-ton, 4 × 4, Utility   **GB**
(Land-Rover 88 Series III)

4-cyl. 2.25-litre diesel engine with 4F1R gearbox and 2-speed transfer box. Wheelbase 2230 mm. 7.00-16 tyres. Weight 1525 kg. 24-Volt electrics. Diesel engine and other modifications for Netherlands Army, for which more than 2000 were ordered in 1975. The Dutch also ordered over 3000 0.75-tonners.

Truck, 0.5-ton, 4 × 4, Utility   **I/F**
(Saviem/Renault TRM500)

4-cyl. 2-litre petrol engine (Renault 829) with 4F1R gearbox and 2-speed transfer box. 16-in. wheels. Wheelbase 2295 mm. Overall dimensions 3770 × 1580 × 1900 mm. Weight 1670 kg. Modified Italian Fiat Campagnola 1107AD, with adapted Renault car (20TS) engine. 10 made for French Army trials in the late 1970s.

Truck, 0.5-ton, 4 × 4, Utility   **F**
(Stemat VELTT)

4-cyl. 1.8-litre petrol engine (Peugeot XM7P) with 4F1R gearbox and 2-speed transfer box. Full-time 4-wheel drive (Tetragrip system). Wheelbase 2040 mm. Overall dimensions 3360 × 1560 × 1770 mm. Weight 1200 kg. Prototypes 1976/77, also diesel, lwb and forward control. Unitary body/chassis.

Truck, 0.6-ton, 4 × 4, AT Gun   **USA/P**
(Jeep CJ6/Bravia Commando Mk II)

4-cyl. petrol (140HC) or diesel (Perkins 4.154) engine with 4F1R gearbox and 2-speed transfer box. Wheelbase 2642 mm. Overall dimensions (less 106-mm recoilless rifle shown) 3937 × 1699 × 1733 mm. Weight 1096 kg. GVW 1700 kg. US Jeep, assembled by Bravia of Lisbon, Portugal, together with swb CJ5 model.

TRUCK, 0.5-TON, 4×4 (MERCEDES-BENZ 230G)   D/A

General Data: The Mercedes G-Series was launched in 1979 and was a co-production of Daimler-Benz in West Germany and Steyr-Daimler-Puch in Austria. It comprised numerous models. Military users included Argentina, Norway and France. Also available in chassis/cab form for the mounting of special bodywork. In 1982 the 230G was superseded by the 230GE with petrol injection engine. The following data apply to the 230G.

Technical Details: Daimler-Benz M115 4-cyl. petrol engine, 2307 cc (93.5 × 83.6 mm), 66kW/90 bhp (net) at 5000 rpm. Dry plate clutch. 4F1R gearbox. 2-speed transfer box with front axle disconnect. 5.33:1 axle gear ratio. Hydraulic brakes. Rigid axles with coil springs. 205R16 tyres. 24-Volt electrics. 70-litre fuel tank. *Note:* Options included diesel engine, diff. locks, etc.

Dimensions and Weights: Wheelbase 2400 mm. Track 1425 mm. Overall length and width 4145 × 1700 mm. Height 1995 mm (canvas top). Ground clearance 240 mm (axles). Angles of approach and departure 39° and 34°. Weight 1700 kg, GVW 2500 kg.

above: 230G; *below left:* early military prototype; *below right:* lwb (2850 mm) 300GD

TRUCK, 0.5-TON, 4×4 (MITSUBISHI JEEP J24A) J

General Data: In addition to the licence-produced US Jeep CJ3B, Mitsubishi introduced a wide variety of models with revised bodywork of their own design, all with extended front wings. The restyled wings were also a feature of the 'Type 73 Small Truck', the Jeep J24A of the Japanese armed forces. The body was longer than that of the CJ3B-based model and a diesel engine was standard equipment. Like its predecessor, the J54A, the J24A of the 1970s also appeared as a mobile mount for anti-tank missiles (J24-P), recoilless rifle (J24-M), etc.

Technical Details: Own 4DR5 4-cyl. diesel engine, 2659 cc (92 × 100 mm), 59 kW/80 bhp (JIS) at 3500 rpm. Dry plate clutch.

4F1R gearbox. 2-speed transfer box with front axle disconnect. 5.375:I axle gear ratio. Hydraulic brakes. Semi-elliptic leaf spring suspension. 7.60-15 tyres. 24-Volt electrics. 46-litre fuel tank.

Dimensions and Weights: Wheelbase 2225 mm. Track 1300 mm. Overall length and width 3750 × 1655 mm. Height 1950 mm (canvas top). Ground clearance 210 mm (axles). Angles of approach and departure 47° and 40°. Weight 1420 kg, GVW 1900 kg.

above: 6-seater J24A; *below left:* with radio equipment; *below right:* as weapons carrier

TRUCK, 0.5-TON, 4×4 (TOYOTA LAND CRUISER)   J

General Data: Conceived in 1950, the Jeep-inspired Toyota 4 × 4 Model BJ was named Land Cruiser in June 1954 and as such remained in production for many years with periodic detail improvements. Additional variants with lwb and different body styles were introduced and a diesel engine became optional. Although produced only as a commercial vehicle, the Land Cruiser was bought by several governments for military use, exemplified by Australia, where a number were taken into service by the RAAF. Toyota Land Cruisers were also produced in Brazil.

Technical Details: Own 6-cyl. petrol engine, 3878 cc (90 × 101.6 mm), 145 bhp (SAE) at 4000 rpm. Dry plate clutch.

3F1R (later 4F1R) gearbox. 2-speed transfer box with front axle disconnect. 3.70:1 axle gear ratio. Hydraulic brakes. Semi-elliptic leaf springs. 7.10-15 tyres. 12-Volt electrics. 70-litre fuel tank.

Dimensions and Weights: Wheelbase 2285 mm. Track 1400 mm. Overall length and width 3870 × 1665 mm. Height 1950 mm (canvas top). Ground clearance 200 mm (axles). Angles of approach and departure 40° and 36°. Weight 1480 kg. GVW 2050 kg.

above: Australia (FJ40, RAAF); *below left:* Jordan (FJ40 with recoilless rifle); *below right:* Netherlands (FJ43L)

TRUCK, 0.5-TON, 4×4 (VOLKSWAGEN 183 ILTIS)   D

General Data: The Iltis (Polecat) was a modernized version of the old Auto Union Munga, powered by a 1.7-litre 4-stroke engine (Munga had 3-cyl. 2-stroke) and with a more sophisticated transmission system and other more modern features. It was produced by Audi in Ingolstadt from 1978, chiefly for the German *Bundeswehr*, which had ordered 8800 units, to be delivered by 1981. In late 1982 a Canadian version was launched by Bombardier (Model 183YX).

Technical Details: Own 183 4-cyl. petrol engine, 1714 cc (79.5 × 86.4 mm), 55 kW/75 bhp (net) at 5500 rpm. Dry plate clutch. 5F1R gearbox (4-speed with crawler gear) with front axle disconnect. 5.286:1 axle gear ratio. Hydraulic brakes. Independent suspension with transversal leaf springs and wishbones. 6.50R16 tyres. 24-Volt electrics. 85-litre fuel tank.

Dimensions and Weights: Wheelbase 2017 mm. Track, front/rear 1230/1260 mm. Overall length and width 3887 × 1520 mm. Height 1847 mm (roll cage). Ground clearance 225 mm (differentials), Angles of approach and departure 40° and 32°. Weight 1390 kg, GVW 2000 kg.

above: production model; *below left:* pilot model; *below right:* weather protection removed

TRUCK, 0.6-TON, 4×4 (FMC XR311)   USA

General Data: This high-mobility vehicle was designed and produced by FMC Corporation as a private venture in 1969/70. Offered to the US Army for examination, as a military vehicle it proved to be a trendsetter. The XR311 featured a space frame, a rear-mounted engine and extra-large 4-ply tyres of nylon construction. The project was later transferred to AM General Corporation (qv).

Technical Details: Chrysler V-8-cyl. petrol engine, 5200 cc (99.3×84.1 mm), 190 bhp (gross) at 4000 rpm. Chrysler A727 3F1R automatic transmission and chain-drive transfer box with controlled-slip differential and manual lockup. Controlled-slip diffs.

in both axles. 4.89:1 axle gear ratio. Hydraulic disc brakes. Independent suspension with torsion bars. 12.4-16 tyres. 24-Volt electrics. 98-litre fuel tank.

Dimensions and Weights: Wheelbase 3070 mm. Track 1630 mm. Overall length and width 4340×1930 mm. Height 1600 mm (roll cage). Ground clearance 280 mm (chassis). Angles of approach and departure 75° and 50°. Weight 2087 kg, GVW 2767 kg.

above: basic vehicle; *below left:* escort/security version; *below right:* with machine gun and crew armour kit

77

TRUCK, 0.6-TON, 4×4 (PEUGEOT P4 VLTT) F

General Data: Following extensive comparison tests with various modern field cars, the Peugeot P4 was selected to replace the Jeep in the French Army, an order for 15000 units being awarded in early 1981. The P4 was essentially the Austro-German G-Series as produced jointly by Daimler-Benz and Steyr-Daimler-Puch, but with a Peugeot petrol engine, gearbox etc. Final assembly was by Peugeot. Peugeot (PSA) offered the P4 also with diesel engine, long (2850 mm) wheelbase, and other options.

Technical Details: Own XN8 4-cyl. petrol engine, 1971 cc (88 × 81 mm), 65 kW/87 bhp (DIN) at 5000 rpm. Dry plate clutch. 4F1R gearbox. 2-speed transfer box with front axle disconnect.

5.33:1 axle gear ratio. Diff. lock in rear axle. Hydraulic brakes. Coil springs front and rear, with Panhard stabilizing rods. 7.00-16 tyres. 24-Volt electrics. 75-litre fuel tank.

Dimensions and Weights: Wheelbase 2400 mm. Track 1425 mm. Overall length and width 3900 × 1700 mm. Height 1925 mm (canvas top). Ground clearance 240 mm (axles). Angles of approach and departure 45° and 45°. Weight 1680 kg, GVW 2280 kg.

above: basic vehicle; *below left:* with Milan guided-missile launcher; *below right:* lwb radio van (prototype)

TRUCK, 0.6-TON, 4 × 4 (UAZ-469B)   SU

General Data: This 7-seater field car-cum-load carrier (2 people plus 600 kg of cargo) first appeared in 1961 as a prototype (UAZ-469) and eventual replacement for the GAZ/UAZ-69A. It took many years before the vehicle was found ready for quantity production, which commenced in the early 1970s, with designation UAZ-469B. It was supplied to the armed forces of most if not all of the Communist countries and was also exported for civil and military service. The engine was the same as that of the Volga GAZ-21A(E) car. Maximum road speed was 105 km/h. It was also known as 'Tundra'.

Technical Details: UMZ-451 4-cyl. petrol engine, 2445 cc (92 ×

92 mm), 53.3 kW/72 bhp (DIN) at 4000 rpm. Dry plate clutch. 4F1R gearbox. 2-speed transfer box with front axle disconnect. 5.125:1 axle gear ratio. Hydraulic brakes. Semi-elliptic leaf springs. 8.40-15 tyres. 12-Volt electrics. 2 × 38-litre fuel tanks.

Dimensions and Weights: Wheelbase 2380 mm. Track 1442 mm. Overall length and width 4025 × 1785 mm. Height 2015 mm (canvas top). Ground clearance 220 mm (axles). Angles of approach and departure 50° and 40°. Weight 1540 kg, GVW 2290 kg.

above and *below left:* civilian version; *below right:* military version

FIELD CARS/UTILITY TRUCKS

Truck, 0.75-ton, 4 × 4, Command   **BR**
(ENGESA/ENVEMO)

6-cyl. petrol engine with 4F1R gearbox and single-speed transfer box. Freewheel front hubs. Hydraulic brakes. 15-in. wheels. Wheelbase 2400 mm. Overall dimensions 4120 × 1890 × 2025 mm. Weight 1895 kg. Also cargo truck and diesel-engined versions. *c.* 1979/80.

Truck, 0.75-ton, 4 × 4, Utility   **CH**
(Monteverdi Military 230M)

4-cyl. 3.2-litre petrol engine (IHC 4-196) with 4F1R gearbox and 2-speed transfer box. Rigid axle with lockable diffs. Designed and built in prototype form by Monteverdi of Basle, Switzerland, in 1978/79, on basis of International Scout. Sold to Saurer for further development.

Truck, 0.75-ton, 4 × 4, Utility   **CH**
(Saurer F006)

4-cyl. 3.2-litre petrol engine with 4F1R gearbox and 2-speed transfer box. Rigid axles with lockable diffs. Max. payload 750 kg. Another variant, designated F007, had forward control and payload capacity of 1500 kg. Both were designed by Monteverdi. The F006 model became the Saurer 232M (qv) in 1981.

Truck, 0.9-ton, 4 × 4, Utility   **USA**
(Teledyne Cheetah)

V-8-cyl. 5.9-litre petrol engine (Chrysler) mounted at rear with 3F1R automatic transmission. Single-speed transfer box with controlled diff. Wheelbase 3000 mm. This high-mobility unit was built in 1977 by Mobility Technology International and subsequently taken over by Teledyne Continental Motors.

Truck, 0.9-ton, 4 × 4, Utility   **H/S**
(Volvo C202)

4-cyl. 2-litre petrol engine (B20) with 4F1R gearbox and 2-speed transfer box. Vacuum/hydraulic brakes. 16-in. wheels with 280/85-16 tyres. Wheelbase 2100 mm. Successor of the L3314 Laplander, the C202 was produced for Volvo by Csepel of Hungary, as pickup, hardtop (shown) and softtop, from 1975.

Truck, 1-ton, 4 × 4, Utility   **USA**
(AMG XR311/XM966)

V-8-cyl. 5.2-litre petrol engine (Chrysler) with 3F1R automatic transmission. Single-speed transfer box. Full-time 4-wheel drive. No-spin diffs. Wheelbase 3070 mm. Original concept taken over by AM General from FMC and modified to meet the XM966 Combat Support Vehicle specification.

TRUCK, 0.8-TON, 4×4 (SAURER 232M)

General Data: In 1980/81 Adolph Saurer of Arbon, Switzerland, introduced 3 new light cross-country vehicles, the softtop 232M and 260M and the 288M pickup, using glassfibre bodywork and common mechanical components (Volvo). The 232M was a further development of the Monteverdi-designed Military 230M (qv), of which Saurer had acquired the production rights. With slight modifications this had become the Saurer F006. The 232M differed from the latter in many details. By 1983 the project had been terminated.

Technical Details: Volvo B23A 4-cyl. petrol engine, 2315 cc (96 × 80 mm), 70 kW/95 bhp (net) at 4700 rpm. Dry plate clutch.

4F1R gearbox (M45). 2-speed transfer box (FD51) with front axle disconnect. 4.55:1 axle gear ratio. Diff. lock at rear. Hydraulic brakes (discs at front). Semi-elliptic leaf springs. 205R16 tyres. 12-Volt electrics. 70-litre fuel tank.

Dimensions and Weights: Wheelbase 2320 mm. Track not specified. Overall length and width 3893 × 1748 mm. Height 1900 mm (canvas top). Ground clearance 200 mm (axles). Angles of approach and departure not specified. Weight 1600 kg, GVW 2400 kg.

above and below: 232M pilot model

TRUCK, 0.9-TON, 4×4 (VOLVO 4141GV)   S

General Data: The Volvo C303 or 4141 range was developed in the 1960s to succeed the L3314 Laplander series (which continued in production in Hungary as Volvo C202) and put into quantity production during the 1970s for the Swedish, Norwegian and other armed forces. In the Swedish Army there were 3 variants: the TGB 111A MT (C03 4 × 4-1-V), the PVPJTGB 1111A MT (C03 4 × 4-2-V) and the RATGB 1112A MT (CO3 4 × 4-3-V). These were a hardtop multipurpose truck, a softtop anti-tank weapon mount and a hardtop radio van respectively.

Technical Details: Own B30A 6-cyl. twin-carburettor petrol engine, 2980 cc (88.9 × 88 mm), 86 kW/117 bhp (DIN) at 4000 rpm. Dry plate clutch. 4F1R gearbox. 2-speed transfer box with front axle disconnect. 5.99:1 axle gear ratio (incl. drop gear final drive). Vacuum/hydraulic brakes. Semi-elliptic leaf springs. 280/85-16 tyres. 24-Volt electrics. 84-litre fuel tank.

Dimensions and Weights: Wheelbase 2300 mm. Track 1540 mm. Overall length and width 4350 × 1900 mm. Height 2170 mm. Ground clearance 380 mm (axles). Angles of approach and departure 50° and 45°. Weight 2400 kg, GVW 3300 kg.

above: 6-seater TGB 111A MT (or TGB 11); *below left:* PVPJTGB 1111A MT; *below right:* RATGB 1112A MT

TRUCK, 1-TON, 4×4 (LAND-ROVER/SANTANA MIL. 109)   E

General Data: Generally known as the 109 Ligero, this long-wheelbase version of the Land-Rover Santana Military 88 (or 88 Ligero) was a design of the Spanish Land-Rover licencee, Metalurgica de Santa Ana, in cooperation with the Spanish military authorities. Like the commercial short- and long-wheelbase Land-Rovers, the Ligero models differ mainly in tyre size, chassis and body length. Over 2000 of the 109 Ligero or Mil.109 were produced. Most were general service vehicles but some were fitted out as recovery vehicles, ambulances and fire-fighters.

Technical Details: Own 4-cyl. diesel engine, 2286 cc (90.47 × 88.9 mm), 46.2 kW/62 bhp (net) at 4000 rpm. Dry plate clutch. 4F1R gearbox. 2-speed transfer box with front axle disconnect. 4.7:1 axle gear ratio. Hydraulic brakes. Semi-elliptic leaf springs. 7.50-16 tyres. 24-Volt electrics. 90-litre fuel tank. *Note:* also with 2286-cc 81-bhp petrol engine.

Dimensions and Weights: Wheelbase 2768 mm. Track 1330 mm. Overall length and width 4546 × 1650 mm. Height 2070 mm (canvas top). Ground clearance 220 mm (axles). Angles of approach and departure 50° and 40°. Weight 1643 kg, GVW 2743 kg.

above: 1973 prototype; *below:* production model

Truck, 1-ton, 4 × 4, Utility   **S**
(Volvo C303)

6-cyl. 2.98-litre petrol engine with 4F1R gearbox and 2-speed transfer box. Wheelbase 2300 mm. Overall dimensions 4250 × 1900 × 2255 mm. Weight 2250 kg. GVW 3450 kg. Civilian version of Volvo 4140 4 × 4 series, 1976. In 1980 it was offered in the UK as Dosco HS100-4 with cargo body and Rover V8 engine.

Truck, 1.25-ton, 4 × 4, Command   **F**
(ALM/ACMAT VLRA 4 × 4 TPK420VCT)

6-cyl. 5.8-litre diesel engine (Perkins 6.354) with 4F1R gearbox and 2-speed transfer box. Wheelbase 3300 mm. Weight 3850 kg. 12.50-20 tyres. French 'command car' on truck chassis, officially known as VCT (*Véhicule de Commandement et de Transmission*). Sold mainly for export. One of several body styles on this chassis.

Truck, 1.25-ton, 4 × 4, Utility   **USA**
(Chrysler EMV)

V-8-cyl. 5.9-litre petrol engine (360-1) with 3F1R automatic transmission and 2-speed transfer box. Spicer axles. Disc/drum brakes. Coil springs. 14.00-18 tyres. Wheelbase 3150 mm. Overall dimensions 4470 × 2159 × 1956 mm. Entered for CSV competition, 1978. Further developed by General Dynamics (qv).

Truck, 1.25-ton, 4 × 4, Command   **ROK**
(Keohwa M-20GL)

6-cyl. 4.2-litre petrol engine with 4F1R gearbox and 2-speed transfer box. Diff. lock in rear axle. Disc/drum brakes. Wheelbase 3330 mm. Overall dimensions 5580 × 2000 × 2050 mm. Weight 2200 kg. GVW 3450 kg. 6-seater 'Command and Control' vehicle, produced in South Korea in the early 1980s.

Truck, 4 × 4, Patrol   **GB**
(Glover Tuareg)

This prototype 'remote area patrol vehicle' was launched in 1978 by Glover Webb & Liversidge in Britain. It was a purpose-built partly-armoured high-mobility vehicle with Mercedes-Benz 6-cyl. petrol engine and 5F1R gearbox with 2-speed transfer box. Wheelbase 2800 mm. 9.00-20 tyres. Front-mounted winch.

Truck, 6 × 6, Patrol   **GB**
(Land-Rover/Hotspur Sandringham S6E)

V-8-cyl. 3.5-litre petrol engine with 4F1R gearbox and 2-speed transfer box. Lockable interaxle diff. in transfer box. Wheelbase 3175 mm. Conversion of Land-Rover V8, as comprehensively-equipped long-range desert patrol vehicle. Payload 2000 kg. Available as 6 × 4, APC, gun tractor or mobile gun mount. 1982.

TRUCK, 1.25-TON, 4×4 (AMG 'HUMMER') USA

General Data: Prototype for new generation of High-Mobility Multipurpose Wheeled Vehicles (HMMWV or 'Humvee') for the US armed forces. 11 units supplied for testing by the US Army in 1982. The 'Hummer' had a top speed of 110 km/h and a cruising range of 480 km. It featured power steering, power disc brakes, full-time 4-wheel drive and run-flat tyres. Accepted for quantity production 1983.

Technical Details: GM Detroit Diesel V-8-cyl. diesel engine, 6217 cc (101 × 97 mm), 97 kW/130 bhp (net) at 3600 rpm. GM Allison THM400HD (Turbo Hydramatic) 3F1R auto. trans. New Process 2-speed transfer box with lockable differential 2.73:1

axle gear ratio. 1.92:1 final drive gear reduction. Hydraulic disc brakes. Independent suspension with coil springs. 36-12.50-16.5 tyres. 24-Volt electrics. 83-litre fuel tank.

Dimensions and Weights: Wheelbase 3302 mm. Track 1819 mm. Overall length and width 4700 × 2126 mm. Height 1753 mm (windscreen). Ground clearance 406 mm. Angles of approach and departure 70° and 45°. Weight 2855 kg, GVW 3990 kg.

above and below: various prototypes

TRUCK, 1.25-TON, 4×4 (GENERAL DYNAMICS XM998)   USA

General Data: When General Dynamics purchased Chrysler's Defense Group activities (for a reported $348.5 million in 1982), one of the projects involved was the HMMWV (see previous entry) which had started life in 1977/78 as Chrysler's expanded-mobility vehicle. Several variants were built, both with Chrysler V8 petrol engine and with North American Deutz diesel. 11 prototypes were delivered to the US Army in mid-1982 for extensive testing. The vehicle was not accepted.

Technical Details: Deutz F8L 610 V-8-cyl. aircooled diesel engine, 6537 cc (102 × 100 mm), 119 kW/160 bhp (net) at 3200 rpm. Chrysler A727 Torqueflite 3F1R auto. trans. New Process 2-speed transfer box with lockable differential. Dana 44 front axle centre unit with True-Trac. diff. Dana 60 rear axle with No-Spin diff. Hydraulic brakes. Coil spring suspension, independent at front. 37-12.5-16LT tyres. 24-Volt electrics. 105-litre fuel-tank.

Dimensions and Weights: Wheelbase 3414 mm. Track not specified. Overall length and width 4798 × 2159 mm. Height 1752 mm (windscreen). Ground clearance 330 mm (axles). Angles of approach and departure 60° and 46°. Weight 2245 kg, GVW 3400 kg.

above: weapons carrier; *below:* troop carrier/cargo vehicle

TRUCK, 1.25-TON, 4×4 (TELEDYNE HMMWV)

USA

General Data: Developed and built by Teledyne Continental Motors' General Products Division in Muskegon, Michigan, this entry in the US Army's HMMWV competition of the early 1980s (see previous entry) can be traced back to the Cheetah (qv) which was a high-performance vehicle with rear-mounted Chrysler V8 engine. Conceived by MTI in 1977, this vehicle had been further developed by TCM. In 1979 the rear-engine design was replaced by a front-engine configuration. It remained experimental

Technical Details: IHC 420 CID V-8-cyl. diesel engine, 6882 cc (101.6 × 106.2 mm), 127 kW/170 bhp (SAE) at 3400 rpm. GM 475 Turbo Hydramatic 3F1R auto. trans. New Process 208 2-speed transfer box with front axle disconnect. Lockable rear diff., limited-slip front diff. Hydraulic disc brakes. Independent suspension with torsion bars. 36-12.50-16.5LT tyres. 24-Volt electrics. 91-litre fuel tank.

Dimensions and Weights: Wheelbase 3302 mm. Track 1773 mm. Overall length and width 4868 × 2090 mm. Height 1752 mm (roof). Ground clearance 381 mm. Angles of approach and departure 60° and 38.2°. Weight 2270 kg, GVW 4022 kg.

above: 1982 prototype; *below left and right:* 1981 and 1980 prototypes

87

Light 4 × 4 Trucks

Presented in this section are cargo/personnel trucks in the under-2-ton cross-country payload rating class, as well as several derivatives of these vehicles, e.g. weapon mounts and special purpose vans. Many of these trucks were modifications of commercially-available vehicles with various degrees of off-road capability. It should be noted that some variants are to be found elsewhere in this book, for example ambulances and fire-fighters which are covered in their special relevant sections. Smallest of the light 4 × 4 trucks (apart from the field car/utility trucks covered in the previous chapter) are the lightweight platform vehicles, some of which can be controlled by the driver sitting on or walking (or even crawling) behind them. The Faun Kraka (also in this category but lacking four-wheel drive) is dealt with in an earlier chapter, a certain amount of overlap between sections being unavoidable.

Some of the trucks catalogued here were made in very large quantities, others never reached the quantity production stage. Some of the latter, e.g. Chrysler Corporation's RAM 1.25-ton model, were quite interesting in technical concept but perhaps over-engineered and consequently too costly if built only in the limited numbers required.

One of the most outstanding vehicles in this class is the Daimler-Benz Unimog (of which there are numerous versions, differing in size and power). It is also a rather complex vehicle, though, with a very sophisticated transmission system: high technology with a price to suit.

Land-Rover 0.75-ton trucks are among the most widely used although they are not ideal vehicles to let the average conscript loose on. But the ideal conscript-proof vehicle has yet to be invented. In spite of automatic transmission (which would be a necessity) we seem to be drifting further away from the tough no-nonsense military trucks of yore; undoubtedly among the best were the Dodge-built M37 and its derivatives. Alas, the US Government decided that Dodge had been producing military trucks long enough and that other manufacturers should be given a chance. As a result, two new models eventually went into production and service, both rated for a higher (1.25-ton or 'five-quarter') payload, one a

high-mobility six-wheeler and the other a medium-mobility four-wheeler, a modification of Kaiser Jeep Corporation's Gladiator pickup truck. There were ambulance variants of both but of neither could it be said that they were real improvements on the trusty old Dodge, many of which were still soldiering on, in military and civil service, long after the new 'five-quarters' began to be thrown out again. The Kaiser Jeep product (M715 and variants) was replaced by another Dodge, but this was a slightly-modified commercial off-the-shelf model and not comparable with the old three-quarter-ton type. The M715 truck, modified and improved in detail, remained in production not only in the USA but also in the Republic of South Korea, where two firms, Asia Motors and Keohwa made them for military use. By the early 1980s, General Motors, who had been out of the military mass-production business for some time, launched their diesel-engined CUCV (Commercial Utility Cargo Vehicle). This was again a militarized off-the-shelf civilian vehicle of which a large number were ordered in 1982. For high-mobility requirements, the cargo/personnel version of the 'Humvee' was conceived (see previous section).

A relative newcomer in the field of 1.25-ton military tactical trucks is the Philippine CM-125, produced by Canlubang Automotive Resources Corporation of Manila and also known as the 'Carco'. It was configured as a normal control truck with set-back front axle and can be employed as a cargo/weapons carrier, a personnel carrier and a field ambulance, all with the same basic bodywork. It has a Mitsubishi diesel engine as standard equipment with full-synchromesh 5-speed gearbox, front hub locks, 7.50-16 tyres (9.00-16 optional), 257-mm ground clearance, and approach and departure angles of 34° and 38° respectively. The chassis and body, as well as most of the mechanical components, are produced in the Philippines. Other unadorned and functional military trucks in this class originating from developing countries include the Brazilian Engesa EE-15 and the Mexican Rural Ramirez. Like the Israeli AIL M-325 and the Portuguese Bravia Gazela, these trucks make a lot of sense for the military forces of the modern world.

Truck, 0.2-ton, 4 × 4, Platform   I
(Fresia)

2-cyl. 0.4-litre aircooled petrol engine. 4-wheel drive via a closed hydrostatic circuit with 2 hydraulic motors. Overall length and width 1980 × 900 mm. Weight 350 kg. Italian mountain tractor/ load carrier, operated by driver seated or walking and intended to replace the Moto Guzzi 3 × 3 'Mulo Meccanico'. 1979.

Truck, 0.5-ton, 4 × 4, Platform   USA
(Brunswick M274A5)

2-cyl. 0.7-litre aircooled petrol engine with 3F1R gearbox and 2-speed transfer box. 4-wheel drive. 7.50-10 tyres. Wheelbase 1448 mm. Overall dimensions (in form as shown) 3016 × 1264 × 1248 mm. Weight 440 kg. Latest 'mechanical mule' made for US Army and USMC by Willys, Baifield and Brunswick. (1970).

Truck, 0.5-ton, 4 × 4, Platform   F
(Fardier Lohr FL500)

2-cyl. 0.6-litre aircooled petrol engine (Citroën AK2), mounted centrally with 4F1R gearbox. Tubular chassis with independent suspension. Wheelbase 1750 mm. Overall length and width 2350 × 1500 mm. Weight 550 kg. Bodywork of aluminium and polyester. Built for French Army airborne forces.

Truck, 0.5-ton, 4 × 4, Platform   F
(Sodives Crapahut)

2-cyl. 0.4-litre aircooled petrol engine (Kohler) (0.7-litre Kohler 4-stroke optional) with centrifugal clutch and 2F1R gearbox. Wheelbase 1600 mm. Overall dimensions 2500 × 1400 × 710 mm. Weight 550 kg. French amphibious airborne platform vehicle with central driver's position. Large-diameter tyres.

Truck, 0.6-ton, 4 × 4, Platform   BR
(Jamy SAFO-1)

Produced by Jamy of Rio de Janeiro, this was the lightest of 4 military vehicles developed in the late 1970s for the Brazilian Army. Other proposed Brazilian platform vehicles were made by Gurgel (X2) and, for the Marines, by Biselli (with 106-mm recoilless rifle). The Jamy company also produced airport fire/crash trucks.

Truck, 0.6-ton, 4 × 4, Platform   I
(Piaggio)

Single-cyl. 2-stroke petrol engine with 4F1R gearbox. Overall dimensions 2190 × 1370 × 1000 mm. Max. speed 35 km/h. Collapsible for ease of air transport and parachute dropping. Developed for Italian armed forces in the early 1970s. Tubular chassis, no springs, rigidly-mounted rear axle, 'floating' front axle.

TRUCK, 0.5-TON, 4 × 4 (GAZ/UAZ-69M)

SU

General Data: This vehicle first went into quantity production in 1952 as the GAZ-69. A 4-door field car variant was launched at the same time, designated GAZ-69A. Production was transferred from Gorky to Ulyanovsk in 1956. Both types were manufactured for many years and there were several derivatives. In Romania it was produced under licence (UMM/ARO M-461) with detail differences. The GAZ-69 range was in service with the Warsaw Pact forces and in several other countries.

Technical Details: M-21/UAZ-69B 4-cyl. petrol engine, 2433 cc (88 × 100 mm), 48.5 kW/65 bhp (net) at 3800 rpm. Dry plate clutch. 3F1R gearbox. 2-speed transfer box with front axle disconnect. 5.125:1 axle gear ratio. Hydraulic brakes. Semi-elliptic leaf spring suspension. 6.50-16 tyres. 12-Volt electrics. 75-litre fuel tank.

Dimensions and Weights: Wheelbase 2300 mm. Track 1440 mm. Overall length and width 3850 × 1850 mm. Height 2030 mm (canvas top). Ground clearance 210 mm (axles). Angles of approach and departure 45° and 35°. Weight 1525 kg, GVW 2125 kg.

above: basic version; *below left:* 'Snapper' missile launcher; *below right:* 69RS command vehicle

TRUCK, 0.6-TON, 4 × 4 (PEKING BJ-212A)

General Data: The Chinese Peking/Pei-ching BJ-212A was the truck version of the BJ-212 field car. It had 2 doors and a tailgate and was supplied for civil and military service, as well as for export. Like the BJ-212, it retained the military-style blackout driving light on the left-hand front wing when sold for non-military use and other features – the dashboard for example – were also of military pattern. Introduced in the late 1960s, these vehicles remained in production for many years. The BJ-212A had a seating capacity of 6 persons in the rear, on hinged longitudinal benches. The vehicle's speed range was given as 3–98 km/h.

Technical Details: 4-cyl. petrol engine, 2445 cc (92 × 92 mm),

56 kW/75 bhp (net) at 3500–4000 rpm. Dry plate clutch. 3F1R gearbox. 2-speed transfer box with front axle disconnect. 4.55:1 axle gear ratio. Hydraulic brakes. Semi-elliptic leaf springs. 6.50-16 tyres. 12-Volt electrics. 85-litre fuel tank.

Dimensions and Weights: Wheelbase 1300 mm. Track 1440 mm. Overall length and width 3860 × 1750 mm. Height 2015 mm (tarpaulin). Ground clearance 220 mm (axles). Angles of approach and departure 45° and 35°. Weight 1520 kg, GVW 2120 kg.

above and below: standard version

TRUCK, 0.75-TON, 4×4 (KEOHWA M-SERIES)   ROK

General Data: In addition to 0.25-ton models with 2134- and 2390-mm wheelbase, Keohwa of Seoul introduced a range of 2895-mm wheelbase models with the same Jeep CJ-type front end but with different bodywork. 4 body styles were offered: M-7GA1L, a 4-seat 'Mobile Headquarters' (cruising range 1600 km), M-7GA3L 'Reconnaissance and Convoy', M-7GBM 'Broadcasting Mobile' (hardtop van for communications purposes) and M-7GP1, a closed-cab truck for cargo and troop transport. A diesel engine was optional.

Technical Details: AMC 258CID 6-cyl. petrol engine, 4229 cc (95.25 × 99.06 mm), 85 kW/114 bhp (net) at 3200 rpm. Dry plate clutch. 4F1R gearbox. 2-speed transfer box with front axle disconnect. 3.73:1 axle gear ratio. Hydraulic brakes. Semi-elliptic leaf springs. 7.00-15 tyres (9.00-15 Wide Track optional). 12-Volt electrics. 70-litre fuel tank.

Dimensions and Weights: Wheelbase 2895 mm. Track, front/rear 1308/1270 mm. Overall length and width 4825 × 1800 mm. Height 2080 mm (tarpaulin). Ground clearance 240 mm (axles). Angles of approach and departure 45° and 30°. Weight 1740 kg, GVW 2490 kg.

above: M-7GP1; *below left:* M-7GA3L; *below right:* M-7GBM

Truck, 0.5-ton, 4 × 4, Cargo   **R**
(ARO/UMM M461C)

4-cyl. 2.5-litre petrol engine (M207A) with 4F1R gearbox and single-speed transfer box. Rigid axles with 16- or 15-in. wheels. Wheelbase 2335 mm. Overall dimensions 3854 × 1850 (incl. spare wheel) × 2050 mm. Weight 1550 kg. GVW 2200 kg. Patterned on Soviet GAZ/UAZ-69 (qv). Many were exported.

Truck, 0.75-ton, 4 × 4, Cargo   **BR**
(Chevrolet C1404)

6-cyl. petrol engine with 4F1R gearbox and single-speed transfer box. Militarized commercial pickup truck, manufactured by General Motors do Brasil and converted to 4-wheel drive by Engesa ('Total Traction'). Cab with removable doors and folding windscreen. Shown in Brazilian Army service in the mid-1970s.

Truck, 0.75-ton, 4 × 4, Cargo   **BR**
(ENGESA/ENVEMO)

6-cyl. petrol engine with 4F1R gearbox (diesel and automatic transmission optional) with 2-speed transfer box. Rigid axles, leaf springs. 15-in. wheels. Wheelbase 2950 mm. Weight 2250 kg. GVW 3250 kg. Designed and produced by the Brazilian Engesa Group, c. 1980. Chassis also available with other bodywork.

Truck, 0.75-ton, 4 × 4, Light Recovery   **GB**
(Land-Rover 109 Series IIA)

4-cyl. petrol engine with 4F1R gearbox and 2-speed transfer box. Wheelbase 2768 mm. Weight 2350 kg. Max. speed 105 km/h. Range 290 km. Employed by the REME of the British Army. Fitted with 2300-kg front-mounted winch, 2500-kg capacity rear jib, front tow hitch and other recovery and repair equipment.

Truck, 0.75-ton, 4 × 4, General Service   **GB**
(Land-Rover 109 Series III)

4-cyl. 2.25-litre diesel engine with 4F1R gearbox and 2-speed transfer box. Wheelbase 2768 mm. Weight 1750 kg. This vehicle has been in service with the Netherlands Army since the late 1970s when over 5000 diesel-engined Land-Rovers were ordered to replace all their existing light cross-country vehicles.

Truck, 0.75-ton, 4 × 4, Reconnaissance   **GB**
(Land-Rover 109 Series III)

4-cyl. diesel engine with 4F1R gearbox and 2-speed transfer box. Wheelbase 2768 mm. Netherlands Army modification of standard model, featuring radiator brush guard, relocated spare wheel (to tailgate), machine-gun pedestal in rear compartment. Known as *Verkenningsvoertuig*. Shown in operational mode. 1981.

TRUCK, 0.75-TON, 4×4 (LAND-ROVER 109 SERIES IIA)   AUS

General Data: The Australian military long-wheelbase Land-Rovers were locally-assembled/modified products and were acquired in large numbers by Army, RAAF and RAN for a variety of roles. Basically similar to the UK version, they had certain distinguishing features like the straight front wing cutouts, the large brushguard on the front bumper and the protected tail lights. Australian Army versions included GS Gargo, FFR, panel van, ambulance, workshop, recovery unit, fire-fighters, early rescue. Series III vehicles were also procured

Technical Details: Own 4-cyl. petrol engine, 2286 cc (90.47 × 88.9 mm), 53 kW/71 bhp (net) at 4500 rpm. Dry plate clutch. 4F1R gearbox. 2-speed transfer case with front axle disconnect. 4.7:1 axle gear ratio. Hydraulic brakes. Semi-elliptic leaf springs. 7.50-16 tyres. 12-Volt electrics. 2 × 45-litre fuel tanks.

Dimensions and Weights: Wheelbase 2768 mm. Track 1330 mm. Overall length and width 4650 × 1690 mm. Height 2100 mm (roof). Ground clearance 248 mm (axles). Angles of approach and departure 45° and 29°. Weight 1550 kg, GVW 2680 kg.

above: hardtop with windows; *below left:* FFR (fitted for radio); *below right:* platform/workshop

TRUCK, 0.75-TON, 4 × 4 (LAND-ROVER 109 SERIES III)   GB

General Data: The '109' version of the Land-Rover has been in service for many years with numerous armed services around the world. Shown above is a British Army 'FV18062 Truck, General Service, FFR (Rover 11, Series III, 0.75 tonne, 4 × 4)' of 1974. The Series III was introduced in 1971. Early in 1983, a modernized version, the One Ten (wheelbase 110 in., 2794 mm) was added, featuring coil spring suspension, 5F1R overdrive-top gearbox, disc/drum brakes and numerous body detail refinements.

Technical Details: Own 4-cyl. petrol engine, 2286 cc (90.47 × 88.9 mm), 53 kW/71 bhp (net) at 4000 rpm. Dry plate clutch. 4F1R gearbox. 2-speed transfer box with front axle disconnect. 4.7:1 axle gear ratio. Hydraulic brakes. Semi-elliptic leaf springs. 7.50-16 tyres. 24-Volt electrics. 2 × 45-litre fuel tanks. *Note:* also with diesel engine, 12-Volt electrics, single fuel tank.

Dimensions and Weights: Wheelbase 2768 mm. Track 1330 mm. Overall length and width 4650 × 1690 mm. Height 2060 mm (canvas top). Ground clearance 248 mm (axles). Angles of approach and departure 45° and 29°. Weight 1890 kg, GVW 2760 kg.

above: Series III FFR; *below left:* mount for Wombat AT gun; *below right:* GS vehicle of Netherlands Air Force (1981)

TRUCK, 0.8-TON, 4 × 4 (UAZ-452 SERIES)

SU

General Data: First announced in the late 1950s (UAZ-450 Series with 65-bhp engine) this range of light commercials was uprated and fitted with a more powerful engine from 1966 and continued in production for many years for civil and military service. The base models were the 452 panel van, the 452A ambulance, the 452B and V personnel carriers and the 452D truck with open dropside body. Some of the forward-control models were also available with rear-wheel drive only.

Technical Details: ZMZ-451E 4-cyl. petrol engine, 2445 cc (92 × 92 mm), 51.3 kW/72 bhp (net) at 4000 rpm. Dry plate clutch. 4F1R gearbox. 2-speed transfer box with front axle disconnect.

5.125 : 1 axle gear ratio. Hydraulic brakes. Semi-elliptic leaf springs. 8.40-15 tyres. 12-Volt electrics. 56-litre fuel tank (plus 30-litre auxiliary tank on all models except 452D).

Dimensions and Weights: Wheelbase 2300 mm. Track 1442 mm. Overall length and width 4460 × 2044 mm. Height 2070 mm (cab). Ground clearance 220 mm (axles). Angles of approach and departure 36° and 30°. Weight 1670 kg, GVW 2550 kg.

above: UAZ-452D; *below left:* UAZ-452; *below right:* UAZ-452 mobile workshop

Truck, 0.75-ton, 4 × 4, General Service   **F**
(SIMI Cournil)

Conceived c. 1960 by Bernard Cournil of Aurillac, France, and produced ever since with successive improvements under several trade names, incl. SAMO, Fennec (and UMM of Portugal). Choice of several petrol and diesel engines and short (2040-mm) or long (2540-mm; shown) wheelbase. Limited military use.

Truck, 1-ton, 4 × 4, Cargo   **RA**
(Chevrolet KS10)

6-cyl. 3.8-litre petrol engine with 3F1R gearbox and 2-speed transfer box. Wheelbase 2921 mm. Prototype by GM Argentina, 1970/71. Argentine Marine Corps acquired a number for use at naval bases. Developed from commercial K10 4 × 4 pickup. Military pattern cab and fittings, incl. brush guard.

Truck, 1-ton, 4 × 4, Weapon Mount   **RA**
(Chevrolet K10)

6-cyl. 3.8-litre petrol engine with 3F1R gearbox and 2-speed transfer box. Basically a standard commercial Chevrolet Stepside pickup, militarized in Argentina and carrying a multiple rocket launcher by EDESA (Empresa de Desarrollos Especiales) of Buenos Aires from the late 1970s. Note hydraulic outriggers.

Truck, 1-ton, 4 × 4, Cargo   **CDN**
(Dodge W200 Power Wagon)

V-8-cyl. petrol engine (6-cyl. optional) with manual or automatic transmission and 2-speed transfer box with lockable diff. Militarized commercial pickup truck of the Canadian Army, supplied by Chrysler Canada in the mid-1970s. Standard Canadian camouflage of charcoal black, olive drab green and khaki.

Truck, 1-ton, 4 × 4, Cargo   **AUS**
(Ford)

6-cyl. 4-litre petrol engine with 4F1R gearbox and 2-speed transfer box. 16-in. wheels. Wheelbase 2581 mm. Track 1784 mm. Overall length and width 4420 × 2134 mm. Prototypes built in 1971/72 by Ford (and International) to meet Australian Army requirement for tactical 1-ton GS truck, but not proceeded with.

Truck, 1-ton, 4 × 4, Cargo   **E**
(Land-Rover/Santana 1300)

4-cyl. 2.28-litre petrol or diesel engine with 4F1R gearbox and 2-speed transfer box. Wheelbase 2770 mm. Overall dimensions 4840 × 1680 × 2190 mm. Weight 1760 kg (diesel 1840 kg). Spanish forward-control version of Land-Rover 109. Used by Spanish forces with full-length canvas top. Other bodystyles existed.

Truck, 1-ton, 4 × 4, Fueller   **GB**
(Land-Rover FC110 SIIB)

4-cyl. 2.28-litre diesel engine with 4F1R gearbox and 2-speed transfer box. 4.7:1 axle gear ratio. Vacuum/hydraulic brakes. Wheelbase 2794 mm. In service with Danish forces, fitted with tank, pump and dispensing equipment for petrol and diesel fuel (650 litres each). Land-Rover FC110 saw very limited military use.

Truck, 1-ton, 4 × 4, Cargo   **IND**
(Nissan Carrier)

6-cyl. 3.9-litre petrol engine with 4F1R gearbox and 2-speed transfer box. Wheelbase 2800 mm. GVW 4200 kg. This Japanese truck was licence-produced by the Ordnance Factory in Jabalpur, India, for the Indian Army. This factory also built the Japanese Nissan Patrol (qv) under licence, under the marque name Jonga.

Truck, 1-ton, 4 × 4, Cargo   **F**
(Peugeot P4 Long)

4-cyl. petrol or diesel engine (several options) with 4F1R gearbox and 2-speed transfer box. Wheelbase 4350 mm. Bodywork by Heuliez. Front-mounted winch (shown) optional. Derived from Mercedes G-Series lwb version, also with panel van bodywork. Personnel carrying capacity 11. Private venture by PSA, 1981.

Truck, 1-ton, 4 × 4, Cargo   **MEX**
(Rural Ramirez)

6-cyl. 3.68-litre petrol engine (GM/Automex 225) or Perkins diesel with 3F1R gearbox (Warner) and 2-speed transfer box (Spicer). Spicer axles. Ross steering. Wheelbase 2890 mm. Overall dimensions 4390 × 1740 × 1800 mm. Weight 1700 kg. Produced from 1971 by Trailers de Monterrey, Mexico, replacing 0.75-ton model.

Truck, 1-ton, 4 × 4, Cargo   **P**
(UMM/Cournil Entrepreneur)

4-cyl. 2.1- or 2.3-litre diesel engine (Indenor) with 4F1R gearbox and 2-speed transfer box. Rigid axles. Diff. lock at rear. Wheelbase 2525 mm. Overall dimensions 3865 × 1570 × 2030 mm. Weight 1500 kg. GVW 2600 kg. Commercially available, also with 2040-mm wheelbase, hardtop, PTO, winch, etc.

Truck, 1-ton, 4 × 4, Cargo   **D**
(Unimog 421)

4-cyl. 2.4-litre diesel engine (OM 616) with 6F2R transmission. Portal axles with 18-in. wheels. Wheelbase 2605 mm. Overall dimensions 4740 × 1825 × 2200 mm (cab). Weight 2500 kg. GVW 4000 kg. Diff. locks front and rear. Speed range 2.5–80 km/h. All-steel cab. 1974. Later redesignated U600L (421).

TRUCK, 1-TON, 4×4 (BRAVIA GAZELA)   P

General Data: The Gazela was designed to meet the specifications for the NATO 1-ton class tactical truck and produced for the Portuguese Army by Bravia of Lisbon. It was also offered commercially and there was a choice of engines and body types. In addition to the open cab shown here, a hardtop variant could be fitted. Bravia trucks, armoured cars and many other types of military equipment were marketed by Trace of Vaduz, in the Principality of Liechtenstein.

Technical Details: Dodge H225 6-cyl. petrol engine, 3687 cc (86.5 × 104.8 mm), 112 kW/150 bhp (net) at 4000 rpm. Dry plate clutch. 4F1R gearbox. 2-speed transfer box with front axle disconnect. 4.88:1 axle gear ratio. Hydraulic brakes. Semi-elliptic leaf springs. 9.00-16 tyres. 12-Volt electrics. 150-litre fuel tank. *Note:* optional equipment included Perkins 4.236 diesel engine, 10.50-16 tyres, 24-Volt electrics, 4.5-ton Braden winch.

Dimensions and Weights (chassis/cab, with winch): Wheelbase 3365 mm. Track, front/rear 1720/1665 mm. Overall length and width 5780 × 2165 mm. Height 2500 mm (approx.). Ground clearance 250 mm (axles). Angles of approach and departure 35° and 33°. Weight 3100 kg, GVW 5300 kg.

above and below: cargo trucks with tarpaulin

TRUCK, 1-TON, 4×4 (LAND-ROVER 101)   GB

General Data: Designed to meet a military requirement for a high power-to-weight ratio helicopter-liftable general service load carrier with a payload rating of 1000 kg, this vehicle featured a 2490 × 1729-mm body with hinged removable sides and tailgate. It could be supplied with (a) rear seating for 8 men in full kit, (b) 24-Volt electrical system, fully suppressed for radio and (c) side-mounted capstan winch. Special bodies included ambulances and vans. Among foreign users were Australia, Egypt, Luxembourg and the USAF (in the UK). Produced in the mid-1970s.

Technical Details: Own V-8-cyl. petrol engine, 3528 cc (88.9 × 71.1 mm), 92.5 kW/124 bhp (net) at 5000 rpm. Dry plate clutch. 4F1R gearbox. 2-speed transfer box with differential for full-time 4-wheel drive. 5.57:1 axle gear ratio. Hydraulic brakes. Semi-elliptic leaf springs. 9.00-16 tyres. 12- or 24-Volt electrics. 114-litre fuel tank.

Dimensions and Weights: Wheelbase 2566 mm. Track, front/rear 1525/1550 mm. Overall length and width 4280 × 1842 mm. Height 2185 mm (canvas top). Ground clearance 254 mm (axles). Angles of approach and departure 50° and 51°. Weight 1860 kg, GVW 3650 kg.

above: with power-axle trailer, 1972; *below:* British GS trucks.

TRUCK, 1-TON, 4×4 (STEYR-DAIMLER-PUCH PINZGAUER 710 SERIES)   A

General Data: The Pinzgauer range of tactical 4 × 4 and 6 × 6 vehicles was developed in the 1960s and series-produced from 1971. They could be called enlarged editions of the Haflinger, which the Pinzgauer replaced in production. Like the Haflinger, it had a sophisticated specification and many unusual features. The Swiss Army was its first customer followed by several other countries. Hardtop, softtop and special bodies were available.

Technical Details: Own 4-cyl. aircooled twin-carburettor petrol engine, 2499 cc (92 × 94 mm), 67 kW/92 bhp (DIN) at 4000 rpm. Dry plate clutch. 5F1R gearbox. 2-speed transfer box with front axle disconnect. 2.846:1 axle gear ratio plus 2.266:1 spur gear ratio. Hydraulic brakes. Coil springs. 245-16 or 7.50-16 tyres. 24-Volt electrics. 75- or 125-litre fuel tank. *Note:* a less powerful engine with 7.5 v. 8.0:1 compression ratio was available.

Dimensions and Weights: Wheelbase 2200 mm. track 1440 mm. Overall length and width 4175 × 1760 mm. Height 2045 mm (canvas top). Ground clearance 335 mm (axles). Angles of approach and departure 45° and 45°. Weight 1950 kg, GVW 3050 kg.

above and *below left:* 710M cargo/personnel; *below right:* 710K command/radio vehicle

TRUCK, 1.2-TON, 4×4 (RENAULT TRM 1200/SAVIEM TP3 L39)   F

General Data: This light on/off-road truck was designed in the late 1960s and entered quantity production in 1970/71. It was essentially a 4-wheel drive conversion of the contemporary Renault/Saviem SG3 commercial truck. Most of these vehicles carried the Saviem name. In addition to the militarized cargo truck with softtop cab and folding windscreen there were several versions with all-steel cab and with integral van-type bodywork, including the 6-stretcher ambulance (qv).

Technical Details: Saviem 817 04 4-cyl. petrol engine, 2600 cc (93 × 96 mm), 58.2 kW/78 bhp (net) at 3600 rpm. Dry plate clutch. 4F1R gearbox. 2-speed transfer box with front axle disconnect.

6.28:1 axle gear ratio. Vacuum-assisted hydraulic brakes. Semi-elliptic leaf springs. 9.00-16 tyres. 24-Volt electrics. 120-litre fuel tank.

Dimensions and Weights: Wheelbase 2640 mm. Track, front/rear 1641/1661 mm. Overall length and width 4997 × 1996 mm. Height 2510 mm (cab). Ground clearance 270 mm (axles). Angles of approach and departure 31° and 40°. Weight 2580 kg (chassis/cab), GVW 3950 kg.

above: cargo truck; *below left:* TRM PC radio command van (*Gendarmerie*); *below right:* all-steel cab

Truck, 1.25-ton, 4 × 4, Cargo   **ROK**
(Asia Motors KM450)
6-cyl. 4-litre diesel engine (MZB) with 5F1R gearbox and 2-speed transfer box. Rigid axles. Wheelbase 3200 mm. Overall dimensions 5328 × 2008 × 2370 mm. Weight 2550 kg. GVW 4080 kg. 3400-kg capacity winch optional. Patterned on US M715 Jeep truck, licence-produced in Seoul, South Korea.

Truck, 1.25-ton, 4 × 4, Cargo   **PI**
(Canlubang/CARCO CM-125)
4-cyl. diesel engine (Mitsubishi 4DR50A, Perkins or Isuzu) with 5F1R gearbox and 2-speed transfer box. Dana-Spicer axles. Diff. lock at rear. Wheelbase 2770 mm. Overall dimensions 4785 × 1600 × 2190 mm. Winch at front. Designed and built by Canlubang Automotive Resources Corp., Philippines, early 1980s.

Truck, 1.25-ton, 4 × 4, Cargo   **CDN**
(Chevrolet K20)
V-8-cyl. 5.7-litre petrol engine with automatic transmission. Power-assisted steering and brakes. Wheelbase 3340 mm. Militarized commercial pickup of the late 1970s by GM of Oshawa, Ontario, for Canadian Army.

Truck, 1.25-ton, 4 × 4, Cargo   **CDN**
(Chrysler/Dodge RAM)
V-8-cyl. 5.2-litre petrol engine with 3F1R automatic transmission and 2-speed transfer box. Independent suspension. Wheelbase 2820 mm. Overall length and width 4572 × 2160 mm. Weight 2825 kg. GVW 4846 kg. 6 (of 7 ordered) built for and tested by Canadian Government but not proceeded with.

Truck, 1.25-ton, 4 × 4, Cargo   **USA**
(GM/Chevrolet K30903/M1008)
V-8-cyl. 6.2-litre diesel engine with 3F1R automatic transmission and 2-speed transfer box. Wheelbase 3340 mm. Overall length and width 5499 × 2022 mm. Also M1009 Utility (Blazer), M1010 Ambulance, M1028 Cargo Shelter Carrier, M1031 Chassis/Cab. Commercial Utility Cargo Vehicle (CUCV) for US Army, 1982.

Truck, 1.25-ton, 4 × 4, Cargo   **ROK**
(Keohwa M-20G1)
6-cyl. 4-litre petrol engine with 4F1R gearbox and 2-speed transfer box. Wheelbase 3330 mm. Overall dimensions 5360 × 2295 × 2290 mm. Weight 2200 kg. GVW 3450 kg. Max. speed 130 km/h. Power steering. Produced under US licence in S. Korea, also with ambulance and command car bodywork. Early 1980s.

TRUCK, 1.25-TON, 4×4 (AMG AM715)

USA

General Data: In the mid-1960s, the US Army placed a large order with Kaiser Jeep Corporation for 1¼-ton trucks. These vehicles were militarized versions of the makers' Gladiator pickup truck and were made as cargo trucks, M715, maintenance trucks, M726, and ambulances, M725 (qv). When deliveries were completed, the suppliers, who had formed a new company – AM General Corporation – offered the truck to other military customers as AM715, AM726, etc. A heavier type, the AM720, was also introduced, as were many variations. The following data apply to the AM715 of the mid-1970s.

Technical Details: Own 6-258 6-cyl. petrol engine, 4229 cc (95.25 × 99.06 mm), 82 kW/110 bhp (net) at 3600 rpm. Dry plate clutch. 4F1R gearbox. 2-speed transfer box with front axle disconnect. 3.73:1 axle gear ratio. Hydraulic brakes. Semi-elliptic leaf springs. 7.50-16 tyres. 12-Volt electrics. 72-litre fuel tank.

Dimensions and Weights: Wheelbase 3320 mm. Track, front/rear 1626/1638 mm. Overall length and width 5321 × 2032 mm. Height 2228 mm (tarpaulin). Ground clearance 220 mm (axles). Angles of approach and departure 41° and 25°. Weight 2132 kg, GVW 3537 kg.

above and *below left:* AM715; *below right:* M715

TRUCK, 1.25-TON, 4 × 4 (DODGE W200/M880)
USA

General Data: In 1973 the M880 (originally XM861, then XM880) 1¼-ton Commercial Truck Program was initiated. It consisted of a low-cost militarized commercial Dodge pickup-type truck with either 4- or 2-wheel drive, intended to be issued to US Army tactical units as a one-for-one replacement for M37 (Dodge) and M715 (Kaiser Jeep) Series vehicles. In addition to the pickup body there were an ambulance and a contact maintenance version. The basic vehicle was Chrysler Corporation's Dodge W200 Sweptline pickup of 1975/76. Also 4 × 2 version.

Technical Details: Chrysler 318 V-8-cyl. petrol engine, 5211 cc (99.3 × 84.07 mm), 112 kW/150 bhp (net) at 4000 rpm. Torque

converter with Loadflite 3F1R auto. trans. 2-speed transfer box with lockable differential. 4.10:1 axle gear ratio. Hydraulic disc/drum brakes. Semi-elliptic leaf springs. 9.50R16.5 tyres. 12-Volt electrics. 87-litre fuel tank.

Dimensions and Weights: Wheelbase 3327 mm. Track, front/rear 1670/1610 mm. Overall length and width 5563 × 2019 mm. Height 1874 mm (cab). Ground clearance 206 mm (axles). Weight 2110 kg, GVW 3632 kg.

above and *below left:* M880 of 1976/77; *below right:* M886 with 1975-pattern grille

TRUCK, 1.25-TON, 4×4 (DODGE XW350)

CDN

General Data: The XW350 truck was designed and developed by Chrysler Canada's Research and Special Products Division. Prototypes were built in 1972/73. The intention was to make a more economical and less complex version of the late-1960s Chrysler RAM truck for the Canadian armed forces. However, the military decided to purchase militarized commercial Dodge Power Wagon trucks and the whole programme was terminated in 1974/75.

Technical Details: Chrysler LA318-3 V-8-cyl. petrol engine, 5211 cc (99.3 × 84.1 mm), 120 kW/161 bhp (net) at 4000 rpm. Dry plate clutch. 4F1R gearbox. 2-speed transfer box with front axle disconnect. 6.8:1 axle gear ratio. Hydraulic brakes. Semi-elliptic leaf springs. 9.00-20 tyres. 24-Volt electrics. 2 × 115-litre fuel tanks.

Dimensions and Weights (vehicle with winch): Wheelbase 3073 mm. Track 1803 mm. Overall length and width 5334 × 2134 mm. Height 2438 mm (cab). Ground clearance 300 mm (axles). Angles of approach and departure 37° and 41°. Weight 3557 kg, GVW 5577 kg.

above and *below left:* military truck with and without winch; *below right:* civilian version with 12.50-20 radial tyres

Truck, 1.25-ton, 4 × 4, Weapon Mount   **RA**
(Unimog 421)

4-cyl. 2.2-litre diesel engine (OM615) with 6F2R transmission. Axles with stepdown final drive. 18-in. wheels. Wheelbase 2250 mm. Overall length and width 4210 × 1750 mm. Built in Argentina for Argentine Army, early 1970s. Carried Cobra AT missiles. Unimog U406 and U416 were also produced.

Truck, 1.5-ton, 4 × 4, Cargo   **I**
(Fiat 40PM)

4-cyl. 2.5-litre turbocharged diesel engine with 5F1R gearbox and 2-speed transfer box. Rear diff. lock. Wheelbase 2800 mm. Overall dimensions 4700 × 1980 × 2200 mm. Weight 2500 kg. GVW 4000 kg. Airdroppable multipurpose truck, seating 2 + 10. Developed in the early 1980s.

Truck, 1.5-ton, 4 × 4, Cargo   **PRC**
(Leap Forward/Yuejin NJ230)

6-cyl. 3.5-litre petrol engine (NJ70A) with 4F1R gearbox and 2-speed transfer box. 9.75-18 tyres. Wheelbase 3300 mm. Overall dimensions 5545 × 2280 × 2245 (cab) mm. GVW 4850 kg. Front-mounted winch optional (NJ230A). Developed from Chinese version of Soviet GAZ-63. Shown with N. Vietnamese Army.

Truck, 1.5-ton, 4 × 4, Cargo   **I**
(OM Leoncino 4 × 4 NF)

4-cyl. 4.4-litre diesel engine (CO2D/12) with 5F1R gearbox and 2-speed transfer box. Wheelbase 2500 mm. Overall length and width 4450 × 2060 mm. Weight 2750 kg. GVW 4300 kg. Front-mounted winch optional. Originally introduced in 1965 (Tipo CL65) and continued into the 1970s. Commercially available.

Truck, 1.5-ton, 4 × 4, Cargo   **GB**
(Stonefield P3000)

V-6-cyl. petrol engine (Ford; Chrysler V8 optional) with automatic transmission and Ferguson transfer box. Full-time 4-wheel drive. Rigid axles with leaf springs. Wheelbase 2800 mm. Overall length and width 4940 × 1990 mm. Softtop cab shown. Space frame construction of rectangular tubing. Also 6 × 4 version. Late 1970s.

Truck, 1.8-ton, 4 × 4, Cargo   **DDR**
(Robur LO1801A)

4-cyl. 3.3-litre aircooled petrol engine (LO4/1) with 5F1R gearbox and 2-speed transfer box. Wheelbase 3025 mm. Weight 3375 kg. Payload 1875 kg. Winch capacity 2500 kg. Produced in the DDR from 1968 until 1973, superseding LO1800A (1961–67). Also other body types, incl. house-type vans.

TRUCK, 1.5-TON, 4×4 (ENGESA EE-15)   BR

General Data: Developed in the early 1960s, the EE-15 (EE for Engenheiros Especializados, the Brazilian Engesa Group) was a straightforward and rugged general-purpose cargo and troop carrier for military and civilian use. It was sold in Brazil and several export markets, especially in developing countries. In addition to the cargo truck, the manufacturers offered several variants, including ambulance, tanker, van and fire-fighter. The truck could carry up to 3000 kg payload on highways, half that weight in off-road conditions.

Technical Details: Daimler-Benz OM352 6-cyl. diesel engine, 5675 cc (97 × 128 mm), 149 bhp (gross) at 2800 rpm. Dry plate clutch. Daimler-Benz G40 5F1R gearbox. 2-speed transfer box with front axle disconnect. 4.625:1 axle gear ratio. Air/hydraulic brakes. Semi-elliptic leaf springs. 9.00-20 tyres. 12-Volt electrics. 120-litre fuel tank.

Dimensions and Weights: Wheelbase 3260 mm. Track 1710 mm. Overall length and width 5400 × 2144 mm. Height 2400 mm (cab). Ground clearance 290 mm (axles). Angles of approach and departure 48° and 40°. Weight 4200 kg, GVW 7200 kg.

above and below: EE-15 GS cargo/personnel

TRUCK, 1.5-TON, 4 × 4 (NISSAN CARRIER 4W73U)   J

General Data: The Nissan Carrier was first made in the 1950s, as a Japanese version of the wartime US Weapons Carrier. It was subsequently improved and remained in production for many years both in Japan and – under licence – in India, for military and commercial purposes. The later production model, as shown, was not unlike the US M37 in appearance and general design, and, as with the Dodge product, a field ambulance with integral bodywork was also manufactured. The military truck was designated D4W73U (right-hand drive only). The 4W73U and the F4W73U fire-truck derivatives were available with left-hand drive.

Technical Details: Own Model P 6-cyl. petrol engine, 3956 cc (85.7 × 114.3 mm), 145 bhp (SAE) at 3800 rpm. Dry plate clutch. 4F1R gearbox. Single-speed transfer box with front axle disconnect. 6.14:1 axle gear ratio. Hydraulic brakes. Semi-elliptic leaf springs. 7.50-20 tyres. 12-Volt electrics. 110-litre fuel tank.

Dimensions and Weights: Wheelbase 2800 mm. Track 1600 mm. Overall length and width 4730 × 2045 mm. Height 2355 mm (tarpaulin). Ground clearance 260 mm (axles). Angles of approach and departure not specified. Weight 2690 kg, GVW 4190 kg.

above and below: 4W73U c. 1975

TRUCK, 1.5-TON, 4 × 4 (TAM 110T7BV)

General Data: Produced by the country's largest truck manufacturing plant, Tovarna Avtomobilov in Motorjev Maribor (TAM) in Marburg, Yugoslavia, this high-mobility tactical truck first appeared in 1976. It was patterned on the German Magirus-Deutz 130T7FAL (qv) and was also produced in 6 × 6 configuration, designated TAM150T11BV (qv). Both were powered by aircooled diesel engines (4- and V-6-cyl. resp.) which were built under German KHD (Deutz) licence.

Technical Details: TAM F4L-413R 4-cyl. aircooled diesel engine, 5880 cc (120 × 130 mm), 85 kW/115 bhp (DIN) at 2650 rpm. Dry plate clutch. 5F1R gearbox (Z5-35S). 2-speed transfer box

(R28NP) with front axle disconnect. ZF self-locking differentials. 4.78:1 axle gear ratio. Air/hydraulic brakes. Semi-elliptic leaf springs. 12.00-18 tyres with variable pressure. 24-Volt electrics. 100-litre fuel tank.

Dimensions and Weights: Wheelbase 2850 mm. Track 1860 mm. Overall length and width 4850 × 2270 mm. Height 2470 mm (cab). Ground clearance 300 mm (axles). Angles of approach and departure 49° and 45°. Weight 4500 kg, GVW 7000 kg.

above and *below left:* cargo truck; *below right:* tilting cab

TRUCK, 1.5-TON, 4 × 4 (UNIMOG 404.0)   D

General Data: The Mercedes-Benz Unimog 404.0 was one of the few models from a very wide range of high-mobility multipurpose trucks to be powered by a petrol engine. As such, it replaced the Unimog S404 (1955–72, with 2.2-litre M180/II engine), of which the West German armed forces used large numbers. Both engines were in-line 6-cylinder units and both trucks had 2900-mm wheelbase size and were used for the mounting of various types of bodywork. Introduced in the early 1970s.

Technical Details: Daimler-Benz M130 6-cyl. petrol engine, 2748 cc (86.5 × 78.8 mm), 81 kW/110 bhp (net) at 4800 rpm. Dry plate clutch. 6F2R gearbox, incorporating transfer box with front

axle disconnect. Hydraulic brakes. Rigid portal axles with coil-spring suspension. 10.50-20 tyres. 24-Volt electrics. 120-litre fuel tank.

Dimensions and Weights: Wheelbase 2900 mm. Track 1630 mm. Overall length and width 5100 × 2120 mm. Height 2300 mm (cab). Ground clearance 400 mm (axles). Angles of approach and departure 45° and 46°. Weight 2900 kg, GVW 5000 kg.

above and *below left:* cargo truck and shop van of Netherlands Air Force; *below right:* 1955–72 S404

TRUCK, 1.8-TON, 4×4 (AIL COMMANDCAR M-325S)   IL

General Data: This Israeli product started life as a locally-assembled Dodge WM300 Power Wagon with certain detail modifications. When Chrysler discontinued the WM300, Automotive Industries continued production of their own version, designated M-325, later also known as 'Commandcar'. In 1979 the M-325S appeared, with a number of improvements. For 1982 there were improvements again. The following data apply to the 1979 M-325S.

Technical Details: Chrysler 225-2 6-cyl. petrol engine, 3682 cc (86.36 × 104.77 mm), 78 kW/105 bhp (DIN) at 3600 rpm. Dry plate clutch. 4F1R gearbox. 2-speed transfer box with front axle disconnect. 4.88:1 axle gear ratio. Hydraulic disc/drum brakes. Semi-elliptic leaf springs. 9.00-16 tyres. 24-Volt electrics. 144-litre fuel tank.

Dimensions and Weights: Wheelbase 3200 mm. Track 1980 mm. Overall length and width 5030 × 2080 mm. Height 2350 mm (tarpaulin). Ground clearance 240 mm (axles). Angles of approach and departure 52° and 25°. Weight 2550 kg, GVW 4315 kg.

above: M-325 desert patrol version, 1974; *below left:* M-325S, 1979; *below right:* 1982 model with closed cab

Medium and Heavy 4 × 2 Trucks

Military four-wheeled trucks with a non-driven front axle (4 × 2) have been in service since the earliest days of army motorization and, although they are probably the least spectacular in terms of 'military appearance', they have always outnumbered all the armed forces' other types by a considerable margin.

Known as 'non-tactical' or 'administrative' vehicles, the 4 × 2 category encompasses a wide range of cars, ambulances, light, medium and heavy trucks, and with few exceptions they have always been commercial off-the-shelf types. A military-pattern truck with rear-wheel drive only would be rather pointless except in time of war when there is a demand for road-going high-speed trucks of sturdier than normal design and finish. During the Second World War, the US armed forces had several military-pattern 4 × 2 trucks (e.g. the Federal 2G, Mack EH, International H-542-9 and H-542-11) in addition to 6 × 4 modifications of 6 × 6 tactical trucks, exemplified by the 5-ton 6 × 4 GMC, International and Studebaker. Such trucks, intended for the rear area supply routes, were also known as 'semi-tactical' types. The Canadians had 4 × 2 versions of several Canadian Military Pattern (CMP) trucks in the 8-, 15- and 60-cwt (3-ton) class, plus several 4 × 2 types which were known as 'Modified Conventional Vehicles'. In fact, over 50 per cent of the military vehicles produced by the Canadian automotive industry during 1939–45 for the war effort comprised 4 × 2 types, and nearly half of those were 3-tonners. In the United Kingdom during the same period, the number of 4 × 2 trucks also outnumbered the all-wheel-drive types but this was more by accident than by design: British 4 × 4 production could never keep up with demand, caused partly by the fact that when war broke out in 1939 there were no 4 × 4 types ready for mass production. It was not until 1940/41 that large-scale manufacture of 3-ton 4 × 4 trucks in Britain began in earnest. Until then, tens of thousands of militarized 4 × 2 trucks were made and additional supplies of these (and other types) arrived from Canada and the USA.

The Axis powers also used mainly 4 × 2 types. Several German trucks were built with either a driven or a non-driven front axle, depending on requirements. France, Russia, Italy, Japan and other truck-producing countries did have vehicles with front-wheel drive, but chiefly for special applications like artillery tractors. A rear-drive-only military truck is of course perfectly usable if it does not have to leave metalled roads. In peacetime this is no problem and even during armed conflicts most of the logistical transport can make use of roads of one description or another.

As will be seen on the following pages, all but one of the trucks shown feature commercial-type front ends and cabs, and except for colour scheme they hardly differ from their civilian counterparts. The exception is the International ACCO-Series GS load carrier, which sports what could be described as a civilianized military-pattern cab. An exclusive of International Harvester Australia, this cab was first used on the makers' 2.5-ton 4 × 4 Mk III truck when it appeared in 1963 to supersede the Mk I and II of the 1950s which differed in detail. Being practical and proven, it was decided to employ an adapted version of this unit for a new range of commercial forward-control trucks which the Australian company launched in the early 1960s, i.e. more or less simultaneously with the Mk III version of the 2.5-ton 4 × 4 (and a 5-ton 6 × 6 derivative, the Mk V – see relevant section). The new commercial edition was known as the AACO (Australian Army Cab-Over) and later, with modifications, became the ACCO (Australian Commercial Cab-Over), the ACCO-A Series, and finally, in the late 1970s, the ACCO-B Series. Several militarized commercial vehicles 'down under' were and are based on models from these series, including 6 × 4 fueller trucks for the RAAF and for export. In the Australian armed forces' current fleet of 4 × 2 trucks, many are Internationals with conventional cab mounting. The cab is essentially the same as used on contemporary normal-control Australian Dodge trucks. During the 1970s, however, the Australian military replaced most of these conventional trucks with forward-control models, mostly from Ford (D-Series), some from Leyland.

This section catalogues a representative assortment of 4 × 2 medium and heavy trucks in order of payload rating (and then alphabetically by make), with some of the most numerous body styles: cargo, van, tank, tipper (dump), tractor. The latter are used in conjunction with various types of single- and tandem-axle semi-trailers, chiefly cargo and tanker types.

MEDIUM AND HEAVY 4×2 TRUCKS

Truck, 1.7-ton, 4 × 2, Cargo/Personnel   **D**
(Volkswagen LT35D)

6-cyl. 2.4-litre ohc diesel engine with 5F1R gearbox. Independent front suspension. 185-14 tyres, dual rear. Wheelbase 2950 mm. Overall dimensions 5330 × 2140 × 2090 (cab) mm. GVW 3500 kg. 5-seat crew cab. Also available with lower GVW rating and with 4-cyl. petrol engine. Used by Netherlands Air Force from 1982.

Truck, 2-ton, 4 × 2, Cargo   **D**
(Magirus-Deutz 90M6FL)

4-cyl. 4-litre aircooled diesel engine (Deutz F4L 913) with 5F1R gearbox (ZF S5-24). Rear-wheel drive. 10.50R20 tyres, single rear. Wheelbase 3000 mm. Chassis/cab dimensions 5090 × 2135 × 2533 mm. Weight 2820 kg. GVW 5600 kg. Tilting cab. Example shown was supplied to the Danish Army. Note roof platform.

Truck, 2-ton, 4 × 2, Aircraft Fueller   **D**
(Mercedes-Benz L508D/29)

4-cyl. 3.8-litre diesel engine (OM314V) with 5F1R gearbox. Wheelbase 2950 mm. GVW 5000 kg. Fitted with 2000-litre tank, pumping, metering and dispensing equipment for AVGAS (aviation gasoline). One of 18 used by the Netherlands Air Force from 1972. Van and ambulance variants were also in service.

Truck, 2-ton, 4 × 2, Cargo   **D**
(Mercedes-Benz L508DG MA)

4-cyl. 3.8-litre diesel engine (OM314V) with 5F1R gearbox. Wheelbase 2950 mm. Overall dimensions 5300 × 2320 × 2680 mm. Weight 3415 kg. GVW 5600 kg. Dropside body, measuring 3150 × 2200 mm, with tarpaulin. Used in considerable numbers by the German *Bundeswehr* from the early 1970s.

Truck, 2.5-ton, 4 × 2, Cargo   **USA**
(Dodge D500)

6-cyl. 3.7-litre (or V-8-cyl. 5.2-litre) petrol engine with 4- or 5-speed gearbox (auto. trans. optional). Wheelbase 3988 mm. Standard commercial Dodge medium-duty truck of 1972/73, used by US Army. Styling shown was current from early 1960s to 1973, with periodic detail changes.

Truck, 2.5-ton, 4 × 2, Van   **USA**
(Dodge D600)

V-8-cyl. 5.2-litre petrol engine with 4F1R gearbox (5F1R and automatic optional). Rockwell hypoid rear axle (Eaton planetary spiral bevel type optional). Wheelbase 4597 mm. Commercial-type medium-duty truck of 1976, used by US Army with Mark van body. Front end styling and cab were current from 1974.

114

Truck, 2.5-ton, 4 × 2, Cargo   **GB/AUS**
(Ford D400)

6-cyl. petrol engine with 4F1R gearbox. 500 of these general service trucks with dropside body were supplied to the Australian Army in 1969. A batch of more than 300 diesel-engined Ford D0911 trucks of similar appearance followed in the early 1980s. They were assembled at Broadmeadows, Victoria.

Truck, 2.5-ton, 4 × 2, Cargo   **USA**
(Ford F350)

6-cyl. 4.9-litre engine with 4F1R gearbox (V-8-cyl. with auto. trans. optional). Typical mid-1970s North American pattern commercial stake/platform truck for general purposes, shown in service with Colombian Army. These Fords featured 'Twin-I-Beam' independent front suspension.

Truck, 2.5-ton, 4 × 2, Cargo   **USA**
(GMC 6000 Series)

V-8-cyl. 5.7-litre petrol engine with 4F1R gearbox (other engines and power trains, incl. auto. trans., were optional). One of a wide range of GMC medium-duty conventional trucks of the 1970s. Truck shown, used by the US Army in Germany, had upper centre section of radiator grille missing (accident damage).

Truck, 2.5-ton, 4 × 2, Van   **USA**
(GMC CE61403)

Supplied to the US Navy by GMC Truck & Coach Division in 1974, this truck's official nomenclature was 'Truck, Van, GED, 16000 GVW, 4 × 2'. GED indicated 'Gasoline Engine Driven'. GVW was in pounds. The van body was by Mark and had a hydraulic tail-lift. Chassis from GMC's 6000 Series, with V8 petrol engine.

Truck, 3-ton, 4 × 2, Cargo   **F**
(Citroën KO6 480)

Perkins 3.86-litre diesel engine (petrol engine or MAN diesel optional) with 4F1R gearbox. Rear-wheel drive. Servo-assisted hydraulic brakes (as on DS-Series car). Wheelbase 3000 mm (2700 and 3900 mm optional). Several hundred were supplied to the French forces in 1971/72.

Truck, 4-ton, 4 × 2, Cargo   **GB**
(Bedford TK/KD)

6-cyl. 5.4-litre diesel engine (330-98D) with 4F1R gearbox. Wheelbase 4293 mm. General service truck of the Belgian Air Force, with Belgian dropside body and hydraulic self-loading crane. Supplied by GM Continental, Antwerp, in the early 1970s. Also with other bodystyles, including fire engine.

Truck, 4-ton, 4 × 2, Cargo   **GB**
(Bedford TK 1000/KEL)

6-cyl. 5.4-litre diesel engine (330D or 5.4/100D) with 4F1R gearbox. Air/hydraulic brakes. Wheelbase 3835 mm. Overall dimensions 6830 × 2207 × 2255 (cab) mm. Weight 2853 kg. GVW 10000 kg. One of a large batch acquired by the British Army in the early 1970s.

Truck, 4-ton, 4 × 2, Cargo   **SU**
(GAZ-53A)

V-8-cyl. 4.25-litre petrol engine with 4F1R gearbox. Conventional chassis design. Vacuum-assisted hydraulic brakes. Wheelbase 3700 mm. Overall dimensions 6395 × 2380 × 2220 mm. Weight 3250 kg. GVW 8250 kg. 12-Volt electrics. Soviet commercial truck, used by the forces of the Soviet Union and the DDR.

Truck, 4-ton, 4 × 2, Tipper   **D**
(MAN 11.136HK)

6-cyl. 5.5-litre diesel engine with 5F1R gearbox. Wheelbase 3700 mm. GVW 11000 kg. In 1981, 131 of these tippers were ordered by the Belgian Army. Body was made by AJK of Belgium. Chassis had most mechanical components in common with the Army's 4 × 4 Model 11 136HA (qv).

Truck, 4-ton, 4 × 2, Van   **D**
(MAN 11.136H)

6-cyl. 5.5-litre diesel engine with 5F1R gearbox. Wheelbase 5000 mm. GVW 11000 kg. Assembled in Belgium for Belgian Army. Refrigerated van body (frigo and pallet installation) by Baeten (Shelters) of Melle, Ghent. Hydraulic tail-lift. Also existed with covered cargo body, for driving instruction purposes.

Truck, 4.5-ton, 4 × 2, Cargo   **DDR**
(IFA W50-L/A)

4-cyl. 6.5-litre diesel engine (4VD14.5/12-1SRW) with 5F1R gearbox. Rear axle with lockable diff. Wheelbase 3200 mm. Overall dimensions 6530 × 2500 × 3200 mm. Weight 5080 kg. GVW 9800 kg. Max. speed 83 km/h. Basically a civilian truck, made in the DDR and widely used by the military also.

Truck, 4.5-ton, 4 × 2, Cargo   **D**
(Magirus-Deutz 130D9L)

6-cyl. 6.1-litre aircooled diesel engine (Deutz F6L 913) with 5F1R gearbox. Air/hydraulic brakes. Exhaust brake optional. Wheelbase 4200 mm. Chassis/cab dimensions 6900 × 2450 × 2820 mm. Weight 4850 kg. GVW 10500 kg. Commercially-available truck of the late 1970s, shown with 4250 × 2350 mm dropside body.

Truck, 5-ton, 4 × 2, Water Tank   **E**
(Avia 7000N)

6-cyl. diesel engine (Perkins 6.305) with 5F1R gearbox. Double-reduction rear axle. Wheelbase 3400 mm. Overall length and width 6245 × 2217 mm. GVW 11200 kg. Commercial chassis/cab with bulk water tank made by TAVI in the late 1970s. Spanish Army used Avia 7000L (3800-mm wb) with military cargo body.

Truck, 5-ton, 4 × 2, Cargo   **USA**
(Chevrolet C60)

Standard commercial US Chevrolet medium-range chassis/cab with cargo/personnel body, in service with the Netherlands Marines in Curacao from 1979/80. The Dutch also had the US-style 'schoolbus' on lwb Chevrolet chassis. The C60 was available with various types of petrol and diesel engines.

Truck, 5-ton, 4 × 2, Cargo   **NL**
(DAF FA1400DF)

6-cyl. diesel engine (DF615) with 5F1R gearbox and dual-ratio rear axle. GVW 11600 kg. Delivered in 1974 as one of a large batch for the Netherlands Air Force. Some had Meiller hydraulic loading ramp at the rear, others had hydraulic loading crane behind the cab. Shown is a dropside body with tarpaulin.

Truck, 5-ton, 4 × 2, Cargo   **E**
(Ebro P137)

6-cyl. 5.8-litre diesel engine (Perkins 6.305) with 5F1R gearbox. Air brakes. Wheelbase 3700 mm. Overall dimensions of chassis/cab 6868 × 2393 × 2400 mm. Weight of chassis/cab 4160 kg. GVW 13700 kg. Commercial chassis with 3-seat tilting cab. Also available with 3200- and 4300-mm wheelbase. 1980.

Truck, 5-ton, 4 × 2, Ammunition   **USA**
(GMC 7000 Series)

Equipped with a steel body with hinged tailgate and removable side boards this GMC medium-duty conventional truck was supplied to the US Navy in 1979. Used for handling ammunition, with a speedloader device of a hydraulically-actuated crane with 2 hydraulic outriggers.

Truck, 5-ton, 4 × 2, Tipper   **USA**
(GMC C6D042)

Officially known as 'Truck, Dump, Street Maintenance, 21000 GVW, GED, 4 × 2' this truck from GMC's medium-duty 6000 Series was delivered in 1979. It had a V-8-cyl. petrol engine. A compressor set was mounted between cab and body. Similar trucks for the military had earlier been supplied on Ford F500 chassis.

MEDIUM AND HEAVY 4 × 2 TRUCKS

Truck, 5-ton, 4 × 2, Dump   **USA**
(GMC CE66213)

The US Marine Corps was a frequent customer for these GMC 6000 Series short-wheelbase dump trucks. They were supplied in 1973 (shown), 1974 and 1975 (and probably in other years) and the official nomenclature was 'Truck, Dump, GED, 28000 GVW, 4 × 2' indicating, amongst other things, a GVW rating of 12712 kg.

Truck, 5-ton, 4 × 2, Cargo   **USA**
(GMC CE67013)

Delivered to the US Navy in 1973 this vehicle's official nomenclature was 'Truck, Stake, with Hydraulic Liftgate, 24000 GVW, 4 × 2, GED'. The truck was from the manufacturers' 6500 Series conventionals and had a V-8-cyl. petrol engine and a long wheelbase. Various transmission options were offered.

Truck, 5-ton, 4 × 2, Tilting Platform   **USA**
(GMC HV77013)

Carrying the designation 'Truck, Equipment Transport, Tilt Platform, Ramp, DED' this diesel-engined truck was built and equipped for the transport of special equipment. 3 were supplied to the US Army in 1972. The chassis was a long-wheelbase type from GMC's 7500 Series, featuring a 'butterfly hood' (side-opening bonnet).

Truck, 5-ton, 4 × 2, Refuse Collection   **USA**
(GMC TE66813)

V-8-cyl. 7-litre petrol engine with 5F1R gearbox. Nomenclature: 'Truck, Refuse Collection, Rear Hopper Loading, 16 cu. yd'. Body/equipment by Leach (Model 16 yd PM). Delivered to US Army in 1977. Garwood also supplied refuse collection bodies. Chassis included Dodge, Ford, GMC and IHC.

Truck, 5-ton, 4 × 2, Tractor   **USA**
(IHC Fleetstar 2000D)

6-cyl. 7-litre diesel engine (GM Detroit Diesel 6-71N). Heavy-duty commercial-type tractor truck of which a large fleet was acquired for line haul operations by the US Army's 37th Transportation Group 'Red Ball Express' in West Germany, with deliveries starting in 1973. Replaced the mid-1960s IHC DCO205H 'cab-overs'.

Truck, 5-ton, 4 × 2, Cargo   **USA**
(IHC Loadstar 1600)

V-8-cyl. petrol engine with 5F1R gearbox. Typical example of commercial-type International Loadstar truck, equipped with stake rack body. Many thousands of such trucks were supplied during the 1960s and 1970s by International Harvester to the US armed forces who used them with numerous body styles.

Truck, 5-ton, 4 × 2, Cargo   **GB**
(Leyland Terrier)

6-cyl. diesel engine with 4F1R gearbox. Regular commercial model from Leyland's Redline series of the late 1970s. The Terrier TR750 was used by the Royal Navy. Similar in appearance was the Boxer, of which some 50 tippers were supplied to the Australian Army in 1981/82 (Model BX5-31, supplied by Leyland Australia).

Truck, 5-ton, 4 × 2, Tractor   **USA**
(Mack MC-Series)

Developed in the late 1970s, the MC Mack (and the MR 6 × 4 derivative) replaced the old MB range in production. The MC and MR shared a modern steel tilting cab with very deep windscreen. Tractor shown was supplied to the US Army in 1980/81 for short-haul transport work. A long-wheelbase chassis was also available.

Truck, 5-ton, 4 × 2, Cargo   **D**
(Magirus-Deutz 168M11FL)

6-cyl. 6.1-litre aircooled diesel engine (Deutz BF6L 913) with 5F1R gearbox. Wheelbase 3600 mm. Overall dimensions 7020 × 2490 × 3180 mm. Weight 6200 kg. GVW 11200 kg. Tilting cab. Dropside body. 7000 ordered by West German *Bundeswehr*. First delivered in 1980. Danish Army had heavier 168M13FL.

Truck, 5-ton, 4 × 2, Cargo   **D**
(Mercedes-Benz L1213/36)

6-cyl. 5.67-litre diesel engine (OM352) with 5F1R gearbox. Wheelbase 3600 mm. Chassis/cab dimensions 6770 × 2460 × 2800 mm. Weight 4020 kg. GVW 11800 kg. In service with Danish Army as 'LVGM, VEJ: Mercedes-Benz, 1213, 4 × 2, D', with dropside cargo body and with removable shelter on platform.

Truck, 5.5-ton, 4 × 2, Cargo   **H**
(Csepel D452)

4-cyl. 5.5-litre diesel engine (D414.62) with 5F1R gearbox. Rear axle with diff. lock. Wheelbase 3200 mm. Overall dimensions 6000 × 2650 × 2400 mm. Weight 4380 kg. GVW 10100 kg. Hungarian truck with French design cab (Chausson) as used also for Polish Star trucks. D452 had dual-circuit air brakes.

Truck, 6-ton, 4 × 2, Tractor   **F**
(Berliet 950K BT6)

6-cyl. 8.8-litre diesel engine (MID 06.20.30) with 6F1R overdrive gearbox. Dual-ratio rear axle with hub reduction gearing. Air brakes. Procured by Netherlands Air Force (from 1977) for towing various types of semi-trailers, including aircraft transporters. The heavier Berliet/Renault TR280 was also acquired.

MEDIUM AND HEAVY 4 × 2 TRUCKS

Truck, 6-ton, 4 × 2, Cargo   **AUS**
(IHC ACCO C1820)

V-8-cyl. 5.6-litre petrol engine with 5F1R gearbox. Cast spoke wheels. Vacuum-assisted hydraulic brakes. Typical general service load carrier of the Royal Australian Navy, photographed in 1974. Supplied by International Harvester Australia, also with other body styles. Army and RAAF also used conventional IHC trucks.

Truck, 6-ton, 4 × 2, Cargo   **E**
(Pegaso 1100L)

4-cyl. 4.37-litre diesel engine with 6F1R overdrive gearbox. Single-reduction rear axle. Vacuum-assisted hydraulic brakes. Wheelbase 3600 mm. Chassis/cab length and width 6497 × 2250 mm. GVW 9600 kg. Fixed-side wooden body with troop seats and tarpaulin. Common Spanish Army truck of the 1970s.

Truck, 6-ton, 4 × 2, Cargo   **PL**
(Star 200)

6-cyl. 6.8-litre diesel engine (359) with 5F1R gearbox. Air/hydraulic brakes. Wheelbase 3400 mm. Overall length and width 6510 × 2330 mm. Replaced the Star 28/29 in the mid-1970s. Variants included long-wheelbase L200, tractor truck C200 and special chassis for tipper, crane, shop van, etc.

Truck, 6-ton, 4 × 2, Cargo   **SU**
(ZIL-130)

V-8-cyl. 6-litre petrol engine (ZIL-130) with 5F1R gearbox. Double-reduction rear axle. 20-in. 8-stud wheels. Wheelbase 3800 mm. Overall dimensions 6675 × 2500 × 2350 mm. Weight 4500 kg. Produced in large numbers for military and civil service from the mid-1960s. Many variants (incl. 6 × 4 and 6 × 6).

Truck, 7-ton, 4 × 2, Cargo   **D**
(Magirus-Deutz 170D14FL)

V-6-cyl. 8.5-litre aircooled diesel engine (Deutz F6L 413) with 6F1R gearbox. Rear axle with planetary hub reduction gearing. Wheelbase 4600 mm. Chassis/cab dimensions 7955 × 2300 × 2815 mm. Weight 4830 kg. GVW 13000 kg. Used by the West German *Bundeswehr* mid-1970s.

Truck, 7-ton, 4 × 2, Cargo   **D**
(MAN 15.192F)

5-cyl. 9.5-litre diesel engine (D2565MF) with 6F1R gearbox. Rear axle with lockable diff. and planetary hub reduction gearing. Air brakes. Wheelbase 4100 mm. Overall dimensions 7650 × 2500 × 2850 (cab) mm. Max. speed 84 km/h. Tilting cab. Produced from 1980 for the West German *Bundeswehr*.

Truck, 7-ton, 4 × 2, Cargo   **D**
(Mercedes-Benz L1419)

V-6-cyl. 9.75-litre diesel engine (OM401) with 4F1R gearbox. Wheelbase 3600 mm. Militarized commercial truck of the mid-1970s. West German *Bundeswehr* used Models 1017 and 1017A (4 × 2 and 4 × 4 resp.) which were of similar external appearance but somewhat lighter (*Lkw 5 t*) and had OM352A 6-in-line engine.

Truck, 8-ton, 4 × 2, Tanker   **YU**
(FAP-13/AC-7B)

6-cyl. diesel engine with 5F1R gearbox. Wheelbase 4600 mm. Overall dimensions 7870 × 2350 × 2725 mm. Weight 8150 kg. 7000-litre tank for oil transport and distribution. Pumping equipment with a capacity of 240–500 litres/min. Conventional truck with normal control, built in Yugoslavia under Saurer licence.

Truck, 8-ton, 4 × 2, Cargo   **PL**
(Jelcz 315MA)

6-cyl. 11.1-litre diesel engine (SW680/1) with 5F1R gearbox. Air brakes. Wheelbase 4100 mm. Overall dimensions 7053 × 2500 × 3520 mm. Weight 8000 kg. Militarized version of Polish Jelcz 315 truck, which existed also in several other forms, including 6 × 4. The engine was a licence-produced Leyland design. From 1973.

Truck, 9-ton, 4 × 2, Cargo   **F**
(Unic P270A)

V-8-cyl. 10.7-litre diesel engine with 2 × 4F1R gearbox. Single-reduction rear axle. Cast spoke wheels. Wheelbase 5600 mm. Tilting cab. 1000 units delivered to the French Army in 1974–77. Similar-looking chassis/cab (Model 130NC) was supplied to the Air Force with runway sweeping equipment.

Truck, 10-ton, 4 × 2, Tractor   **GB**
(AEC Mercury 2TGM4R)

6-cyl. diesel engine (AV505) with 6F1R gearbox. Air brakes. Wheelbase 2890 mm. Weight 4285 kg. GCW 25000 kg. Used by Royal Air Force in conjunction with various types of semi-trailers. Later supplies were under the Leyland marque name. Similar trucks were in service with the Royal Navy.

Truck, 10-ton, 4 × 2, Dump   **F**
(Berliet GLR200)

6-cyl. diesel engine with 11F2R gearbox. Rear-wheel drive with lockable diff. Overall dimensions 7650 × 2500 × 2900 mm. Weight 8210 kg. Edbro hydraulic end tipper with cab protector. Militarized commercial truck, in service with the Netherlands Air Force, starting with 5 units in 1976.

121

Truck, 10-ton, 4 × 2, Tractor   **F**
(Berliet TLM12)

6-cyl. diesel engine (M635) with 10F1R gearbox. Air brakes. GVW 35000 kg. In service with the French Air Force, towing several types of semi-trailers. Various types of these commercial Berliets, including long-wheelbase load carriers, were employed by all the French armed forces throughout the 1970s.

Truck, 10-ton, 4 × 2, Tractor/Aircraft Fueller   **NL**
(DAF FA/FT1600DF)

6-cyl. diesel engine (DF615) with 5F1R gearbox. Wheelbase 3600 mm. Lockable cabinet with pumping equipment behind cab. Used by Netherlands Air Force from the early 1970s for re- and defuelling of aircraft. Semi-trailer (DAF RE8-14) tank capacity 12000 litres. Also used with earlier Strüver semi-trailer.

Truck, 10-ton, 4 × 2, Tractor   **NL**
(DAF FT2305DHU)

6-cyl. turbocharged diesel engine with intercooling and 12F1R gearbox. Rear axle with planetary hub reduction gearing. Air brakes. Wheelbase 3250 mm. One of 24 ordered (first units delivered in late 1981) for Netherlands Army. Shown coupled to a DAF YTT1004 10-ton ammunition van semi-trailer.

Truck, 10-ton, 4 × 2, Tractor   **GB**
(Leyland Mastiff MS2600)

V-8-cyl. diesel engine (Perkins) with 5F1R gearbox and 2-speed rear axle. Used by the British RAF, fitted with Dunlop Maxaret anti-skid braking with Westinghouse air drying system. Automatic chassis lubrication. Basically a commercial tractor unit with detail modifications. New in 1978.

Truck, 12-ton, 4 × 2, Aircraft Fueller   **GB**
(Ford D1616)

6-cyl. diesel engine. Wheelbase 4550 mm. Overall dimensions 7660 × 2450 × 2700 mm. GVW 16000 kg. Bodied and equipped by Acomal of Malines, 1975/76, for Belgian Air Force and Navy. Two versions: 10000-litre overwing/underwing aircraft fueller (shown) and 11000-litre roadgoing tanker.

Truck, 15-ton, 4 × 2, Aircraft Fueller   **D**
(Magirus-Deutz 232D19FL)

V-8-cyl. 11.3-litre aircooled diesel engine (Deutz F8L 413) with 6F1R gearbox. Hub reduction rear axle. Wheelbase 4800 mm. Chassis/cab dimensions 7970 × 2300 × 2730 mm. Weight 5980 kg. GVW 19000 kg. Early 1970s' chassis with 14000-litre tank and equipment by Strüver for Imperial Iranian Air Force.

Medium and Heavy 4 × 4 Trucks

Medium and heavy four-wheeled trucks with all-wheel drive, known as 'four-by-fours', take up a considerable part of this book, indicating their importance in the world's tactical military vehicle fleets. It will be noted that the majority of entries are of West European origin, American trucks in this load class (2-ton and over) being predominantly six-wheelers. As with the other types of military load carriers, it will be seen that many of the medium 4 × 4 trucks are modifications of commercial designs. During the Second World War and up to the 1960s, most military tactical trucks were purpose-built to special military designs. Some of them had a softtop military-pattern cab, designed to comply with NATO specifications. These cabs, with their tops removed and windscreens folded, made for a low silhouette which had advantages from a military tactical point of view, but since the tops and side screens were *in situ* most of the time to keep the cold out and to prevent loss, it was later deemed an unnecessary feature.

Today's models in the main have a modern and comfortable all-steel closed cab with a good heater and well-sprung seats. It is interesting to note that the British have never bothered much with softtop cabs on their tactical trucks since before the war. With the main exception of light trucks in the 8- and 15-cwt class, most of these vehicles as built from the war onwards had an enclosed cab with the upper part detachable at waist level. This was for two main reasons: when shipping the trucks in crates to overseas theatres of war their height could be reduced to the top level of the body sides (cab roof, wheels, etc. would be stowed in the body, making for an acceptable crate height) and, secondly, the complete roof could be removed in those circumstances where either a low profile was necessary or where, due to the ambient temperatures, it was not needed for weather protection. This also applied to practically all the Canadian Military Pattern (CMP) vehicles of the Second World War, which were made to conform as much as possible with established British design. The CMP cabs could be split by undoing a number of bolts and nuts, and the windscreen assembly could also be unbolted. Yet this was seldom done during the war itself: once removed

and stored somewhere, nobody could guarantee that a driver would be able to pick them up afterwards. One big and clearly underestimated advantage of military-pattern softtop cabs (apart from considerable savings in steel, which during the war was an important aspect) is that they are much simpler to repair and otherwise work on. With mostly flat panels (including the windscreen glass) and no compound curves, accident damage is much easier to repair in field conditions and less costly in peacetime. Added to the fact that many modern military load carriers as used by the industrialized nations are derived from commercial state-of-the-art models, or at least assembled using a maximum amount of off-the-shelf componentry, it is not difficult to see that they are much more suitable for professional drivers than for handling by careless conscripts ('I always keep the handbrake half-applied – it makes the engine labour and thus keeps the cab warmer').

With a few exceptions (the French ALM/ACMAT range among them), it is felt that the military trucks which are most effective all round, i.e. with acceptable performance in relation to acquisition and operating costs, are now being made in developing countries. The South African Samil 20, the Brazilian Engesa EE-25, the Greek NAMCO Milicar may be somewhat crude by some people's standards but they are no-nonsense and practical vehicles. Obviously, if money is no object, industry can design superb cross-country trucks which provide a beautiful ride and tremendous pulling power and performance in terrain which on the actual battle front will be hard to find. It is all a matter of putting priorities in sensible order.

One recognized and distinct advantage of modern designs is the widespread use of full-time all-wheel-drive systems and differential locks which can be engaged without stopping the vehicle. The latter, if applied properly, can result in the prevention of a lot of unnecessary wear and tear. Some of today's vehicles in this category were actually designed and built before 1970 and these are, with a few exceptions, not repeated here as they are covered in the *Observer's Military Vehicles Directory – from 1945.*

TRUCK, 2-TON, 4×4 (FIAT 75PM14)

I

General Data: In the mid-1970s, Fiat developed the 'Bolzano' range of medium 4 × 4 trucks, the 65P, 75P, 90P and derivatives. The 75PM14 was the military version of the 75PC. Through the IVECO organization it was available in Switzerland under the Saurer-OM name and in France it was entered in Army trials for 2-ton trucks as the Unic 75PM. The Italian Army bought the truck under the Lancia 6611 designation and called it the ACL75 (*Autocarro Leggero 1975* – Truck, Light, 1975 model).

Technical Details: Own 8060.04 6-cyl. diesel engine, 5499 cc (103 × 110 mm), 95.6 kW/130 bhp (DIN) at 3200 rpm. Dry plate clutch. 5F1R gearbox. 2-speed transfer box with front axle disconnect. Portal axles with 7.583:1 overall gear ratio. Air/hydraulic brakes. Semi-elliptic leaf springs. 12.50-20 tyres. 24-Volt electrics. 145-litre fuel tank.
Note: 6.81:1 axles and other tyre sizes optional.

Dimensions and Weights: Wheelbase 2750 mm. Track 1852 mm. Overall length and width 5218 × 2270 mm. Height 2681 (cab) mm. Ground clearance 445 mm (axles). Angles of approach and departure 45°. Weight 5100 kg, GVW 7100 kg.

above: 75PM14; *below left:* Lancia 6611/ACL75; *below right:* Unic 75PM

TRUCK, 2-TON, 4 × 4 (GAZ-66 SERIES)

General Data: Developed during the 1960s, the GAZ-66 range succeeded the normal-control GAZ-63 and -63A models. The 66 was produced for military and civilian use and appeared in many variants, e.g. with tropical equipment, winch, screened ignition system or combinations thereof; with cargo body, various types of shop vans, tipper, etc. GAZ-66A models had a softtop cab, a central tyre pressure regulation system and a tilting cab. Used in Warsaw Pact countries and overseas.

Technical Details: ZMZ V-8-cyl. petrol engine, 4250 cc (92 × 80 mm), 84.6 kW/115 bhp (net) at 3200 rpm. Dry plate clutch. 4F1R gearbox. 2-speed transfer box with front axle disconnect. 6.83 : 1 axle gear ratio. Vacuum/hydraulic brakes. Semi-elliptic leaf springs. 12.00-18 tyres. 12-Volt electrics. 2 × 105-litre fuel tanks.

Dimensions and Weights: Wheelbase 3300 mm. Track, front/rear 1800/1750 mm. Overall length and width 5655 × 2342 mm. Height 2440 mm (cab). Ground clearance 315 mm (axles). Angles of approach and departure 41° and 32°. Weight 3440 kg (with winch 3640 kg), GVW 5650 kg.

above: cargo truck; *below left:* artillery repair (GAZ-66A); *below right:* radio van

MEDIUM AND HEAVY 4 × 4 TRUCKS

Truck, 2-ton, 4 × 4, Cargo   **F**
(Berliet/Citroën 380K)

4-cyl. 3.86-litre diesel engine (Perkins 4.236) with 5F1R overdrive-top gearbox and 2-speed transfer box. Wheelbase 3055 mm. GVW 6500 kg. Citroën design, offered commercially by Berliet in 1973. Softtop cab with folding windscreen was optional. A number of these trucks were sold to at least one African country.

Truck, 2-ton, 4 × 4, Cargo   **NL**
(DAF YA2442)

6-cyl. 6.17-litre diesel engine (DF615) with 5F1R gearbox and 2-speed transfer box. Wheelbase 3200 mm. Overall length and width 5480 × 2440 mm. Weight 5120 kg. GVW 7320 kg. 5 prototypes delivered to Netherlands Army for tests in late 1974 but no quantity production. Shown with machine-gun ring mount.

Truck, 2-ton, 4 × 4, Cargo   **E**
(Land-Rover/Santana S-2000)

6-cyl. 3.43-litre petrol or diesel engine with 4F1R gearbox and 2-speed transfer box. 4.7 : 1 axles. 9.00-16 tyres. Wheelbase 2565 mm. Overall length and width 4918 × 1925 mm. Weight 2360 kg. GVW 4360 kg. Launched in 1979. One application was an open-cab mobile mount for Oerlikon 20-mm cannon (1982).

Truck, 2-ton, 4 × 4, Cargo   **D**
(Magirus-Deutz 130M7FAL)

6-cyl. 6.1-litre aircooled diesel engine (Deutz F6L 913) with 5F1R gearbox and 2-speed transfer box. Portal axles. Wheelbase 2900 mm. Chassis/cab dimensions 5420 × 2313 × 2905 mm. Weight 4960 kg. GVW 7700 kg. Ground clearance 485 mm. 1977 prototype for *Bundeswehr,* quantity-produced in S. Africa.

Truck, 2-ton, 4 × 4, Cargo   **D**
(Magirus-Deutz 130T7FAL)

6-cyl. 6.1-litre aircooled diesel engine (Deutz F6L 413) with 5F1R gearbox and 2-speed transfer box. 12.50-20XL tyres. Wheelbase 2800 mm. Chassis/cab length and width 4820 × 2350 mm. Weight 3750 kg. GVW 6300 kg. Developed in the early 1970s. No quantity production except in Yugoslavia as TAM110T7BV (qv).

Truck, 2-ton, 4 × 4, Cargo   **GR**
(Militrak Super)

4-cyl. 3.86-litre diesel engine (Perkins B4.236). 9.00-16 tyres. Wheelbase 2650 mm. Chassis/cab dimensions 4315 × 1950 × 2290 mm. 24-Volt electrics. Winch optional. Militarized version of Polytrak multipurpose truck by Petros Petropoulos. Alternative body styles included ambulance, radio van, wrecker. 1982.

TRUCK, 2-TON, 4×4 (ROBUR LO2002A)

DDR

General Data: Introduced in 1973 and superseded the 1.8-ton LO1801A. It was derived from a civilian range of 4 × 2 and 4 × 4 variants. It comprised 6 basic body styles: AKSF/MIII cargo/personnel, with winch; AKSF/A1 workshop truck; AKSF/XI telephone construction, with winch; AKF Type I universal house-type van with rear door; AKF Type II universal shop van with side door and double rear door; AKF/KSA expandable van body.

Technical Details: LO4/2 aircooled 4-cyl. petrol engine, 3345 cc (95 × 118 mm), 56 kW/75 bhp (net) at 2800 rpm. Dry plate clutch. 5F1R gearbox. 2-speed transfer box with front axle disconnect.

5.83:1 axle gear ratio. Hydraulic brakes. Semi-elliptic leaf springs. 10.00-20 tyres. 12-Volt electrics. 125-litre fuel tank.

Dimensions and Weights: Wheelbase 3025 mm. Track, front/rear 1636/1664 mm. Overall length and width 5400 × 2370 mm. Height 2780 mm (tarpaulin). Ground clearance 265 mm (axles). Angles of approach and departure not specified. Weight 3400 kg, GVW 5500 kg. The van-bodied truck weighed 3850 kg (empty).

above: AKSF/MIII; *below left:* AKF Type II; *below right:* AKSF/S Pr. (commercial)

TRUCK, 2-TON, 4×4 (SAMIL 20)

General Data: In the early 1980s, the south African Armscor organization introduced a wide range of military vehicles, based on locally-built versions of IVECO/Magirus-Deutz chassis. The Samil 20 models had forward control with military-pattern cab but otherwise resembled the Magirus-Deutz 130M7FAL and, with the main exception of the engine, the Fiat 75PM. The cab featured an all-steel roll cage. A mine-resistant cab-behind-engine configuration was also offered. Body types included cargo/personnel, fire-fighter, light repair workshop and shelter. The shelter could be fitted out as office, command post, etc.

Technical Details: Deutz 6-cyl. in-line aircooled diesel engine,

79 kW/106 bhp (net) at 2650 rpm. Capacity not specified. Dry plate clutch. 5F1R gearbox. 2-speed transfer box with front axle disconnect. Portal-type axles. Air/hydraulic brakes. Semi-elliptic leaf springs. 14.50-20 tyres. 24-Volt electrics. 200-litre tank.

Dimensions and Weights: Wheelbase 2900 mm. Track 1852 mm. Overall length and width 5340 × 2300 mm. Height not specified. Ground clearance 460 mm (axles). Angles of approach and departure not specified. Weight 4580 kg, GVW 7700 kg.

above: shelter/container; *below left:* cargo/personnel; *below right:* light repair workshop

Truck, 2-ton, 4 × 4, Cargo   F
(Renault TRM2000)

4-cyl. 3.6-litre turbocharged diesel engine (720) with 5F1R gearbox and 2-speed transfer box. Portal axles (conventional axles available; ground clearance 425 and 305 mm respectively). Wheelbase 2700 mm. Chassis/cab dimensions 5020 × 2140 × 2713 mm. GVW 6000 kg. In production from 1983.

Truck, 2-ton, 4 × 4, Cargo   ZA
(Samil 20)

6-cyl. aircooled diesel engine (Deutz) with 5F1R gearbox and 2-speed transfer box. Wheelbase 2900 mm. Normal-control version of Samil 20 chassis, with mine-resistant cab. Also a 2 + 10-seat 'Mine-resistant Troop Carrier' with the same front end and an integral full-length hull with armour glass windows. 1982.

Truck, 2-ton, 4 × 4, Cargo   J
(Toyota Type 73)

6-cyl. 4.3-litre diesel engine (Hino DQ100) with 5F1R gearbox and 2-speed transfer box. Rigid axles with leaf springs. Wheelbase 2900 mm. Overall dimensions 5360 × 2090 × 2490 mm. Weight 3200 kg. GVW 5355 kg. Military version of Hino WB500, produced by Toyota partner Hino Motors. Standard Japanese Army chassis.

Truck, 2-ton, 4 × 4, Van   D
(Unimog U125/416)

6-cyl. 5.67-litre diesel engine (OM352; 125-bhp version) with 6F2R gearbox/transfer box. Portal axles with diff. locks. 12.5R20 tyres. Wheelbase 2900 mm. GVW 6000 kg. With special bodywork, this was one of several operated by the Netherlands Army's explosives disposal service, from 1976/77. Optional winch.

Truck, 2-ton, 4 × 4, Cargo   D
(Unimog U800L)

4-cyl. 3.78-litre diesel engine (OM314) with 8F4R transmission. Lockable differentials between axles and between wheels. Air/hydraulic brakes. Hydraulic power steering. Wheelbase 2900 mm. Overall dimensions 5100 × 2150 × 2340 mm. Used as troop carrier, cargo truck and prime mover. From 1979.

Truck, 2-ton, 4 × 4, Tipper   D
(Unimog U900/406.121)

6-cyl. 5.67-litre diesel engine (OM352/353.902) with 6F2R main gearbox and auxiliary box providing 14 forward and 6 reverse gears. Portal axles with diff. locks. Wheelbase 2380 mm. Overall dimensions 4160 × 2000 × 2360 mm. Weight 3700 kg. GVW 6000 kg. GCW 16800 kg. Fixed or tipping body.

TRUCK, 2-TON, 4×4 (UNIMOG 416)

D

General Data: This high-mobility truck in the NATO 2-ton class was used by several armed forces. It could carry 2500 kg or 10–12 men on roads and in rough terrain and could also tow loads of up to 4000 kg in off-road conditions. Its speed range was 3.5–85 km/h and its cruising range about 600 km. It was offered with softtop cab with folding windscreen and with tilting all-steel cab, with or without roof hatch. Continuous ground contact of all wheels was provided by a high degree of axle articulation, with differential locks fitted front and rear.

Technical Details: Daimler-Benz OM352 6-cyl. diesel engine, 5675 cc (97 × 128 mm), 74 kW/100 bhp (net) at 2800 rpm. Dry plate clutch. 6F2R gearbox, combined with transfer box with front axle disconnect. Rigid, portal type axles with coil spring suspension. Air/hydraulic brakes. 12.50-20 tyres. 12-Volt electrics. 90-litre fuel tank.

Dimensions and Weights: Wheelbase 2900 mm. Track 1616 mm. Overall length and width 5100 × 2140 mm. Height 2325 mm (cab). Ground clearance 440 mm (axles). Angles of approach and departure 45° and 46°. Weight 3400 kg, GVW 6000 kg.

above: cargo, softtop cab; *below left:* closed cab (Danish Army); *below right:* Argentine Army (local assembly)

TRUCK, 2-TON, 4×4 (UNIMOG U1300L) D

General Data: In 1976 Daimler-Benz launched a new generation of Unimogs, comprising heavier prime movers, implement carriers and cargo trucks than had been available hitherto. One of the truck versions had already been subjected to tests in competition with a Magirus-Deutz product as a possible replacement for the West German *Bundeswehr*'s 1955-style Unimog S404. As a result, 17000 Unimog U1300L trucks were ordered, to be delivered during 1978–87. In addition to the cargo truck, several other variants were developed.

Technical Details: Daimler-Benz OM352 6-cyl. diesel engine, 5675 cc (97 × 128 mm), 96 kW/130 bhp (net) at 2800 rpm. Dry plate clutch. 8F8R gearbox. Transfer box with front axle disconnect. 6.36:1 axle gear ratio. Portal axles with diff. locks and coil spring suspension. Air/hydraulic brakes. 12.50R20 tyres. 24-Volt electrics. 160-litre fuel tank.

Dimensions and Weights: Wheelbase 3250 mm. Track 1860 mm. Overall length and width 5540 × 2300 mm. Height 2630 mm (cab). Ground clearance 440 mm (axles). Angles of approach and departure 46° and 51°. Weight 5250 kg, GVW 7500 kg.

above and below: U1300L cargo truck of the *Bundeswehr*

MEDIUM AND HEAVY 4 × 4 TRUCKS

Truck, 2-ton, 4 × 4, Cargo   **S**
(Volvo C303/4140 Series)

6-cyl. 2.98-litre twin-carburettor petrol engine (B30) with 4F1R gearbox and 2-speed transfer box. Portal axles with 7.1:1 overall gear ratio. Wheelbase 2530 mm. Overall dimensions 4470 × 1870 × 2150 mm. Weight 2956 kg. GVW 4056 kg. Side-mounted winch optional. Special export model with rhd shown. 1974.

Truck, 2.5-ton, 4 × 4, Shop Van   **BR**
(Engesa EE-25)

6-cyl. 5.67-litre turbocharged diesel engine (Daimler-Benz OM352A) with 5F1R gearbox and 2-speed transfer box. 20-in. wheels. Wheelbase 4200 mm. Air-assisted hydraulic brakes. Integral hydraulic power steering. Brazilian-made military pattern truck with multipurpose shop van body. Early 1980s.

Truck, 2.5-ton, 4 × 4, Lube- and Fuel-Servicing   **USA**
(Ford F600)

V-8-cyl. 5.4-litre petrol engine with 5-speed gearbox and 2-speed transfer box. Wheelbase 3973 mm. GVW 9852 kg. Equipped by Eastern Tank of Peabody, Andover, Mass., for the USMC in 1975. Delivered fuel, lubricants and hydraulic fluids in the field. Designated 'Type B, Style II, 4 × 4, Model E/T931C'.

Truck, 2.5-ton, 4 × 4, Stores   **AUS**
(International Mk IV)

6-cyl. 4.6-litre petrol engine with 5F1R gearbox and 2-speed transfer box. Wheelbase 3683 mm. GVW 7945 kg. Latest in a line of Australian-designed and -built tactical trucks. Also appeared with other body styles, e.g. cargo, self-contained lube unit, house-type van, trackway equipment, etc. Also 6 × 6 versions.

Truck, 2.5-ton, 4 × 4, Cargo   **I**
(Sirmac SAB 2500A)

V-6-cyl. 3.2-litre petrol engine (Fiat 130B.000) with 5F1R gearbox and 2-speed transfer box. Independent air suspension. Wheelbase 2500 mm. Chassis/cab dimensions 4930 × 2140 × 2450 mm. Weight 2750 kg (approx.). Supplied in the late 1970s to the Italian Air Force. Several engine and transmission options were offered.

Truck, 2.5-ton, 4 × 4, Cargo   **D**
(Unimog U1100L)

6-cyl. 5.67-litre diesel engine (OM352) with 8F4R gearbox/transfer box. Portal axles with diff. locks and coil spring suspension. 12.50R20 tyres. Wheelbase 2900 mm. Overall dimensions 5100 × 2150 × 2700 mm. Weight 2860 kg. GVW 6000 kg. Militarized commercial truck replaced the U416 model in the late 1970s.

TRUCK, 2.5-TON, 4 × 4 (ALM/ACMAT VLRA 4 × 4 TPK420)   **F**

General Data: ACMAT (Ateliers de Construction Mécanique de l'Atlantique) was originally founded in 1958 as ALM (Ateliers Legueu à Meaux) when the first prupose-built ALM 4 × 4 trucks were supplied for mineral-prospecting customers. Several African and Middle East armed forces began to acquire them. Known as the VLRA (*Vehicule Léger de Reconnaissance et d'Appui* – light reconnaissance and support vehicle), by the early 1980s they were used by the French and over 30 foreign forces. A Ford 6-cyl. petrol engine was one of the many options available.

Technical Details: Perkins 6.354.4 6-cyl. diesel engine, 5800 cc (98.4 × 127 mm), 120 bhp (SAE) at 2800 rpm. Dry plate clutch.

4F1R gearbox. 2-speed transfer gearbox with lockable differential. 5.83:1 axle gear ratio. Air/hydraulic brakes. Semi-elliptic leaf springs. 12.50-20 tyres. 24-Volt electrics. 2 × 180-litre fuel tanks.

Dimensions and Weights: Wheelbase 3600 mm. Track, front/ rear 1760/1660 mm. Overall length and width 5995 × 2070 mm. Height 1826 mm (cab). Ground clearance 287 mm (axles). Angles of approach and departure 43° and 41°. Weight 4300 kg, GVW 6800 kg.

above: TPK420SMT2 cargo/personnel; *below left:* missile launcher (Nord-Aviation); *below right:* TPK420SC fuel tanker

TRUCK, 2.5-TON, 4 × 4 (ENGESA EE-25 4 × 4)   BR

General Data: The EE-25 was a product of the Brazilian Engesa Group, introduced in the mid-1970s and offered for military and civilian purposes with bodywork to suit. Among the various body types offered by the manufacturers were ambulance, shop van, water and fuel tankers, recovery vehicle and field lubrication unit. For increased off-road mobility, the EE-25 was available with 'Boomerang' single-axle 4-wheel rear bogie, a conversion system that was initially offered for commercial trucks.

Technical Details: Mercedes-Benz OM352A 6-cyl. turbo-charged diesel engine, 5675 cc (97 × 128 mm), 174 bhp (gross) at 2800 rpm. Dry plate clutch. 5F1R gearbox. 2-speed transfer box with front axle disconnect. Axle gear ratios 5.14:1 front, 6.83:1 rear. Air/hydraulic brakes. Semi-elliptic leaf springs 12.00-20 tyres. 12-Volt electrics. 200-litre fuel tank.

Dimensions and Weights: Wheelbase 4200 mm. Track 1800 mm. Overall length and width 6820 × 2250 mm. Height 2500 mm (cab). Ground clearance 350 mm (axles). Angles of approach and departure 52° and 31°. Weight 5100 kg, GVW 10100 kg.

above: cargo/personnel; *below left:* lube vehicle; *below right:* 4500-litre fuel tanker

TRUCK, 2.5-TON, 4 × 4 (SISU A-45)   SF

General Data: Conceived in the 1960s as Model KB-45, this somewhat unorthodox cross-country truck went into quantity production for the Finnish Army as Model A-45, with a number of changes. Instead of the Leyland 0.400 engine and Kirkstall axles of the KB-45, the manufacturers (Oy Suomen Autoteollisuus of Helsinki) used Finnish-made components for the A-45. The engine was behind the cab and the winch on the right-hand side.

Technical Details: Valmet 6-cyl. diesel engine, 103 kW/140 bhp (DIN) at 2600 rpm. Engine cubic capacity not specified. Dry plate clutch. 5F1R gearbox. 2-speed transfer box with front axle disconnect. 7.46:1 axle gear ratio (including planetary hub reduction). Air brakes. Semi-elliptic leaf springs. 14.50-20 tyres. 24-Volt electrics. 210-litre fuel tank.

Note: turbocharged diesel also available (100 kW/150 bhp).

Dimensions and Weights: Wheelbase 3400 mm. Track 1890 mm. Overall length and width 5700 × 2300 mm. Height 2440 mm (cab). Ground clearance 340 mm (axles). Angles of approach and departure 38° and 38°. Weight 5500 kg. GVW 9500 kg.

above and *below left:* A-45 with winch; *below right:* KB-45 of the 1960s

TRUCK, 2.5 TON, 4 × 4 (STEYR 680M2)

A

General Data: Introduced in the mid-1960s (as 680M/Allrad) this truck was in production for a number of years and used in the Austrian and Nigerian armies. Variants included double-cab version for driving-instruction, radar vehicle and an airfield tanker. A slightly different version (A680g) was built for the Swiss Army. A 6 × 6 derivative (680M3) was also produced (qv). Both the 4 × 4 and the 6 × 6 were licence-produced in Greece as Steyr Hellas 680MH and 680MH3.

Technical Details: Own WD609r 6-cyl. diesel engine, 5975 cc (105 × 115 mm), 89.4 kW/120 bhp (DIN) at 2800 rpm. Dry plate clutch. 5F1R gearbox. 2-speed transfer box with front axle

disconnect. 6.5:1 axle gear ratio. Air/hydraulic brakes. Semi-elliptic leaf springs. 9.00-20 tyres. 24-Volt electrics. 160-litre fuel tank. *Note:* also built with WD610.23 direct-injection engine.

Dimensions and Weights: Wheelbase 3700 mm. Track, front/rear 1810/1670 mm. Overall length and width 6570 × 2400 mm. Height 2650 mm (cab). Ground clearance 250 mm (axles). Angles of approach and departure 28° and 28°. Weight 5430 kg (with winch 5830 kg), GVW 10500 kg.

above: 680M2; *below left:* 680MH (Greece); *below right:* A680g (Switzerland)

Truck, 2.8-ton, 4 × 4, Gun Mount   **F**
(ALM/ACMAT VLRA 4 × 4 TPK435VPC)

6-cyl. 5.8-litre diesel engine (Perkins 6.354.4) with 4F1R gearbox and 2-speed transfer box with lockable differential. Wheelbase 4300 mm. Basically the VLRA long-wheelbase cargo truck but fitted out as VPC (*Véhicule de Protection de Convois* – convoy protection vehicle). There were several other body options.

Truck, 3-ton, 4 × 4, Trackway (MLC30)   **GB**
(Bedford RLC)

Danish Army GS truck carrying Assault Class 30 trackway equipment as supplied to several NATO member countries by Laird (Anglesey). It was used on soft ground for wheeled and tracked vehicles up to 30 tons. Earlier R-type trucks of the Danish Army had a modified cab with reverse-slope windscreen.

Truck, 3-ton, 4 × 4, Water Tank   **GB**
(Bedford RLC3Z)

Late production type of the R-type Bedford, fitted with mine-resistant cab and 2728-litre water tank produced by Thompson Tankers for the British Army. The tank had 2 compartments, each with a manhole cover, and a 227-litre/min self-priming positive-driven pump. Truck shown was new in 1970/71.

Truck, 3-ton, 4 × 4, Cargo   **F**
(Berliet 680T)

4-cyl. 5.9-litre diesel engine (M420.30) with 5F1R gearbox (overdrive top) and 2-speed transfer case with lockable differential. Air brakes. Wheelbase 3800 mm. GVW 9035 kg. Softtop cab with folding windscreen. 24-Volt electrics. Offered in early 1970s as low-cost derivative from the 6-ton Model GBD 4 × 4.

Truck, 3-ton, 4 × 4, Cargo   **NL**
(DAF V1600BB358)

6-cyl. 4.77-litre petrol engine (BB475) with 5F1R gearbox and 2-speed transfer box. 20-in. wheels, single rear tyres (9.00 or 11.00-20). Wheelbase 3580 mm. Overall length and width 5600 × 2250 mm (approx.). GVW 12100 kg. Model V1300BA390 similar in appearance. Both were used by the Netherlands Marines.

Truck, 3-ton, 4 × 4, Cargo   **E**
(Pegaso 3045)

6-cyl. 4.77-litre petrol engine (DAF BB475) with 5F1R gearbox (ZF) and 2-speed transfer box. Axles with hub reduction gearing and 11.00 or 12.00-20 tyres, single or dual rear. Wheelbase 3700 mm. Dimensions 6470 × 2480 × 3200 mm. GVW 11700 kg. DAF design (YA414) licence-produced by ENASA, 1970.

TRUCK, 3-TON, 4 × 4 (EBRO E70/1)

E

General Data: Introduced in 1978 by Motor Iberica of Barcelona, the Ebro E70/1 was a low-cost commercially-available off-road truck, assembled mainly from 'off-the-shelf' commercial components and intended for military use in certain export markets. In addition to a cargo truck with fixed or hinged sides it was supplied as a mobile workshop and as a recovery vehicle or wrecker. Other body types were also offered. In order to achieve a flat body floor, the truck was exceptionally tall, with sizeable spacers between axles and springs. The Perkins engines used in Ebro (and Avia) vehicles were licence-produced by Motor Iberica.

Technical Details: Perkins 4.236 4-cyl. diesel engine, 3860 cc

(98.4 × 127 mm), 56.7 kW/76 bhp (DIN) at 2800 rpm. Dry plate clutch. 5F1R gearbox. 2-speed transfer box with front axle disconnect. 4.857:1 axle gear ratio. Hydraulic brakes. Semi-elliptic leaf springs. 7.00-20 tyres. 12-Volt electrics. 75-litre fuel tank.

Dimensions and Weights: Wheelbase 2935 mm. Track, front/rear 1653/1540 mm. Overall length and width 5130 × 2000 mm. Height 2575 mm (cab). Ground clearance 295 mm (axles). Angles of approach and departure 57° and 52°. Weight (chassis/cab) 3296 kg, GVW 7000 kg.

above: cargo/personnel; *below left:* cargo; *below right:* workshop

TRUCK, 3-TON, 4 × 4 (IFA W50LA/A)   DDR

General Data: This 3-ton 4 × 4 range of trucks, built by VEB IFA-Automobilwerke Ludwigsfelde, was one of the few remaining series of indigenous military vehicles in East Germany, most of the others being of chiefly Czech and Soviet origin. The basic type of the IFA was the W50L 4 × 2, of which there were several versions. The 4 × 4 modification was known as the W50LA (Allrad) and again there existed a range of models to meet a number of military (and civil) requirements.

Technical Details: 4VD14,5/12-1SRW 4-cyl. diesel engine, 6560 cc (120 × 145 mm), 92 kW/125 bhp (net) at 2300 rpm. Dry plate clutch. 5F1R gearbox. 2-speed transfer box with front axle

disconnect. 6.07:1 axle gear ratio. Air/hydraulic brakes. Semi-elliptic leaf springs. 16.00-20 tyres. 24-Volt electrics. 150-litre fuel tank.

Dimensions and Weights: Wheelbase 3200 mm. Track, front/rear 1900/1950 mm. Overall length and width 5750 × 2500 mm. Height 2600 mm (cab). Ground clearance 340 mm (axles). Angles of approach and departure not specified. Weight 6300 kg, GVW 9300 kg.

above: W50LA/A cargo truck; *below left:* W50LA/A/C shop van; *below right:* W50LA/PV cargo (dual rear tyres)

TRUCK, 3-TON, 4×4 (PEGASO 3045D)

E

General Data: Widely used by the Spanish (and other) armed forces, this truck was originally built, as Model 3045, under Dutch DAF licence, with certain alterations. Later it was made with a diesel engine and redesignated 3045D. The resemblance to the DAF YA314 truck was noticeable, although it was recognizable by its different wheels and dual rear tyres. In addition to the steel cargo body there were other versions, e.g. dump, tanker, wrecker. Model 3050 was a 6×6 derivative and the 3045DV was a wadeproof version for the Spanish Marines.

Technical Details: Own 9026/13 6-cyl. diesel engine, 6550 cc (107.25 × 120.65 mm), 93 kW/125 bhp (net) at 2400 rpm. Dry

plate clutch. 6F1R gearbox (overdrive top). 2-speed transfer box with front axle disconnect. 6.933:1 axle gear ratio (including hub reduction gearing). Air brakes. Semi-elliptic leaf springs. 11.00-20 tyres. 24-Volt electrics. 2 × 140-litre fuel tanks.

Dimensions and Weights: Wheelbase 3700 mm. Track, front/rear 1900/1818 mm. Overall length and width 6470 × 2480 mm. Height 2720 (cab). Ground clearance 320 mm (axles). Angles of approach and departure 46° and 33°. Weight 6750 kg, GVW 11700 kg.

above: cargo truck/AA gun; *below left:* tanker; *below right:* dump

Truck, 3-ton, 4 × 4, Cargo   **E**
(Pegaso 3046/50)

6-cyl. 6.5-litre diesel engine (9.135/13) with 6F1R gearbox (overdrive top) and 2-speed transfer box. Air brakes. 13.00-20 tyres. Wheelbase 3400 mm. Overall length 5675 mm. Weight 6500 kg. GVW 11500 kg. Max. payload on roads 5000 kg. Made by ENASA, introduced in 1979 and sold also to Egypt.

Truck, 3-ton, 4 × 4, Cargo   **GB**
(Reynolds Boughton RB44)

V-6-cyl. 3-litre petrol engine (Ford 2614E) with 5F1R gearbox (ZF) and own transfer box with lockable differential. Wheelbase 3302 mm. Launched in 1978 (as RB510) this truck, derived from the Ford A-Series, was offered with choice of alternative engines (incl. Rover V8), transmissions, axles, wheelbase sizes, etc.

Truck, 3-ton, 4 × 4, Cargo   **PL**
(Star 244)

6-cyl. 6.9-litre diesel engine (359) with 5F1R gearbox and 2-speed transfer box. Rigid axles. 20-in. wheels. Air/hydraulic brakes. Wheelbase 3400 mm. GVW 10650 kg. The Star 244 was an all-wheel-drive derivative from the Star 200 standard medium truck and used certain components from the 266 6 × 6 model (qv).

Truck, 3-ton, 4 × 4, Cargo   **USA**
(White WM460)

V-8-cyl. 10.4-litre diesel engine (Caterpillar 3208) with auto. trans. (Allison AT545). Eaton axles. Air brakes. Wheelbase 3632 mm. Overall dimensions 6223 × 2438 × 3505 mm. Weight 6169 kg. Prototype only, 1980. White also prototyped a remanufactured M813 5-ton 6 × 6 with power package/drive train conversion.

Truck, 4-ton, 4 × 4, Cargo   **I**
(Astra BM201MC1)

6-cyl. 8.1-litre diesel engine (Fiat 8360) with 6F1R gearbox and 2-speed transfer box with lockable differential. Hub reduction axles with diff. locks. Wheelbase 3450 mm. Overall dimensions 6600 × 2500 × 2850 (cab) mm. Weight 7120 kg. GVW 11120 kg. Alternative body types are dump truck and tanker.

Truck, 4-ton, 4 × 4, Aircraft Fueller   **GB**
(Bedford MK)

6-cyl. 5.4-litre multifuel diesel engine (330-93) with 4F1R gearbox and 2-speed transfer box. Wheelbase 3960 mm. 4500-litre tank and ancillary equipment by Gloster Saro for servicing Harrier VTOL aircraft of the British Royal Air Force. Fuel delivery rate 227 litre/min. Note window curtains and front-mounted exhaust. 1978.

TRUCK, 4-TON, 4 × 4 (BEDFORD MKP2BMO)   GB

General Data: The Bedford MK 4 × 4 or M-type was produced from May 1970 for the British Army (FV13801) and later also for other services (RAF, RN) and several overseas governments, e.g. Denmark, Nigeria, Rhodesia and South Africa. The cargo truck was the most numerous but there were several special-purpose types, some with dual rear tyres. The winch-equipped chassis was designated MKP2WMO.

Technical Details: Own 330-93 6-cyl. multifuel diesel engine, 5408 cc (103.2 × 107.9 mm), 73 kW/98 bhp (net) at 2700 rpm. Dry plate clutch. 4F1R gearbox. 2-speed transfer box with front axle disconnect. 6.8:1 axle gear ratio. Air/hydraulic brakes. Semi-

elliptic leaf springs. 12.00-20 tyres. 24-Volt electrics. 150-litre tank.
Note: from 1977 turbocharged engine optional.

Dimensions and Weights: Wheelbase 3960 mm. Track, front/rear 2050/2032 mm. Overall length and width 6540 × 2440 mm. Height 2590 mm (cab). Ground clearance 340 mm (axles). Angles of approach and departure 41° and 38°. Weight 4860 kg, GVW 9450 kg.

above: cargo truck; *below left:* RAFG (Harrier) shelter; *below right:* CB300 Series shelter/container

Truck, 4-ton, 4 × 4, Cargo   **GB**
(Bedford MK)

6-cyl. diesel engine with 4F1R gearbox and 2-speed transfer box. Wheelbase 3960 mm. M-type chassis with fixed-side steel body and mine-resistant cab with canopy, produced by Reynolds Boughton in England for Sultanate of Oman through Vauxhall Motors in the mid-1970s.

Truck, 4-ton, 4 × 4, Drone Launcher   **GB**
(Bedford RLC)

6-cyl. 4.9-litre petrol engine with 4F1R gearbox and 2-speed transfer box. Wheelbase 3962 mm. Long-time British Army 'work-horse', superseded by M-type in 1969/70. Shown as launcher for Canadair 'Midge' recce drone. Drone's max. operational speed was 740 km/h, at altitude of 300–1200 m. Range 160 km. 1974.

Truck, 4-ton, 4 × 4, Cargo   **F**
(Berliet GBC8KT)

5-cyl. 7.9-litre m/f diesel engine (MK520) with 6F1R gearbox and 2-speed transfer box. Air brakes. Wheelbase 4050 mm. Weight 6960 kg. 2-axle version of the more numerous GBC8KT 6 × 6, supplied mainly for export, e.g. Algeria (shown) and Portugal. French Army had about 60 units in service as fire trucks.

Truck, 4-ton, 4 × 4, Cargo   **R**
(Bucegi SR114)

V-8-cyl. 5.03-litre petrol engine (SR211) with 5F1R gearbox and 2-speed transfer box. Diesel optional. Wheelbase 4000 mm. Overall dimensions 6570 × 2540 × 2310 mm. GVW 8750 kg. Commercial and military (SR114M) versions. Carpati SR132(M) and 3BR2S 3-tonner looked similar but had 9.75-18 tyres, single rear.

Truck, 4-ton, 4 × 4, Tipper   **H**
(Csepel D469.05)

6-cyl. 8.27-litre diesel engine (D614.35) with 5F1R gearbox and 2-speed transfer box (with integral differential and twin propeller shafts for the front-axle drive). Wheelbase 3500 mm. Overall dimensions 5840 × 2410 × 2550 mm. Weight 6000 kg. 3-way tipping body. Made by Csepel of Budapest, mid-1970s.

Truck, 4-ton, 4 × 4, Cargo   **R**
(DAC 6.135RA)

6-cyl. 5.5-litre diesel engine (797-05; Saviem licence) with 5F1R gearbox (AK5-35) and 2-speed transfer box (G450): 20-in. wheels. Wheelbase 4000 mm. Chassis/cab length and width 6915 × 2350 mm. 24-Volt electrics. Several body variants (tractor, tipper) for military and civil service. Also 4 × 2 versions. 1978.

TRUCK, 4-TON, 4×4 (DAF YA4440)

NL

General Data: Launched in the mid-1970s, this DAF truck replaced earlier vehicles like the DAF 3-ton 4 × 4 YA314 and 6 × 6 YA328 in their load-carrying role. It was designed with maximum use (65%) of commercial truck componentry, including the tilting cab. The first orders for the YA4440 were placed in 1976 and 1977 and were for 6500 units for the Netherlands Army. Another 688 were ordered in 1981. Others users included the Netherlands Marines.

Technical Details: Own DT615 6-cyl. turbocharged diesel engine, 6170 cc (104.2 × 120.6 mm), 114 kW/153 bhp (DIN) at 2400 rpm. Dry plate clutch. ZF 5F1R gearbox and 2-speed transfer box with front axle disconnect. 5.72:1 axle gear ratio. Air brakes. Semi-elliptic springs. 12.00-20 tyres. 24-Volt electrics. 200-litre fuel tank.

Dimensions and Weights: Wheelbase 4050 mm. Track 1910 mm. Overall length and width 7050 × 2440 mm. Height 2790 mm (cab). Ground clearance 291 mm (axles). Angles of approach and departure 41° and 30°. Weight 6840 kg, GVW 11500 kg.

above: cargo (Marines); *below left:* shelter (Army); *below right:* YAK4440 with loading crane

Truck, 4-ton, 4 × 4, Cargo/Driving Instruction   **NL**
(DAF YAL4440)

6-cyl. 6.17-litre diesel engine (DT615) with 5F1R gearbox and 2-speed transfer box. Differed from standard Model YA4440 (qv) in having an extended cab with 4 seats. It was used chiefly for drivers' tuition. The first DAF YA4440 pilot models appeared in 1974. The tarpaulin could be lowered, as shown.

Truck, 4-ton, 4 × 4, Cargo   **I**
(Fiat 90PM16)

6-cyl. 5.5-litre diesel engine (8062.24) with 5F1R gearbox and 2-speed transfer box. Portal axles with rear diff. lock. Power steering. Air/hydraulic brakes. Wheelbase 3700 mm. Overall dimensions 6413 × 2270 × 2681 (cab) mm. Weight 5700 kg. Italian Army designation ACM80 (*Autocarro Medio 1980*). 4-ton rear winch.

Truck, 4-ton, 4 × 4, Cargo   **D**
(Mercedes-Benz LA911)

6-cyl. 5.67-litre diesel engine (OM352 II) with 5F1R gearbox and 2-speed transfer box. Air-assisted hydraulic brakes and exhaust brake. Militarized commercial truck with cargo/personnel body, acquired in some quantity by the Danish Army when the R-type Bedford was discontinued in 1969/70.

Truck, 4-ton, 4 × 4, Cargo   **GR**
(NAMCO Milicar)

4-cyl. 3.77-litre aircooled diesel engine (Deutz F4L 912) with 5F1R gearbox and 2-speed transfer box (both ZF). 'Powermaster' portal axles with diff. locks and disc brakes. Wheelbase 2900 mm. Overall dimensions 5100 × 2060 × 2400 mm. Weight 3100 kg. GVW 8500 kg. Prototypes, 1982. Also with crew cab, 6 × 6, etc.

Truck, 4-ton, 4 × 4, Cargo   **F**
(Unic XU-4 × 4)

6-cyl. 5.2-litre diesel engine (Fiat 8060.02) with 5F1R gearbox and 2-speed transfer box. Wheelbase 3800 mm. Chassis/cab length and width 6250 × 2250 mm. Weight of chassis/cab 5850 kg. GVW 10000 kg. Trailer weight 6000 kg. Developed for the French Army, which ordered 1000 units in 1976.

Truck, 4-ton, 4 × 4, Cargo   **D**
(Unimog U1700L)

6-cyl. 5.67-litre diesel engine (OM352A, with exhaust gas turbocharger) with 8F8R gearbox/transfer box. Portal axles with diff. locks and coil springs. Wheelbase 3250 mm. Overall dimensions 5580 × 2320 × 3020 mm. Weight 4900 kg. In 1981 the Australian Army ordered 1295 units, to be assembled in Australia.

TRUCK, 4-TON, 4 × 4 (MAN 11.136HA)

D

General Data: In 1975 the Belgian Army ordered 3000 of these militarized commercial trucks. In addition to the 4 × 4 type, a quantity of 4 × 2 variants was ordered, including 131 tippers in 1981 (qv). All these trucks were assembled in Belgium by MAN importers Hocke. The 4 × 4 chassis were fitted with cargo and tanker bodies.

Technical Details: MAN-Saviem 797.06 6-cyl. diesel engine, 5488 cc (102 × 112 mm), 101 kW/136 bhp (DIN) at 3000 rpm. Dry plate clutch. 5F1R gearbox. 2-speed transfer box with lockable differential. Axles with separate drive shafts and spur gear hub reduction. Air/hydraulic brakes front, full air rear, plus exhaust

brake. Semi-elliptic leaf springs. 9.00R20 tyres. 24-Volt electrics. 200-litre fuel tank.

Dimensions and Weights: Wheelbase 4400 mm. Track, front/rear 1824/1632 mm. Overall length and width 7420 × 2500 mm. Height 2650 mm. (cab). Ground clearance 330 mm (axles). Weight 6248 kg, GVW 11400 kg.
Note: tanker truck dimensions: 7200 × 2480 × 2740 mm, weight 7204 kg.

above: cargo truck; *below left:* cargo truck with shelter; *below right:* tanker truck

TRUCK, 4-TON, 4 × 4 (RENAULT TRM4000/SAVIEM SM8)   F

General Data: The Renault TRM4000 started life as Saviem SM8 and early prototypes were provided with a military pattern cab and later with a softtop version of the commercial-type tilting cab. The Saviem SM8 was offered also with dual rear tyres. In 1977 the French Army ordered between 15000 and 20000 units, with the single rear tyre equipment and all-steel enclosed cab. Several body options were called for, including tipper trucks, tankers and recovery vehicles (wreckers). A fire-fighting version with 4-door crew cab was manufactured for the French Air Force.

Technical Details: Own 797 6-cyl. diesel engine, 5491 cc (102 × 112 mm), 98 kW/133 bhp (DIN) at 2900 rpm. Dry plate clutch. 5F1R gearbox. 2-speed transfer box with torque-equalizing differential. 6.833:1 axle gear ratio. Air brakes. Semi-elliptic leaf springs. 12.00-20 tyres. 24-Volt electrics. 150-litre fuel tank.

Dimensions and Weights: Wheelbase 3850 mm. Track, front/rear 1836/2018 mm. Overall length and width 6180 × 2190 mm. Height 2750 mm (cab). Ground clearance 280 mm (axles). Angles of approach and departure 37° and 45°. Weight (chassis/cab) 4660 kg, GVW 10000 kg.

above: TRM4000; *below left:* SM8 pilot model; *below right:* SM8 with dual rear tyres

147

TRUCK, 4.5-TON, 4×4 (SCANIA SBA 111A134)   S

General Data: Officially known by the Swedish armed forces as TGB (*Terrängbil*) 311A MT, this truck was first launched in 1970 (with model designation LBA110) and taken into series production in the mid-1970s, together with a 6 × 6 version, both with several body variants. A number were exported to Finland. The chassis/cab was also commercially available, designated SBA 111 40.

Technical Details: Own D11LB28 6-cyl. diesel engine, 11000 cc (127 × 145 mm), 133 kW/208 bhp (DIN) at 2200 rpm. Automatic 6F1R gearbox. 2-speed transfer box with front axle disconnect. 5.58:1 axle gear ratio (incl. hub reduction). Diff. locks front and rear. Air brakes. Semi-elliptic leaf springs. 14.00-20 tyres. 24-Volt electrics. 170-litre fuel tank.

Note: turbocharged engine (DS11LB27) optional.

Dimensions and Weights: Wheelbase 4000 mm. Track 2020 mm. Overall length and width 6750 × 2490 mm. Height 2890 mm (cab). Ground clearance 380 mm (axles). Angles of approach and departure 45° and 40°. Weight 8820 kg, GVW 13700 kg.

above: cargo with crane; *below left:* with personnel cab; *below right:* with radar equipment

TRUCK, 5-TON, 4×4 (DAF V1600BB425)

NL

General Data: A considerable number of these militarized commercial trucks were supplied to the Netherlands Air Force during the 1960s and early 1970s. They were gradually superseded in later years by the new generation DAF YA5441. The V1600 Series chassis/cab (including V1600DD diesel) was used with a variety of body types, both open and closed. Some had a winch at the front or a crane at the rear and others had attachment points for a snowplough. Netherlands Marines had V1600BB390 with front-mounted winch (1973).

Technical Details: Own BB475 6-cyl. petrol engine, 4769 cc (100.6 × 100 mm), 99 kW/134 bhp (DIN) at 3500 rpm. Dry plate clutch. ZF AK5-35/2 5F1R gearbox. 2-speed transfer box with front axle disconnect. 7.2:1 axle gear ratio. Air/hydraulic brakes. Semi-elliptic leaf springs. 9.00-20 tyres. 12-Volt electrics. 120-litre fuel tank. *Note:* certain models had air/mechanical brakes.

Dimensions and Weights: Wheelbase 4250 mm. Track, front/rear 1772/1730 mm. Overall length and width 6500 × 2500 mm. Height 2750 mm (cab). Ground clearance and angles of approach and departure not specified. Weight 5620 kg, GVW 11500 kg.

above: cargo; *below left:* bomb-handling crane; *below right:* mobile control tower

TRUCK, 5-TON, 4 × 4 (DAF YA5441)

NL

General Data: The DAF YA5441 (military truck, 5-ton, 4 × 4, 1st series) was taken into service by the Royal Netherlands Air Force in a variety of roles (from 1975) and by the Army (1978, 20 only, mainly for the transport of Lance rocket components). It was a heavier edition of the Dutch Army's YA4441 4-tonner, with dual rear tyres. As with the YA2442 (2-ton) and YA4441, maximum use was made of 'off-the-shelf' componentry from commercial production. The 5-ton models had a taller, tilting cab, with 3 seats.

Technical Details: Own DT615 6-cyl. turbocharged diesel engine, 6170 cc (104.2 × 120.6 mm), 114 kW/153 bhp (DIN) at 2400 rpm. Dry plate clutch. ZF 5F1R gearbox and 2-speed transfer box with front axle disconnect. 5.72:1 axle gear ratio. Air brakes. Semi-elliptic leaf springs. 10.00-20XL tyres. 24-Volt electrics. 200-litre fuel tank.

Dimensions and Weights: Wheelbase 3850 mm. Track, front/rear 1938/1729 mm. Overall length and width 7505 × 2305 mm. Height 2960 mm (cab). Ground clearance 270 mm (axles). Angles of approach and departure 32° and 23°. Weight 7290 kg, GVW 13000 kg.

above: cargo (Army); *below left:* crane and rear winch (Air Force); *below right:* explosives van (Air Force)

TRUCK, 5-TON, 4 × 4 (FIAT 6602CM)   I

General Data: First launched in 1962 as the Carro Pesante CP62, this heavy-duty general purpose truck was later redesignated in the Italian Army as the 6602CM. It remained in production, with periodic improvements, for many years and several alternative body styles were introduced, including a dump truck and an aircraft refueller. The cargo truck was fitted with a power winch at the rear, with a capacity of 9200 kg and provided with an automatic safety brake. The 6602CM was originally designed to meet the NATO requirements for 6-ton tactical trucks, with softtop cab and folding windscreen.

Technical Details: Own 8202.02 6-cyl. diesel engine, 9816 cc (122 × 140 mm), 142 kW/190 bhp (DIN) at 2500 rpm. Dry plate clutch. 5F1R gearbox. 2-speed transfer box with front axle disconnect. 6.682:1 axle gear ratio. Air brakes. Semi-elliptic leaf springs. 11.00-20 tyres. 24-Volt electrics. 230-litre fuel tank.

Dimensions and Weights: Wheelbase 3570 mm. Track, front/rear 1873/1785 mm. Overall length and width 6650 × 2460 mm. Height 2700 mm (cab). Ground clearance 271 mm (axles). Angles of approach and departure 45° and 35°. Weight 7407 kg, GVW 12550 kg.

above and *below left:* cargo/personnel; *below right:* dump truck

151

TRUCK, 5-TON, 4×4 (MAN N4610W)

D

General Data: Developed by the Gemeinschaftsburo (joint design office in which Büssing, Henschel, KHD, Krupp and MAN participated) this *Lkw 5 t gl* was produced during the late 1970s for the West German *Bundeswehr*. Some 3000 units were made, approximately one-third of which were Model N4510 with winch. Both had many components in common with 6 × 6 7-ton and 8 × 8 10-ton variants (qqv).

Technical Details: Deutz F8L 413F V-8-cyl. aircooled diesel engine, 12763 cc (125 × 130 mm), 188 kW/256 bhp (net) at 2650 rpm. Hydraulic torque converter plus dry plate clutch. ZF S6-65 6F1R gearbox. Transfer box with lockable differential. Diff. lock

in rear axle. 6.734:1 axle gear ratio (incl. hub reduction). Air/hydraulic brakes. Rigid axles with coil springs. 14.00R20M tyres. 24-Volt electrics. 270-litre fuel tank.

Dimensions and Weights: Wheelbase 4500 mm. Track 2066 mm. Overall length and width 8020 × 2500 mm. Height 2860 mm (cab). Ground clearance 415 mm (axles). Angles of approach and departure 45° and 40°. Weight 9860 kg, GVW 14500 kg.

above: N4610W, 1978; *below left:* pre-production model; *below right:* Contraves Fieldguard fire-control system

Truck, 4.9-ton, 4 × 4, Cargo   CH
(Saurer 2DM)

6-cyl. 8.1-litre diesel engine (CT3D) with 2 × 8F1R gearbox and 2-speed transfer box with lockable differential. Trilex wheels with 20-in. rims. Wheelbase 4200 mm. Overall dimensions 7370 × 2300 × 3200 mm. Weight 7100 kg. GVW 12000 kg. 1964–73. Also with special bodywork. Co-produced with Berna (Model 2VM).

Truck, 5-ton, 4 × 4, Cargo   F
(Berliet 770K B)

4-cyl. 6-litre diesel engine with 5F1R gearbox and 2-speed transfer box. Rear axle diff. lock optional. 12.00-20XL tyres (10-22.5, dual rear, optional). Wheelbase 3300 mm. Overall length and width 6035 × 2300 mm. GVW 10990 kg. Front winch and rhd optional. Militarized version of Berliet 770KB 4 × 2 of the mid-1970s.

Truck, 5-ton, 4 × 4, Cargo   F
(Berliet L64/8R)

6-cyl. 7.9-litre diesel engine (M520) with 6F1R gearbox and 2-speed transfer box. 20-in. wheels, single or dual rear tyres. Wheelbase 3930 mm. Chassis/cab dimensions 6555 × 2480 × 2999 mm. Weight 6820 kg. GVW 13500 kg. Supplied, chiefly for export, with cargo, tipper and other bodywork. 1973.

Truck, 5-ton, 4 × 4, Tipper   H
(Csepel D564)

6-cyl. 8.27-litre diesel engine (D614.35) with 5F1R gearbox and 2-speed transfer box. Portal axles. Air brakes. Wheelbase 3668 mm. Overall dimensions 6470 × 2500 × 2780 (cab) mm. Weight 6100 kg. GVW 11100 kg. Speed range 2.2–87.9 km/h. 3-way tipping dropside body. 24-Volt electrics. 4-seat cab. Early 1970s.

Truck, 5-ton, 4 × 4, Tanker   AUS
(International ACCO 610A)

V-8-cyl. 5.7-litre petrol engine with 4F1R gearbox and 2-speed transfer box. 17-in. cast spoke wheels. Wheelbase 3430 mm. Square-shape 3700-litre water tank, one of 18 built by Gilbarco (Australia) for the Royal Australian Air Force, for fire control purposes and as drinking-water units. 1982.

Truck, 5-ton, 4 × 4, Dump   USA
(International Loadstar 1700 4 × 4)

V-8-cyl. 5.6-litre petrol engine (V345) with 5F1R gearbox and 2-speed transfer box. Wheelbase 3226 mm. Although numerous IHC Loadstar trucks were delivered to all the US forces, this swb dump truck of the Marine Corps was relatively rare. Loadstar trucks were in production for many years and in many variants.

TRUCK, 5-TON, 4×4 (SAMIL 50)   ZA

General Data: Marketed by Nimrod International (Pty) of Pretoria, South Africa, the Samil 50 was one of a range of South African military vehicles built by Armscor (Krygkor in Afrikaans). The range comprised 2-, 5- and 10-ton types, all resembling certain German IVECO/Magirus-Deutz models. A wide range of body styles was developed, those for the Samil 50 chassis including cargo/personnel, wrecker, welding workshop, fuel tanker, pantry vehicle and mine-resistant ambulance.

Technical Details: Deutz V-6-cyl. aircooled diesel engine, 108 kW/145 bhp (net) at 2650 rpm. Cubic capacity not specified. Dry plate clutch. 6F1R gearbox. 2-speed transfer box with front axle disconnect. Rear axle with hub reduction gearing. Air brakes. Semi-elliptic leaf springs. 14.00-20 tyres. 24-Volt electrics. Fuel tank capacity not specified.

Dimensions and Weights: Wheelbase 4900 mm. Track, front/rear 1985/2030 mm. Overall length and width 7730 × 2500 mm. Height 3100 mm. Ground clearance 355 mm (axles). Angles of approach and departure not specified. Weight 6340 kg, GVW 12400 kg. GCW 18400 kg.

above: shelter body; *below left:* cargo/personnel; *below right:* water tanker/sprinkler

Truck, 5-ton, 4 × 4, Tanker (Magirus-Deutz 130D13AL)   D

6-cyl. 6.1-litre aircooled diesel engine (Deutz F6L 913) with 5F1R gearbox and 2-speed transfer box. Banjo-type axles. Air/hydraulic brakes. Exhaust brake optional. Wheelbase 4200 mm. Chassis/cab dimensions 6270 × 2290 × 2220 mm. Weight 4990 kg. GVW 12300 kg. Also built as tipper (130D13AK 4 × 4, 130D13K 4 × 2).

Truck, 5-ton, 4 × 4, Cargo (Magirus-Deutz 170D10FAL)   D

V-6-cyl. 8.5-litre aircooled diesel engine (Deutz F6L 413V) with 5F1R gearbox and 2-speed transfer box with lockable planetary differential. 13.00-20XL tyres. Wheelbase 3500 mm. Chassis/cab length and width 6035 × 2480 mm. Weight 5460 kg. GVW 10600 kg. Commercially available military truck of 1974.

Truck, 5-ton, 4 × 4, Cargo (Magirus-Deutz 192D12AL)   D

V-6-cyl. 9.6-litre aircooled diesel engine (Deutz F6L 413F) with 6F1R gearbox and 2-speed transfer box. Wheelbase 4200 mm. Chassis/cab dimensions 6880 × 2450 × 2860 mm. Weight 5880 kg. GVW 11700 kg. Models 130D9AL and 170D10AL externally similar in general appearance.

Truck, 5-ton, 4 × 4, Chassis (Magirus-Deutz 232D16AL)   D

V-8-cyl. 11.3-litre aircooled diesel engine (Deutz F8L 413) with 6F1R gearbox and 2-speed transfer box with lockable planetary differential. Hub reduction gearing. 14.00-20XL tyres. Wheelbase 4650 mm. Chassis/cab length and width 6780 × 2450 mm. Weight 5635 kg. GVW 15500 kg. In Norwegian Army from early 1970s.

Truck, 5-ton, 4 × 4, Cargo (Mercedes-Benz L1017A)   D

6-cyl. 5.67-litre diesel engine with exhaust gas turbocharger (OM352A) with 6F1R gearbox and 2-speed transfer box. Wheelbase 3600 mm. GVW 11660 kg. Shown with 9.00-20 tyres, dual rear (for *Bundeswehr*, 1977) but offered also with 13.00-20, single rear. By late 1970s L1017A was replaced by L1217A.

Truck, 5-ton, 4 × 4, Cargo (Tata 1210SA)   IND

6-cyl. 4.79-litre diesel engine with 5F1R gearbox and 2-speed transfer box. Wheelbase 3625 mm. Weight 3750 kg (approx.) GVW 12180 kg. Produced by Tata Engineering & Locomotive Co. (TELCO), originally as a joint venture with Daimler-Benz but from the late 1970s with own styling and 98% local content.

Truck, 5-ton, 4 × 4, Cargo/Crane   **S**
(Volvo BM)

6-cyl. diesel engine with semi-automatic transmission. Hydrauli-cally-actuated steering by articulation. Hydraulic self-loading crane on front unit. In service with the Swedish forces for transport of ammunition. Derived from 'Skogs-Lisa' tractor/carrier, built by Bolinder-Munktell (member of the Volvo Group).

Truck, 5-ton, 4 × 4, Cargo/Prime Mover   **S**
(Volvo F88 4 × 4)

6-cyl. 9.6-litre diesel engine with 8F1R gearbox and 2-speed transfer box. Wheelbase 4200 mm. Derived from commercial Volvo F88 tilt-cab truck in the mid-1970s this vehicle was intended chiefly for heavy artillery towing. It was sold to the Swedish forces and for export. Also appeared as wrecker.

Truck, 5-ton, 4 × 4, Cargo/Prime Mover   **S**
(Volvo L48546A)

6-cyl. 6.7-litre diesel engine (D67C, or turbocharged T-D67C) with 5F1R gearbox and 2-speed transfer box. Wheelbase 4400 mm. Overall dimensions 7550 × 2450 × 2850 mm. Weight 6680 kg. GVW 12000 kg. Known as 'Ltgbil 939E' this was one of several models, used by the Swedish Coast Artillery.

Truck, 6-ton, 4 × 4, Cargo   **D**
(MAN 14.240FAEG)

6-cyl. 11.1 diesel engine (D2566MFG) with torque converter, 6F1R gearbox and transfer box with lockable differential. Hub reduction axles, with diff. lock at rear. Air/hydraulic brakes. Coil spring suspension. Commercially-available version of MAN 5-ton tactical truck (qv) with own engine and cab. 1976.

Truck, 6-ton, 4 × 4, Cargo   **CH**
(Saurer 6DM)

6-cyl. 11.95-litre turbocharged diesel engine (D4KT) with torque converter, 10-speed semi-auto. gearbox and transfer box with lockable diff. (ZF). Hub reduction axles. Air brakes. Wheelbase 4350 mm. Length and width 7705 × 2500 mm. GVW 16000 kg. 1982/83 model shown.

Truck, 6-ton, 4 × 4, Cargo   **A**
(Steyr 1291M/4 × 4)

6-cyl. 9.7-litre turbocharged diesel engine (WD614.71) with 6F1R gearbox and 2-speed transfer box. Hub reduction axles. Diff. lock at rear. Wheelbase 4200 mm. Overall dimensions 7870 × 2500 × 3100 (cab) mm. Weight 9500 kg. GVW 15500 kg. Also 6 × 6 variant (1491M/6 × 6). Early 1980s.

TRUCK, 6-TON, 4×4 (RENAULT TRM6000/BERLIET GBD)   F

General Data: This vehicle was originated by Berliet but after Berliet's takeover by the Renault Group (RVI – Renault Véhicules Industriels) the name was changed to Renault. 'TRM' stands for all-wheel-drive truck, '6000' for the payload in kg across country. Prototypes, manufactured by Berliet in the early 1970s, had smooth door surfaces and body side panels and other detail differences. Production models could be supplied with either a removable hardtop, as shown, or a canvas-top cab.

Technical Details: Berliet MI620.30 6-cyl. diesel engine, 8820 cc (120 × 130 mm), 131 kW/176 bhp (DIN) at 2400 rpm. Dry plate clutch. 6F1R overdrive-top gearbox. 2-speed transfer box with

lockable differential. Hub reduction axles. 6.83:1 axle gear ratio. Air brakes. Semi-elliptic leaf springs. 12.00-20 tyres. 24-Volt electrics. 200-litre fuel tank.

Dimensions and Weights: Wheelbase 3800 mm. Track, front/rear 1936/1938 mm. Overall length and width 6815 × 2480 mm. Height 2825 mm (cab). Ground clearance 370 mm (rear axle). Angles of approach and departure 45° and 34°. Weight 6400 kg, GVW 15000 kg.

above: cargo truck, 1979; *below left:* Air Force lube truck (Lamberet, 1980); *below right:* prototype, 1973/74

TRUCK, 8-TON, 4 × 4 (BEDFORD TM4-4, WNV-SERIES) GB

General Data: This vehicle was developed for the British Army during the late 1970s to meet a General Staff requirement for a medium-mobility load carrier with a load capacity of 8000 kg and capable of carrying 6 pallets or unit load containers of NATO standard dimensions, general stores, fuel loads and certain container loads. In addition to the standard cargo truck, there were variants with Turner 8000-kg winch, Atlas AK 3500 loading crane, Edbro 6.5-m³ tipper body, light mobile digger, etc.

Technical Details: Own 8.2/205TD 6-cyl. turbocharged diesel engine, 8198 cc (115.9 × 129.5 mm), 151 kW/202 bhp (net) at 2500 rpm. Twin-plate clutch. 6F1R gearbox. 2-speed transfer box with front axle disconnect. 5.887:1 axle gear ratio. Air brakes. Semi-elliptic leaf springs. 15.50/80R20 tyres. 24-Volt electrics. 156-litre fuel tank.

Dimensions and Weights: Wheelbase 4325 mm. Track, front/ rear 2024/2078 mm. Overall length and width 6630 × 2500 mm. Height 2997 mm (cab). Ground clearance 352 mm (axles). Angles of approach and departure 41° and 35°. Weight (chassis/cab) 6300 kg, GVW 16260 kg.

above: cargo truck; *below left:* with loading crane (CALM); *below right:* tipper (with 3880-mm wheelbase)

Truck, 8-ton, 4 × 4, Cargo   **GB**
(Foden MMC)

6-cyl. diesel engine (Rolls-Royce 220 Mk3) with 9F1R gearbox and 2-speed transfer box. Kirkstall axles with hub reduction gearing. 14.00-20 tyres. Wheelbase 4250 mm. Known as 'Medium Mobility Cargo' truck, this limited production model was derived from the makers' 6 × 6 medium-mobility truck (qv) in 1976.

Truck, 8-ton, 4 × 4, Cargo   **GB**
(Leyland Mil. 4 × 4)

V-8-cyl. 8.8-litre diesel engine (Perkins 540) with 6F1R gearbox (Turner) and 2-speed transfer case (Rockwell). Rockwell-Maudslay hub reduction axles. Mid-1970s prototype for British Army's medium-mobility logistic vehicle, produced by Leyland's Scammell division but not accepted for quantity procurement.

Truck, 8-ton, 4 × 4, Cargo   **GB**
(Shelvoke MYC)

6-cyl. turbocharged diesel engine (Leyland 411E) with 6F1R gearbox and 2-speed transfer box. Full-time 4-wheel drive. GKN-Kirkstall axles. Own tilting steel cab. Marshall body. Private venture, launched in 1982. Several power train and body options. Shelvoke & Drewry also supplied military forklift trucks.

Truck, 8-ton, 4 × 4, Cargo   **GB**
(Unipower P44-M)

V-8-cyl. diesel engine (Perkins 510) with 5F1R gearbox and 2-speed transfer case. Air brakes. 20-in. wheels with 12.00-20 tyres. GVW 16256 kg. 24-Volt electrics. Also offered with Rolls-Royce B81 8-cyl. in-line engine. Truck shown, a one-off, was tested by the British Ministry of Defence in 1974/75.

Truck, 9-ton, 4 × 4, Tractor   **D**
(MAN 15.240FAS)

6-cyl. 11.1-litre diesel engine (D2566MF) with 6F1R gearbox and 2-speed transfer box with lockable differential. Diff. lock in rear axle. Air/hydraulic brakes. Wheelbase 3500 mm. A number of these tractors were bought by the *Bundeswehr* in 1980/81, chiefly for towing Blumhardt 15-ton semi-trailers. GCW 29200 kg.

Truck, Heavy, 4 × 4, Mine-Laying   **F**
(Matenin)

During the 1960s, Ets Matenin of Paris designed and produced 2 types of sophisticated excavators for high-speed trench digging. The KX609 model went into service with the French and West German armies. This mine-laying vehicle was based on the same chassis type and entered French Army service in 1981.

Six-Wheeled Trucks

The largest chapter of this Directory is devoted to six-wheeled trucks. The entries have been arranged in alphabetical sequence by payload rating, regardless of drive configuration: 6 × 4 types and even a lonely 6 × 2 have thus been included among the many six-by-sixes. The addition of an extra rear axle increases both the carrying capacity and the tractive effort of a vehicle, but it also has to do with design philosophy and tradition. It is interesting, for example, to observe that in the United States a typical military load carrier like the 2.5-ton 6 × 6 M35A2 (with a highway-payload rating of 4540 kg) rides on ten tyres, whereas the British Bedford TM4-4 carries nearly twice that weight on four. Admittedly, the Bedford's 15.50/80R20 tyres are much more capable than the M35A2's 9.00-20s but the British have never deemed the six-by-six configuration necessary for 'ordinary' load carriers. The US armed forces, on the other hand, have (with some notable exceptions like the articulated 4-wheeled 'Goer') stuck by the 6 × 6 for on- and off-road haulage ever since the trusty GMC 'deuce-and-a-half' of 1940/41 proved its worth in arduous battle service throughout the Second World War (and far beyond). The United States' M-Series 2.5-ton 6 × 6, introduced in the early 1950s and produced almost continually since then, did and still does an even better job and has never changed much. Right from the start it proved a very sound vehicle and, apart from a few detail modifications, late production models still look the same as in 1951. Only recently have some basic improvements been introduced for a Product Improved Package (PIP), including a Caterpillar V8 diesel engine with automatic transmission, a wider cab and larger front end. All these modifications made the vehicle nearly 20 per cent heavier and although the automatic transmission may be a good thing for prolonging engine and drive-line life, it is less appropriate for a cross-country machine because with a severely jolting vehicle it is hard to 'play' the accelerator pedal properly, and thus control the up and down shifts, unless one keeps low range selected, which is not always practical. This was also a problem with the GMC M135 (and variants) which was produced concurrently with the early M35 (and variants) in the 1950s. The GMC had a dual-range four-speed Hydramatic transmission with a single-speed transfer box and was also in service for many years with the Canadian Army.

In 1977 the Armor Engineer Board of the US Army evaluated a number of commercial trucks (Dodge, Ford, International) to see whether any of these would be suitable to replace the rather more costly M-Series 2.5- and 5-ton 6 × 6 trucks, if only for restricted use. The six-wheelers used for these trials were from Ford and International. The 6 × 4 Ford, shown in this section, featured a Caterpillar engine with Allison automatic transmission (not unlike the product-improved 2.5-ton 6 × 6 XM963). The results of these tests were not exactly favourable. Inadequate ground clearance caused damage to fuel tanks and exhaust systems, cooling systems were not up to the job, and many other defects also indicated that none of these commercial models could possibly compete with the military designs for the rough work.

As will be seen in the following pages, a fair number of 6 × 6 vehicles were or are still also available with two axles, as 4 × 4. And again, in several instances central differentials in the transfer box, with manual locking device, are replacing the old-established type where the front axle drive had to be (dis)connected manually. Differential locks in the axles also feature rather more often. Relatively few of these trucks have independent suspension, the notable exception being the Tatra models with their swing axles (which they have used since time immemorial), the Steyr-Daimler-Puch Pinzgauer (which, through Dr Hans Ledwinka, can be linked with the Tatra) and another central European truck the Hungarian Csepel D566 which uses individual wheel stations not unlike those of the British Alvis Stalwart and related vehicles, enabling the manufacturer to construct 4 × 4 and 8 × 8 variants with relative ease (see the chapter on 'Tractors and Wreckers' for an 8 × 8 derivative).

Some old East European trucks like the Soviet ZIL-157K and Czech Praga V3S have been updated. Of the former, a (probably remanufactured) diesel-engined version, known as the ZIL-157KD, appeared in 1978 and the Praga V3S was superseded in production by a modernized version, the M1, with more powerful engine (88-kW Tatra T912.4), new transmission, relocated headlamps (in the front bumper) and, like the ZIL-157KD, having improved performance and carrying capacity.

TRUCK, 1.25-TON, 6×6 (CONSOLIDATED DIESEL 2252/M561)   USA

General Data: Commonly known as the 'Gama Goat', this articulated 6-wheeler was an integrated tractor-carrier unit, joined through a flexible connection permitting vehicle articulation and maintaining ground contact and traction at all driving wheels in the roughest terrain. Standardized as M561 in 1966, over 14000 were made during 1969–73 by Consolidated Diesel Division of Condec Corporation. The vehicle, which in the field proved unsatisfactory, could swim, using its wheels for propulsion.

Technical Details: GM Detroit Diesel 3-53 3-cyl. 2-stroke diesel engine, 2610 cc (98.4 × 114.3 mm), 103 bhp (gross) at 2800 rpm. Dry plate clutch. 4F1R gearbox. 2-speed transfer box with front axle disconnect. Limited-slip diffs. 5.57:1 axle gear ratio. Hydraulic brakes with sealed drums. Independent suspension (coil springs front and rear; leaf spring on centre swing axle). 11.00-18 tyres. 24-Volt electrics. 2 × 76-litre fuel tanks.

Dimensions and Weights: Wheelbase 2050+2154 mm. Track 1829 mm. Overall length and width 5756 × 2134 mm. Height 2075 mm. Ground clearance 381 mm. Angles of approach and departure 62° and 45°. Weight 3315 kg, GVW 4630 kg.

above: cargo truck M561; *below left:* XM561 (pilot, LTV); *below right:* M561 with shelter (USMC)

TRUCK, 1.5-TON, 6×6 (STEYR-DAIMLER-PUCH PINZGAUER 712 SERIES)   A

General Data: This 6-wheeled derivative of the Pinzgauer was developed in conjunction with the Swiss and Austrian armed forces and provided exceptionally high mobility. Like the makers' smaller Haflinger, the Pinzgauer was particularly suited to operation in mountainous areas. A central tube chassis was used, with transaxles. All axles had differential locks, which could be engaged and disengaged hydraulically on the move, and step-down gearing.

Technical Details: Own 4-cyl. aircooled twin-carburettor petrol engine, 2499 cc (92 × 94 mm), 67 kW/92 bhp (DIN) at 4000 rpm. Dry plate clutch. 5F1R gearbox. 2-speed transfer gear with front axle disconnect. 2.846:1 axle gear ratio and 2.266:1 spur gear

ratio. Hydraulic brakes. Coil springs at front, leaf springs at rear. 245-16 or 7.50-16 tyres. 24-Volt electrics. 75- or 125-litre fuel tank. *Note:* also available with 64 kW/87 bhp engine.

Dimensions and Weights: Wheelbase 2490 mm. Track 1440 mm. Overall length and width 4955 × 1760 mm. Height 2045 mm (canvas top). Ground clearance 335 mm. Angles of approach and departure 45° and 45°. Weight 2350 kg, GVW 3900 kg.

above and *below left:* 712M cargo/personnel; *below right:* 712K radio vehicle

TRUCK, 1.5-TON, 6×6 (VOLVO 4143GV)   S

General Data: Developed simultaneously with the 4 × 4 4141 range (qv), these 6-wheelers were designed for increased mobility and payload for the Swedish armed forces. In 1975 quantity production began, with the following variants: TGB 131A MT (multipurpose), RLTGB 1312A MT (radio link van), STABSTGB 1313A MT (command), RATGB 1316A MT (radio) and BPLTGB 1317A MT (battery command post). For higher payloads there was the 5700-kg GVW TGB 221A MT with 5F1R gearbox and 3245-mm wheelbase. Certain types were for export.

Technical Details: Own B30A 6-cyl. petrol engine, 2980 cc (88.9 × 88 mm), 86 kW/117 bhp (DIN) at 4000 rpm. Dry plate clutch. 4F1R gearbox. 2-speed transfer box with front axle disconnect. 5.99:1 axle gear ratio (including drop gear final drive). Vacuum/hydraulic brakes. Semi-elliptic leaf springs, inverted at rear. 280/85-16 tyres. 24-Volt electrics. 84-litre fuel tank.

Dimensions and Weights: Wheelbase 2825 mm. Track 1540 mm. Overall length and width 5350 × 1900 mm Height 2170 mm. Ground clearance 380 mm (axles). Angles of approach and departure 50° and 45°. Weight 2820 kg. GVW 4400 kg.

above: 6-seat TGB 131A MT (or TGB 13); *below left:* BPLTGB 1317A MT; *below right:* RLTGB 1312A MT

Truck, 2.5 ton, 6 × 6, Cargo   **CDN**
(Bombardier M35CDN)

V-8-cyl. 8.2-litre diesel engine (Detroit Diesel 4087/7101) with
4F1R auto. trans. (Allison MT643) and 2-speed transfer box.
11.00-20 tyres. Wheelbase 3900 mm. Overall length and width
7080 × 2500 mm. Weight 6523 kg. GVW 11068 kg. Canadian
version of US M35A2C truck, with certain modifications. 1982.

Truck, 2.5-ton, 6 × 6, Cargo   **PRC**
(Dongfeng/Aeolus EQ240)

6-cyl. 5.4-litre petrol engine (EQ6100) with 5F1R gearbox and 2-
speed transfer box. 11.00-18 tyres. Wheelbase 3740 mm. Overall
dimensions 6218 × 2255 × 2385 (cab) mm. Weight 4850 kg. GVW
9060 kg. Made from 1973. From 1978 also 3.5-ton version
(EQ245) with 5.9-litre petrol engine. Aeolus was export name.

Truck, 2.5-ton, 6 × 6, Cargo   **PRC**
(Liberation/Jiefang CA30)

6-cyl. 5.5-litre petrol engine (CA30A) with 5F1R gearbox and 2-
speed transfer box. 12.00-18 tyres. Wheelbase 4225 mm. Overall
dimensions 6680 × 2315 × 2360 (cab) mm. Weight 5340 kg. GVW
9840 kg. Winch at front optional (CA30A). Patterned on Soviet
ZIL-157K, built in Changchun from the mid-1960s.

Truck, 2.5-ton, 6 × 6, Cargo   **USA**
(USA XM963)

In 1978/79 a PIP (Product Improvement Package) version of the
old US M-Series 2.5-ton 6 × 6 was produced, using a Caterpillar
3208 V-8-cyl. diesel engine with Allison MT643 4F1R auto. trans.,
new axles with large tyres, redesigned suspension, brakes, steering,
etc. Experimental only.

Truck, 2.75-ton, 6 × 6, Cargo   **S**
(Volvo C306/4140 Series)

6-cyl. 2.98-litre twin-carb. engine (B30) with 4F1R gearbox and
2-speed transfer box. Portal axles with 7.05:1 overall gear ratio.
Wheelbase 3245 mm. Side-mounted winch. Export model (Far
East) with rhd and large-capacity dropside cargo/personnel body.
Same country bought 4 × 4 cargo and ambulance versions. 1974.

Truck, 3-ton, 6 × 6, Cargo   **YU**
(TAM 150T11BV)

V-6-cyl. 9.57-litre aircooled diesel engine (Deutz/TAM F6L 413F)
with 5F1R gearbox and 2-speed transfer box. Rigid axles with
self-locking differentials. 12.00-18 tyres. Wheelbase 3700 mm.
Overall length and width 6550 × 2275 mm. Weight 6400 kg. GVW
11400 kg. Built under German KHD licence, from 1977/78.

TRUCK, 2.5-TON, 6×6 (AMG M44A2 SERIES)   **USA**

General Data: Dating back to the early 1950s and the Reo 'Eager Beaver', the 2.5-ton 6 × 6 M-Series was produced in considerable numbers by several US truck manufacturers and improved in detail. Many body types existed, on several chassis variants (variations being in wheelbase, tyres, engines). From 1973 (M44A2 Series) multifuel engines were used, except in the 'austere' M602 models which retained the petrol unit. The most numerous model was the M35A2 cargo truck. M35A2C was a dropside cargo truck.

Technical Details: Own LDT-465-1C 6-cyl. multifuel diesel engine, 7833 cc (115.8 × 124 mm), 97 kW/130 bhp (net) at 2600 rpm. Dry plate clutch. 5F1R gearbox. 2-speed transfer box with front axle disconnect. 6.27:1 axle gear ratio. Air/hydraulic brakes. Semi-elliptic leaf springs, inverted at rear. 9.00-20 tyres. 24-Volt electrics. 190-litre fuel tank.

Dimensions and Weights (without winch): Wheelbase 3912 mm. Track, front/rear 1721/1778 mm. Overall length and width 6712 × 2438 mm. Height 2470 mm (cab). Ground clearance 324 mm (axles). Angles of approach and departure 48° and 40°. Weight 5925 kg, GVW 10456 kg.

above: M35A2, 1972; *below left:* M342A2 dump (US Navy), 1978; *below right:* M109A3 shop van, 1978

TRUCK, 2.5-TON, 6×6 (ENGESA EE-25)   BR

General Data: Derivative of the Engesa EE-25 4 × 4, which had the same payload rating, namely 5000 kg on paved roads, 2500 kg cross-country. Early models (1974) had a Chevrolet 4.3-litre petrol engine with a Chrysler V8 optional (as well as Mercedes, Perkins and MWM diesel power). Later the Mercedes-Benz OM352A diesel engine became standard, with a Chrysler V8 petrol unit or a GM Detroit Diesel 4-53 optional.

Technical Details: Mercedes-Benz OM352A 6-cyl. turbo-charged diesel engine, 5675 cc (97 × 128 mm), 174 bhp (gross) at 2800 rpm. Dry plate clutch. 5F1R gearbox. 2-speed transfer box with front axle disconnect. Axle gear ratios 5.15:1 front, 6.83:1 rear. Air/hydraulic brakes. 'Boomerang'-type rear bogie with single axle and walking beams with helical gears. 11.00 or 12.00-20 tyres. 12-Volt electrics. 200-litre fuel tank.

Dimensions and Weights: Wheelbase 4200 mm. Track 1800 mm. Overall length and width 6820 × 2250 mm. Height 2500 mm (cab). Ground clearance 350 mm (axles). Angles of approach and departure 52° and 52°. Weight 6800 kg, GVW 11800 kg.

above: cargo/personnel, 1980; *below left:* 1974 model with winch; *below right:* shop van with optional tandem rear axles, 1982

TRUCK, 2.5-TON, 6×6 (MERCEDES-BENZ LG1213)   **BR**

General Data: Founded in 1956, Mercedes-Benz do Brasil is a member of the German Daimler-Benz concern and became one of South America's largest producers of trucks of various types. The LG1213 was originally built only for military purposes but later became available also for civilian transportation. The company also produces the 4 × 4 Model 1113 in LA, LAK and LAS versions, which, except for the number of axles, are similar to the LG1213. Engesa of Brazil have also produced 6 × 6 variants.

Technical Details: Own OM352 6-cyl. diesel engine, 5675 cc (97 × 128 mm), 97 kW/130 bhp (DIN) at 2800 rpm. Dry plate clutch. 5F1R gearbox. 2-speed transfer box with front axle disconnect. 6.857:1 axle gear ratio. Air/hydraulic brakes. Semi-elliptic leaf springs, inverted at rear. 9.00-20 tyres (11.00-20, single rear, optional). 12-Volt electrics. 140-litre fuel tank.

Dimensions and Weights: Wheelbase 4250 mm. Track, front/rear 1976/1885 mm. Overall length and width 7577 × 2465 mm. Height 2595 mm (cab). Ground clearance 264 mm (axles). Angles of approach and departure not specified. Weight (chassis/cab) 5270 kg, GVW 12000 kg.

above and *below left:* cargo/personnel; *below right:* with 11.00-20 tyres

TRUCK, 3-TON, 6×6 (BRAVIA LEOPARDO MK III)   P

General Data: Bravia of Lisbon, Portugal, produced a variety of military soft-skin and armoured vehicles for the Portuguese armed forces and for export. The Leopardo model was originally based on Chrysler components. Later company sales literature showed and described it to be the US Army pattern 2.5-ton 6 × 6 (G742) truck, reworked and fitted with Detroit Diesel 4-53T engine and Allison AT545 automatic transmission. 4 × 2 and 4 × 4 Leopardos were also offered.

Technical Details: Chrysler 318-3 V-8-cyl. petrol engine, 5211 cc (99.3 × 79.2 mm), 113 kW/165 bhp (net) at 3900 rpm. Dry plate clutch. 5F1R gearbox. 2-speed transfer box with front axle disconnect. 6.8:1 axle gear ratio. Vacuum/hydraulic brakes. Semi-elliptic leaf springs. Hendrickson walking-beam rear suspension. 9.00-20 tyres. 12-Volt electrics. 150-litre fuel tank.

Dimensions and Weights (chassis/cab): Wheelbase 4140 mm. Track, front/rear 1700/1727 mm. Overall length and width 6833 × 2172 mm. Height 2500 mm. Ground clearance 292 mm (axles). Angles of approach and departure not specified. Weight 4000 kg. GVW 11800 kg.

above: Leopardo Mk III; *below left:* Leopardo prototype; *below right:* 4 × 4 derivative

TRUCK, 3.5-TON, 6 × 6 (ISUZU SKW440M)   J

General Data: Known in the Japanese armed forces as the Type 73 medium truck, this forward-control tactical load carrier was introduced in the early 1970s and eventually superseded the earlier normal-control Isuzu 2.5-ton 6 × 6 models. It featured a military-pattern softtop cab and a much longer cargo body than the preceding TWD20 model. Alternative body styles included dump, fuel tanker, water tanker, crane and wrecker. Shop van requirements were met by the use of removable shelters.

Technical Details: Own 8PA1 V-8-cyl. diesel engine, 9971 cc (115 × 120 mm), 130 kW/175 bhp at 2800 rpm. Dry plate clutch. 5F1R gearbox. 2-speed transfer box with front axle disconnect.

5.571:1 axle gear ratio. Air/hydraulic brakes. Semi-elliptic leaf springs, inverted at rear (with helper springs). 9.00-20 tyres. 24-Volt electrics. 140-litre fuel tank.

Dimensions and Weights: Wheelbase 3850 mm. Track, front/rear 1800/1820 mm. Overall length and width 6670 × 2410 mm. Height 3020 mm (tarpaulin). Ground clearance 250 mm (axles). Angles of approach and departure 45° and 40°. Weight 6650 kg, GVW 12650 kg.

above: cargo truck; *below left:* shelter with AA radar equipment; *below right:* SKW490M with 4350-mm wheelbase

TRUCK, 3.5-TON, 6×6 (STAR 266)

PL

General Data: In 1973 the Star 266 high-mobility truck replaced the old Star 2.5-ton 6 × 6 range (1958–73) in production, chiefly for the Polish armed forces. It had the sleeper version of the standard cab, used also for the Star 4 × 2 trucks, albeit with 2-piece opening windscreen and other detail differences. Designed by Chausson of France, this cab was also employed by Csepel of Hungary. Other licence-produced West European componentry used included German ZF gearboxes and power steering.

Technical Details: Own 359 6-cyl. diesel engine, 6842 cc (110 × 120 mm), 112 kW/150 bhp (net) at 2800 rpm. Dry plate clutch. 5F1R gearbox. 2-speed transfer box with front axle disconnect. 6.33:1 axle gear ratio. Air/hydraulic brakes. Semi-elliptic leaf springs, inverted at rear. 12.00-20 tyres. 24-Volt electrics. 2 × 150-litre fuel tanks.

Dimensions and Weights: Wheelbase 3595 mm. Track 1970 mm. Overall length and width 6800 × 2500 mm. Height 2640 mm (cab). Ground clearance 325 mm (axles). Angles of approach and departure 37° and 47°. Weight 7200 kg, GVW 12200 kg.

above: cargo truck; *below left:* commercial (export) model; *below right:* shop van

TRUCK, 3.5-TON, 6×6 (STEYR 680M3)   A

General Data: The Steyr 680M3 was developed from the makers' 680M2 4×4 truck and entered production in the late 1960s. It was produced during several years, chiefly for the Austrian Army and with various types of bodywork, including cargo/prime mover, rocket launcher (130-mm, 32-round), dump, tanker and fire appliance. Certain models, e.g. the rocket launcher, had an extended 4-door cab. Steyr-Hellas in Greece licence-produced both the 4×4 and the 6×6, as 680MH and 680MH3.

Technical Details: Own WD609er 6-cyl. turbocharged diesel engine, 5975 cc (105×115 mm), 112 kW/150 bhp (DIN) at 2800 rpm. Dry plate clutch. 5F1R gearbox. 2-speed transfer box with front axle disconnect. 6.50:1 axle gear ratio. Air/hydraulic brakes. Semi-elliptic leaf springs, inverted at rear. 9.00-20 tyres. 24-Volt electrics. 180-litre fuel tank.

Dimensions and Weights: Wheelbase 3360 mm. Track, front/rear 1810/1720 mm. Overall length and width 6730 × 2400 mm. Height 2630 mm (cab). Ground clearance 300 mm (axles). Angles of approach and departure 28° and 32°. Weight (without optional winch) 6500 kg, GVW 13000 kg.

above: cargo/prime mover; *below left:* early cargo truck; *below right:* Greek-built 680MH3, 1982

171

SIX-WHEELED TRUCKS

Truck, 3.5-ton, 6 × 6, Decontamination   **J**
(Isuzu Type 73)
V-8-cyl. 9.97-litre diesel engine (8PA1) with 5F1R gearbox and 2-speed transfer box. Air/hydraulic brakes. Wheelbase 3850 mm. Closed-cab version of military Type 73 medium truck (qv). The cab was a militarized version of the commercial type as used on Isuzu SPZ580/650, etc.

Truck, 3.5-ton, 6 × 6, Cargo   **SU**
(ZIL-131)
V-8-cyl. 6-litre petrol engine with 5F1R gearbox and 2-speed transfer box. Wheelbase 3975 mm. Overall length and width 7040 × 2500 mm. Weight 6925 kg. GVW 10425 kg. (Without winch 140 mm shorter, 240 kg lighter.) Successor to the ZIL-157, from the late 1960s. Various types of bodywork.

Truck, 4-ton, 6 × 6, Cargo   **DZ**
(Sonacome M210)
Produced under Berliet licence in Rouïba, Algeria, this truck resembled the Berliet GBC 8KT with the main exception of the engine which was an aircooled V-8-cyl. 210-bhp Deutz diesel. Sonacome trucks finished first, third and fourth in their class in the 1980 Paris–Dakar rally. A prototype is shown.

Truck, 5-ton, 6 × 6, Cargo   **R**
(DAC 665T)
6-cyl. 10.3-litre diesel engine (D2156HMN8) with 6F1R gearbox and 2-speed transfer box with lockable differential. Diff. lock at rear. Wheelbase 3750 mm. Overall length and width 7570 × 2500 mm. Weight 9940 kg. GVW 14940 kg. Produced from 1979 for Romanian Army and export (e.g. Iraq, with rocket launcher).

Truck, 5-ton, 6 × 6, Cargo   **BR**
(ENGESA EE-50)
6-cyl. turbocharged diesel engine (Scania D11) with 5F1R gearbox and 2-speed transfer box. 'Boomerang' rear suspension with walking beams. 20-in. cast spoke wheels. Wheelbase 4500 mm. Air brakes. Weight 12000 kg. Overall length and width 7850 × 2600 mm. On-road max. payload rating 10000 kg.

Truck, 5-ton, 6 × 6, Cargo   **I**
(Fiat 6607CM/CP70)
6-cyl. 9.8-litre diesel engine with 5F1R gearbox and 2-speed transfer box. Double reduction axles. Wheelbase 4195 mm. Overall dimensions 7824 × 2430 × 2700 mm. Weight 8840 kg. GVW 13985 kg. Italian Army truck. Air-transportable. Employed for transport of cargo and personnel and also as missile carrier. 1974.

TRUCK, 4.3-TON, 6×6 (ALM/ACMAT VLRA 6×6 TPK640SM2)   **F**

General Data: Introduced in 1981, this was a 6-wheel-drive version of the more familiar VLRA 4×4 truck which was sold to the armed forces of more than 30 countries, particularly in Africa. It was made mainly with a cargo body with tilt and as a platform truck for the conveyance of portable shelters (TPK660SH), but other body styles also existed, including a hydraulic revolving crane. In the early 1960s, when the company was still at Meaux, a heavier 6×6 chassis was made (PKS-6RS2).

Technical Details: Perkins 6.354 6-cyl. turbocharged diesel engine, 5800 cc (98.4 × 127 mm), 138 bhp (SAE) at 2800 rpm. Dry plate clutch. 5F1R gearbox. 2-speed transfer box with front axle disconnect. 6.66:1 axle gear ratio. Air/hydraulic brakes. Semi-elliptic leaf springs, inverted at rear. 12.50-20 tyres. 24-Volt electrics. 2 × 210-litre fuel tanks.

Dimensions and Weights: Wheelbase 4100 mm. Track, front/rear 1760/1800 mm. Overall length and width 6943 × 2250 mm. Height 1900 mm (cab). Ground clearance 287 mm (axles). Angles of approach and departure 43° and 41°. Weight 5700 kg, GVW 10000 kg.

above: TPK640SM2; *below left:* TPK660SH; *below right:* TPK640SPP (Trackway)

V.L.R.A. Version véhicule porte shelter TPK 660 SH.

TRUCK, 5-TON, 6×6 (AMG M809 SERIES)

General Data: The M-Series 5-ton 6 × 6 range first appeared in 1950 and remained in production for more than three decades with detail improvements and modifications. In the 1960s the petrol engine was replaced by a diesel unit and from 1970 (M809 Series) a commercial Cummins diesel was employed. There were numerous variations in chassis length and bodies, e.g. cargo, dump, tractor, shop van, wrecker and many special purpose types. AM General Corporation was the main contractor for many years.

Technical Details: Cummins NHC250 6-cyl. diesel engine, 14011 cc (139.7 × 152.4 mm), 168 kW/225 bhp (net) at 2100 rpm. Dry plate clutch. 5F1R (overdrive top) gearbox. 2-speed transfer box with automatic front axle engagement. 6.443:1 axle gear ratio. Air/hydraulic brakes. Semi-elliptic leaf springs, inverted at rear. 11.00-20 tyres. 24-Volt electrics. 295-litre fuel tank.

Dimensions and Weights (without winch): Wheelbase 4547 mm. Track, front/rear 1880/1829 mm. Overall length and width 7652 × 2476 mm. Height 2946 mm (cab). Ground clearance 267 mm (axles). Angles of approach and departure 46° and 38°. Weight 9743 kg, GVW 18823 kg.

above: M813 cargo; *below left:* M817 dump; *below right:* M818 tractor (New Zealand Army)

TRUCK, 5-TON, 6×6 (AMG M939 SERIES)

USA

General Data: This 'Product-Improved' (PIP) 5-ton 6 × 6 truck was developed in the early 1980s to replace the existing M809 Series in the US Army. The first unit was delivered by AM General Corp on 14 June 1982. The initial order was for 11394 units. Compared with its predecessor, the M939 Series' main improvements included a 3-seat cab, 5-speed automatic transmission, full air brakes, a full-load speed of 86 km/h, a cruising range of 560 km and a 1.5-metre fording ability.

Technical Details: Cummins NHC250 6-cyl. diesel engine, 14011 cc (139.7 × 152.4 mm), 168 kW/225 bhp (net) at 2100 rpm. Allison MT654CR 5F1R automatic transmission. 2-speed transfer box. Rockwell axles and air brakes (Stopmaster). Semi-elliptic leaf springs, inverted at rear. 11.00-20 tyres. 24-Volt electrics. 295-litre fuel tank.

Dimensions and Weights (M926): Wheelbase 4547 mm. Track, front/rear 1880/1830 mm. Overall length and width 8287 × 2476 mm. Height 2946 mm (cab). Ground clearance 267 mm (axles). Angles of approach and departure 34° and 38°. Weight 10442 kg, GVW 19922 kg.

above and *below left:* M926 cargo truck with winch; *below right:* M924 cargo truck with 'Enhanced Mobility System'

TRUCK, 5-TON, 6×6 (CSEPEL D566)

General Data: This high-mobility tactical truck, developed in the late 1960s and produced by the Csepel Automobile Works at Szigethalon, Hungary, first appeared in 1970. Quantity production commenced in 1971. The vehicle was rather unusual in having independent suspension on all wheels. For the large tyres there was a central pressure regulation system. On roads, the truck could carry 8 tons and tow 10 tons. The maximum road speed was 80 km/h. Although the cargo truck was the most common, other variants appeared, e.g. shop vans and a recovery vehicle.

Technical Details: Rába-MAN 2156HM6/01 6-cyl. diesel engine, 10350 cc (121 × 150 mm), 149 kW/200 bhp (DIN) at 2200 rpm.

Dry plate clutch. 6F1R gearbox. 2-speed transfer box (built in unit with middle axle/differential) with front axle disconnect. Spur gear reduction in wheel hubs. Hydro-pneumatic inboard disc brakes. Torsion bar independent suspension. 14.00-20 tyres. 24-Volt electrics. 250-litre fuel tank.

Dimensions and Weights: Wheelbase 3600 mm. Track 2050 mm. Overall length and width 7100 × 2500 mm. Height 2740 mm (cab). Ground clearance 465 mm. Angles of approach and departure 40° and 40°. Weight 9000 kg, GVW 17500 kg.

above and *below left:* cargo truck; *below right:* shop van

TRUCK, 5-TON, 6×6 (SCANIA SBAT 111SA 166)   S

General Data: Introduced in prototype form (designated LBAT 110S) in 1970, the Scania Terrängbil TGB 411AL MT – as it is known in the Swedish Army – went into quantity production in 1976, together with its 4×4 counterpart. Several variants were developed, including cargo, cargo with loading crane (HIAB, 1270- and 3500-kg), cargo with canvas tarpaulin, artillery tractor with crew cab, fire/crash truck, wrecker, radar vehicle, etc. The 4×4 version was designated SBA 111A134(qv).

Technical Details: Own DS11LB27 6-cyl. turbocharged diesel engine, 11000 cc (127×145 mm), 213 kW/290 bhp (DIN) at 2200 rpm. Automatic 6F1R gearbox. 2-speed transfer box with front axle disconnect. 5.58:1 axle gear ratio (including hub reduction gearing). Air brakes. Semi-elliptic leaf springs, inverted at rear. 14.00-20 tyres. 24-Volt electrics. 167-litre fuel tank.

Dimensions and Weights: Wheelbase 4290 mm. Track 2020 mm. Overall length and width 7800×2490 mm. Height 2880 mm (cab). Ground clearance 390 mm (axles). Angles of approach and departure 45° and 40°. Weight 11550 kg, GVW 16600 kg.

above and *below left:* cargo/prime mover; *below right:* with crew cab

TRUCK, 5-TON, 6×6 (URAL-4320)

SU

General Data: This Soviet 6×6 truck appeared in 1980 as a replacement for the URAL-375D (and variants) which had been in production since the early 1960s. In the mid-1970s a diesel engine had been made available. The new power unit (engine, clutch and gearbox) was, in fact, the same as in the then-new KAMAZ 6×4 and 6×6 trucks. With further modifications the model designations became URAL-4320 and -4420 for cargo and tractor truck respectively. The URAL-43202 and -44202 were generally similar. All had a revised radiator grille design.

Technical Details: JAMZ-740 V-8-cyl. diesel engine, 10850 cc (120 × 120 mm), 155 kW/210 bhp (net) at 2600 rpm. Twin dry plate clutch. 5F1R gearbox. 2-speed transfer box with central differential. Air brakes. Semi-elliptic leaf springs, inverted at rear. 14.00-20 tyres. 24-Volt electrics. 270-litre fuel capacity.

Dimensions and Weights: Wheelbase 4225 mm. Track 2000 mm. Overall length and width 7366 × 2500 mm. Height 2870 mm (tarpaulin). Ground clearance 400 mm (axles). Angles of approach and departure 45° and 40°. Weight 8020 kg, GVW 13425 kg. *Note:* winch-equipped models were 420 kg heavier.

above and *below left:* URAL-4320; *below right:* petrol-engined URAL-375D

Truck, 5-ton, 6 × 4, Cargo   **USA**
(Ford L-Series)

In 1977 the US Army (Armor-Engineer Board) evaluated a selection of militarized commercial trucks as possible 2.5- and 5-ton load carriers. Dodge, Ford and IHC models participated; results were reported as 'far from encouraging'. Shown is a 6 × 4 Ford Louisville Line derivative.

Truck, 5-ton, 6 × 6, Cargo   **SU**
(KAMAZ-4310)

V-8-cyl. 10.85-litre diesel engine (JAMZ-740) with 5F1R gearbox and 2-speed transfer box with lockable differential. 1220 × 400-533 tyres with central pressure regulation. Air brakes. Wheelbase 4000 mm. Overall dimensions 7650 × 2500 × 2900 (cab) mm. Weight 8410 kg. Introduced in 1981.

Truck, 5-ton, 6 × 6, Cargo   **D**
(Magirus-Deutz 232D16FAL 6 × 6

V-8-cyl. 11.3-litre aircooled diesel engine (Deutz F8L 413) with 6F1R gearbox and 2-speed transfer box with lockable differential. Hub reduction axles. Wheelbase 4040 mm. Chassis/cab dimensions 7085 × 2500 × 2835 mm. Weight 6785 kg. Produced for undisclosed Middle East country in early 1970s.

Truck, 5-ton, 6 × 6, Cargo   **D**
(Magirus-Deutz 232D16AL 6 × 6)

V-8-cyl. 11.3-litre aircooled diesel engine (Deutz F8L 413) with 6F1R gearbox and 2-speed transfer box. Wheelbase 4890 mm. Chassis/cab dimensions 8115 × 2450 × 3310 mm. Weight 8500 kg. GVW 18000 kg. Shown with dropside body, measuring 5400 × 2410 mm. Militarized commercial truck, 1978.

Truck, 6-ton, 6 × 6, Cargo   **D**
(Magirus-Deutz 310D20AL 6 × 6)

V-10-cyl. 14.7-litre aircooled diesel engine (Deutz F10L 413L) with 6F1R gearbox and 2-speed transfer box. Hub reduction axles. 14.00R20 tyres. Wheelbase 4590 mm. Chassis/cab dimensions 8145 × 2450 × 2830 mm. Weight 9720 kg. GVW 21300 kg. Right-hand drive. Produced for undisclosed African country in 1974.

Truck, 5-ton, 6 × 6, Cargo   **E**
(Pegaso 3051)

6-cyl. diesel engine with 6F1R gearbox and 2-speed transfer box. Rigid axles with hub reduction gearing and 13.00-20 tyres, single rear. Air brakes and differential locks. Modernized version of Pegaso 3050, with same cab as Model 3046/50 3-ton 4 × 4, introduced in 1979/80 by ENASA of Spain.

TRUCK, 6-TON, 6×6 (FIAT 6605N)

General Data: Medium artillery tractor, first introduced in the mid-1960s as TM65 (OM 6605) with 10.67-litre 206-bhp engine. The succeeding TM69 (1969; Fiat 6605N) had a 13.8-litre 216-bhp engine. Derived from the 6605N were the 260-bhp 6605TM prime mover for 155- to 203-mm artillery and 6605FH for the NATO 155-mm FH70 howitzer. The latter vehicle had a hydraulic jib crane between cab and body for ammunition handling. All models had a softtop 4-door cab for a crew of 12 men.

Technical Details: Own 8212.02 6-cyl. diesel engine, 13797 cc (137×156 mm), 161 kW/216 bhp (DIN) at 1900 rpm. Twin plate clutch. 8F2R gearbox. 2-speed transfer box with lockable differential. 7.428:1 axle gear ratio (including hub reduction). Air brakes. Semi-elliptic leaf springs, inverted at rear. 14.00-20 tyres. 24-Volt electrics. 2 × 180-litre fuel tanks.

Dimensions and Weights: Wheelbase 3900 mm. Track 2072 mm. Overall length and width 7330 × 2500 mm. Height 2920 mm (cab). Ground clearance 363 mm (axles). Angles of approach and departure 45° and 40°. Weight 11860 kg, GVW 17000 kg.

above: TM69/6605N; *below left:* TM65/OM6605; *below right:* 6605A 10-ton 6 × 6

TRUCK, 6-TON, 6×6 (PEGASO 3050)

E

General Data: Derived from the DAF-designed Spanish-built Pegaso 3045D 4×4 truck, the 3050 6×6 was used for several special roles, including tractor truck for semi-trailers (e.g. tankers), shop vans and several types of wrecker with hydraulic cranes. The most common type, however, was the cargo/prime mover truck, used for towing artillery such as the M114 155-mm howitzer. These vehicles were built during the 1970s, after which they were replaced in production by the modernized Model 3051, which featured the same new cab as the 3-ton 4×4 3046/50.

Technical Details: Own 9100/40 6-cyl. diesel engine, 10170 cc (118×155 mm), 127 kW/170 bhp (net) at 2000 rpm. Dry plate clutch. 6F1R gearbox (overdrive top). 2-speed transfer box with front axle disconnect. 6.933:1 axle gear ratio (including hub reduction). Air brakes. Semi-elliptic leaf springs, inverted at rear. 13.00 or 14.00-20 tyres. 24-Volt electrics. 250-litre fuel tank.

Dimensions and Weights: Wheelbase 3987 mm. Track 1900 mm. Overall length and width 7200×2500 mm. Height 2720 mm (cab). Ground clearance 325 mm (axles). Angles of approach and departure 47° and 45°. Weight 8500 kg, GVW 18500 kg.

above and *below left:* cargo/prime mover; *below right:* tractor

Truck, 6-ton, 6 × 6, Cargo   **P**
(Bravia Pantera)

V-8-cyl. diesel engine (Perkins 510 or 540) with 5F1R gearbox and 2-speed transfer box. Hendrickson-type rear bogie. Air brakes. Wheelbase 4140 mm. Weight 7715 kg. GVW 17250 kg. Generally similar to the makers' 3-ton Leopardo but heavier chassis and drive line componentry. Several other engine options. 1980.

Truck, 7-ton, 6 × 4, Tractor   **USA**
(International F2010)

This commercial truck from the IHC Fleetstar series was powered by a V-8-cyl. petrol engine and available with several transmission types including Fuller 10-speed and Allison automatic. Produced in the late 1960s and early 1970s for, amongst others, the Greek Army (shown). US Army used similar-looking 2070A diesel (1976).

Truck, 7-ton, 6 × 6, Cargo   **D**
(Mercedes-Benz LG498)

During 1965–71 Daimler-Benz developed a range of high-mobility tactical trucks: LG479 10-ton 8 × 8, LG498 7-ton 6 × 6 and LG499 5-ton 4 × 4. Of each there was also an amphibious version. None were produced in quantity, however. Shown is the amphibious LG498.

Truck, 7.5-ton, 6 × 6, Cargo   **SU**
(KRAZ-255B)

V-8-cyl. 14.86-litre diesel engine with 5F1R gearbox and 2-speed transfer box. Air brakes. Wheelbase 5300 mm. Overall length and width 8645 × 2750 mm. Weight 12175 kg. GVW 20175 kg. Superseded KRAZ-214B in production in 1966 and was used chiefly by Army engineers (bridging equipment, etc.).

Truck, 8-ton, 6 × 4, Elevating, Cargo   **USA**
(GMC 6500 Series)

V-8-cyl. petrol engine with manual or automatic transmission (diesel engine also offered). Elevating-type stake/platform body by Moore & Sons of Memphis, Tennessee, for US Navy in 1976. Body designated MH-2-6 × 4 with a capacity of 8200 kg. Truck's rear suspension was Hendrickson walking-beam type.

Truck, 8-ton, 6 × 4, Telephone Maintenance   **USA**
(International Loadstar/M876)

Replacing the old 2.5-ton 6 × 6 G742-based telephone maintenance and repair trucks, the M876 entered service in 1977. 232 units had been ordered in 1976 from IHC and the firm McCabe Powers who produced the body and equipment which included an auger to drill holes and a derrick to lift and set poles.

TRUCK, 7-TON, 6×6 (MAN N4530)

D

General Data: The MAN-built 7-ton 6 × 6 range of new-generation Class 1 tactical trucks of the West German *Bundeswehr* comprised the following models: N4520 cargo, N4530 tipper, N4550 bridging and N4620 cargo with winch. The tipper was of the 3-way type and over 500 of these were made. In total, between 1977 and 1981 MAN built 3460 of these 7-ton 6 × 6 trucks. Unlike the 4 × 4, the 6 × 6 and 8 × 8 had turbocharged engines.

Technical Details: Deutz BF8L 413F V-8-cyl. aircooled turbocharged diesel engine, 12763 cc (125 × 130 mm), 253 kW/320 bhp (net) at 2650 rpm. Torque converter and dry plate clutch. 6F1R gearbox. Single-speed transfer box with lockable differential.

6.734:1 axle gear reduction (incl. hub reduction). Rear axle differential locks. Air/hydraulic brakes. Rigid axles with coil springs. 14.00R20M tyres. 24-Volt electrics. 270-litre fuel tank.

Dimensions and Weights: Wheelbase 4500 mm. Track 2066 mm. Overall length and width 8065 × 2500 mm. Height 2860 mm (cab). Ground clearance 415 mm (axles). Angles of approach and departure 45° and 42°. Weight 11800 kg, GVW 18800 kg.

above: N4530; *below left:* N4550; *below right:* rocket launcher 110SF2

Truck, 8-ton, 6 × 6, Cargo   J
(Hino ZC121E)

6-cyl. diesel engine (EK100) with 6F1R overdrive-top gearbox and 2-speed transfer box. Singe-reduction axles. Wheelbase 5300 mm. Overall dimensions 9065 × 2490 × 3480 mm. Weight 9795 kg. GVW 22000 kg. One of the Japanese entries in the Australian Army trials for new 8-ton trucks, late 1970s.

Truck, 8-ton, 6 × 6, Cargo   PRC
(Hongyan CQ261)

6-cyl. 14.8-litre diesel engine (6150) with 5F1R gearbox and 2-speed transfer box. 14.00-20 tyres. Wheelbase 4205 mm. Overall dimensions 7975 × 2500 × 3000 (cab) mm. Weight 14200 kg. GVW 26460 kg. Patterned on Berliet GCH (which was imported, together with the Berliet GBC 8MT) and made from 1972.

Truck, 8-ton, 6 × 6, Cargo   AUS
(Leyland Mastiff MS)

V-8-cyl. diesel engine (Perkins 540) with 6F1R gearbox (Turner M6-476) and 2-speed transfer box (Rockwell T226). Hub reduction axles (Kirkstall D65-11-1). Air brakes. Garwood-Olding winch. Tiltable cab. Three pilots built in 1979 by Leyland Australia for Army evaluation but no quantity production followed.

Truck, 8-ton, 6 × 6, Cargo   AUS
(Mack RM6866RS)

6-cyl. 11-litre diesel engine (EM6-285) with 5F1R gearbox (Maxitorque) and 2-speed transfer box. Mack rear tandem. Fabco front axle. Air brakes. Wheelbase 4368 mm. GVW 29510 kg. Three prototypes by Mack Australia in 1979 for Army evaluation. In 1981 the Australian Government placed an order for 940 units.

Truck, 8-ton, 6 × 6, Cargo   D
(Mercedes-Benz 2032A/38)

In the late 1970s, Daimler-Benz offered a range of militarized commercial all-wheel-drive trucks. The 6 × 6 models were the 8-ton 2026A/38 and 2032A/38 (shown, with optional rhd), 9-ton 2028A/38, 10-ton 2632A/41 and 15-ton 2626A/41 and 2632A/41. The 2032A was rated at 20 ton GVW (on roads).

Truck, 8-ton, 6 × 6, Cargo   USA
(Oshkosh F1838-M4)

In the late 1970s, Oshkosh Truck Corp. offered two militarized commercial trucks: 4-ton 4 × 4 P1616 and 5-ton 6 × 6 F1634. Later, the F1838-M Series was offered (derived from commercial F Series), with 7 different models (including cargo, dump, tractor, tanker), all with 6-cyl. CAT 3306DITA diesel engine.

TRUCK, 8-TON, 6×6 (FAP-2220BS)

General Data: Launched in the early 1970s and manufactured by FAP FAMOS in Belgrade. This firm produced vehicles under foreign licences, chiefly from Saurer of Austria and Daimler-Benz of West Germany. Typical Saurer-designed vehicles were the FAP-13 8-ton 4×2 (normal control) and the FAP-18BST/A 12-ton 4×4 (COE). Of the new 6×6 truck there were several versions, including cargo (FAP-2020BS) and 32-round rocket launcher (FAP-2220BS).

Technical Details: FAMOS-2F/002A 6-cyl. diesel engine, 10000 cc (123 × 140 mm), 149 kW/200 bhp (DIN) at 2300 rpm. Dry plate clutch. 6F1R overdrive-top gearbox (ZF S6-80). 2-speed transfer box with front axle disconnect. Air-actuated diff. locks. Axle gear ratios 9.4:1 front, 9.23:1 rear. Air brakes. Semi-elliptic leaf springs. 11.00-20 tyres. 24-Volt electrics. 200-litre tank.
Note: FAP-2020BS had larger, variable-pressure tyres, single rear.

Dimensions and Weights: Wheelbase 4500 mm. Track, front/rear 1970/1745 mm. Overall chassis length and width 7750 × 2460 mm. Height 2970 mm (cab). Ground clearance 300 mm (axles). Weight 8600 kg, GVW 22000 kg.

above: FAP-2220BS; *below left:* FAP-2020BS (with shorter wheelbase and winch); *below right:* FAP-2220BDS bridging truck

TRUCK, 8-TON, 6×6 (TATRA 148 SERIES)

General Data: The T148 Series supplemented the existing Tatra 138 models from 1972. All these types featured a backbone chassis with independent suspension. Several wheelbase lengths and numerous body styles were available, ranging from cargo and tractor trucks to revolving cranes, military and civilian. Czechs and East Germans were main users. The following data apply to the T148N cargo truck with winch.

Technical Details: Own T-2-928-1 V-8-cyl. aircooled diesel engine, 12667 cc (120 × 140 mm), 156 kW/212 bhp (DIN) at 2000 rpm. Twin plate clutch. 5F1R gearbox. 2-speed transfer gear with front axle disconnect. 3.39:1 axle gear ratio. Air brakes.

Swinging axles with torsion bars at front, inverted leaf springs at rear. 11.00-20 tyres. 24-Volt electrics. 150-litre fuel tank.
Note: 232-bhp T-2-928-19 engine optional.

Dimensions and Weights: Wheelbase 4920 mm. Track, front/rear 1966/1770 mm. Overall length and width 8497 × 2442 mm. Height 2500 mm (cab). Ground clearance 290 mm. Angles of approach and departure 45° and 25°. Weight 10500 kg, GVW 23500 kg.

above: tractor (T148CN22; bulk fuel); *below left:* tractor (17-m³ fuel container); *below right:* decontamination apparatus

TRUCK, 9-TON, 6×6 (RENAULT TRM9000/BERLIET GBD)   F

General Data: The Renault TRM9000 started life as Berliet GBD 6 × 6. The name was changed after Berliet was absorbed by Renault Véhicules Industriels (RVI). The TRM9000 was the 6 × 6 version of the 6-ton 4 × 4 TRM6000. The 6 × 6 chassis was made with single and double cab, the latter having 4 doors. Body types included cargo (with tarpaulin), dump, tanker, wrecker, rocket launcher and other special equipment.

Technical Details: Berliet MIDS 06.20.30 6-cyl. turbocharged diesel engine, 8820 cc (120 × 130 mm), 230 bhp (gross) at 2400 rpm. Dry plate clutch. 6F1R overdrive-top gearbox. 2-speed transfer box with lockable differential. Hub reduction. 6.83:1 axle gear ratio. Air brakes. Semi-elliptic leaf springs, inverted at rear. 14.00-20 tyres. 24-Volt electrics. 200-litre fuel tank. Rear-mounted 4500-kg winch optional.

Dimensions and Weights: Wheelbase 4500 mm. Track, front/rear 1936/1938 mm. Overall length and width 7900 × 2480 mm. Height 2825 mm (cab). Ground clearance 370 mm (rear axles). Angles of approach and departure 45° and 40°. Weight 11000 kg, GVW 19440 kg.

above: single-cab cargo; *below left:* early double cab; *below right:* Exocet missiles (coastal defence)

**Truck, 9-ton, 6 × 6, Cargo   SU
(KRAZ-260)**

V-8-cyl. diesel engine (JAMZ-238N) with 8F1R gearbox and 2-speed transfer box with lockable differential. 13.00 × 530-533 tyres. Air brakes. Wheelbase 5300 mm. Overall dimensions 9030 × 2720 × 2985 (cab) mm. Weight 12775 kg. Track 2160 mm. Ground clearance 370 mm. Winch below body floor. Produced from 1980.

**Truck, 10-ton, 6 × 2, Cargo   NL
(DAF FAS2000DHB)**

6-cyl. 8.25-litre turbocharged diesel engine (DHB825) with 12F1R gearbox (ZF; Fuller 9F1R optional) driving leading tandem axle. 31 ordered in 1977 by Netherlands Army for road haulage, together with 116 6-ton 4 × 2 Model FM1600DF trucks. All 10-tonners and 42 of the 6-tonners had hydraulic loading platform.

**Truck, 10-ton, 6 × 4, Aircraft Fueller   USA
(Dodge CT800)**

V-8-cyl. 7.7-litre diesel engine (Cummins V8-185) with automatic transmission (Allison). Hendrickson tandem. USAF Type A/S32R-9 19000-litre fueller by Consolidated on 1972 Dodge LCF (low cab forward) chassis. US Army used shorter CT700 chassis with V8 petrol engine as garbage truck (Lodal L25A Load-A-Matic).

**Truck, 10-ton, 6 × 4, Cargo/Prime Mover   E
(Dodge R3464)**

6-cyl. 11.9-litre turbocharged diesel engine (BS36) with 8F2R gearbox (815SD). Air brakes. 20-in. 10-stud wheels. Wheelbase 4030 mm. Overall length and width 6950 × 2500 mm. Spanish-built heavy-duty chassis with tilting cab, used by the Spanish Army with steel cargo body as artillery prime mover. 1979.

**Truck, 10-ton, 6 × 4, Bulk Fuel Carrier   GB
(Foden 46PO24R2209)**

6-cyl. 12.17-litre diesel engine (RR 220 Mk 3) with 9F1R gearbox. Tyres 12.00-20 front, 14.00-20 rear. Wheelbase 5482 mm. Overall dimensions 8750 × 2497 × 2665 mm. Weight 11980 kg. GVW 26420 kg. 12000-litre steel tank by Butterfield. PTO-driven centrifugal pump, capacity 900 litre/min. British Army.

**Truck, 10-ton, 6 × 4, Bulk Fuel Carrier   USA
(GMC 7500 Series)**

Typical example from GMC's 7500 Series, of conventional cab design and in production for many years. Available in 4 × 2 and 6 × 4 configuration and with choice of V8 petrol engine or V6 Detroit Diesel (6V-53N). Max. GCW ratings to over 27 ton. Full air brakes. This large-capacity fuel tanker was built for US Army.

Truck, 10-ton, 6 × 4, Tractor   **USA**
(GMC DI9692)

Known as the Astro 95 this commercial tractor was used by several US Government departments, including Army and Navy. The example shown was supplied to the USN in early 1976. The Astro 95 models (4 × 2, 6 × 4) had an aluminium tilting cab and GCW ratings of up to nearly 60000 kg.

Truck, 10-ton, 6 × 4, Dump   **USA**
(GMC JV76713)

V-6-cyl. 5.2-litre diesel engine (Detroit Diesel) (available also with V8 petrol engine or Caterpillar diesel). Supplied to the US Navy in 1976, with official nomenclature 'Truck, Dump, DED, 6 × 4, 39500 GVW'. The truck was one of GMC's 7500 Series with Hendrickson rear suspension. US Army bought similar trucks.

Truck, 10-ton, 6 × 4, Aircraft Fueller   **AUS**
(International ACCOF 1910C)

V-8-cyl. 6.4-litre petrol engine with 13-speed gearbox (10-speed manual and 5-speed automatic optional). Air brakes. Wheelbase 4648 mm. GVW 20870 kg. One of 9 supplied by Gilbarco (Australia) to Malaysian Air Force, 1981/82. Fuelling rate 1360 litres/min. Transportable in Hercules C130 aircraft.

Truck, 10-ton, 6 × 4, Tractor   **USA**
(International F2275)

6-cyl. diesel engine (Cummins NTC230) with 10-speed gearbox (Magnum Power) driving the 15-ton rating tandem bogie. GCW 36287 kg. These tractors, from IHC's S-Series, were supplied to the USAF in the late 1970s and early 1980s, in blue and olive drab livery, for hauling fuel tankers and low-bed semi-trailers.

Truck, 10-ton, 6 × 4, Cargo   **D**
(MAN 22.240DF)

6-cyl. 11.1-litre diesel engine (D2566MXF) with 6F1R gearbox driving both rear axles which featured diff. locks and hub reduction gearing. Wheelbase 4525 mm. Overall dimensions 9155 × 2500 × 2846 mm. Weight 9700 kg. GVW 22000 kg. Used by *Bundeswehr* from 1976. Model 22.240DE had loading crane.

Truck, 10-ton, 6 × 4, Cargo   **D**
(Mercedes-Benz 2626K)

V-8-cyl. 12.76-litre diesel engine (OM402) with 5F1R gearbox driving both hub reduction rear axles. GVW 26000 kg. In service with the Danish Army from the late 1970s as 'LVGS, FELT: Mercedes-Benz, 2626K, 6 × 4, D', indicating a truck with limited off-road capability. Shown with loading crane at the rear.

189

TRUCK, 10-TON, 6×6 (DAF 2300 SERIES)

General Data: In 1981 the Netherlands Army ordered nearly 1100 10-ton 6 × 6 trucks from DAF to replace the ageing DAF 6-ton 6 × 6 616-Series. The new chassis were again to be fitted with several body variants. In addition a 4 × 4 tractor derivative was designed to replace the DAF YT514 tractor unit. Series production planned for mid-1980s. Following data apply to prototype cargo truck.

Technical Details: Own DHS825 6-cyl. turbocharged diesel engine, 8250 cc (118×126 mm), 180 kW/245 bhp (DIN) at 2400 rpm. ZF torque converter. 8F1R gearbox in unit with transfer box with lockable differential. Hub reduction axles (Kirkstall front, DAF rear). 5.48:1 axle gear ratio. Air brakes. Semi-elliptic leaf springs, inverted at rear. 12.00-20 or 13R22.5 tyres. 24-Volt electrics. 200-litre fuel tank. *Note:* auto. trans. optional.

Dimensions and Weights: Wheelbase 4850 mm. Track, front/rear 1990/1820 mm. Overall length and width 9580 × 2490 mm. Height 3590 mm (crane). Ground clearance 320 mm (axles). Angles of approach and departure 30° and 20°. Weight 13000 kg, GVW 27500 kg.

above: YAZ2300 cargo truck; *below left:* YKZ2300 dump; *below right:* YTV2300 4 × 4 tractor truck

TRUCK, 10-TON, 6×6 (FIAT 230PM26/35)

I

General Data: The Fiat 230PM26 and 230PM35 models were similar except for engine and transmission. Both had a military-pattern softtop tiltable cab. The artillery tractor differed from the cargo truck version in having a shelter-type crew compartment (fixed or removable), seating 8–10 men. The tractor was suitable for towing medium and heavy artillery. The 260PM26 and 260PM35 were generally similar but with civilian-type cab and longer wheelbase. The following data apply to the 230PM26.

Technical Details: Own 8210.02 6-cyl. diesel engine, 13798 cc (137 × 156 mm), 191 kW/260 bhp (DIN) at 2200 rpm. Dry plate clutch. 2 × 8F1R ZF 16S160A 'Ecosplit' gearbox. Transfer box with lockable differential. 5.709:1 axle gear ratio (including hub reduction). Air brakes. Semi-elliptic leaf springs, inverted at rear. 14.00-20 tyres. 24-Volt electrics. 300-litre fuel tank.

Dimensions and Weights: Wheelbase 3300 mm. Track 2025 mm. Overall length and width 7660 × 2500 mm. Height 3000 mm (cab). Ground clearance 332 mm (axles). Angles of approach and departure 45° and 40°. Weight 11600 kg. GVW 21600 kg.

above: artillery tractor; *below left:* cargo truck; *below right:* 260PM26/35

TRUCK, 10-TON, 6 × 6 (FODEN 46VO26R3009) GB

General Data: The Foden range of 6 × 6 medium-mobility truck chassis was developed in the early 1970s, primarily for the provision of towing and limber vehicles to service the FH70 155-mm howitzer. Following extensive trials with 23 prototypes, Foden (later to become Sandbach Engineering Co.) received an order for 111 units in 1977. The vehicles shared many components with Foden's low-mobility vehicle range (6 × 4, 8 × 4). The tractor version featured a crew compartment behind the cab.

Technical Details: Rolls-Royce Eagle Mk 3 6-cyl. turbocharged diesel engine, 12170 cc (130.2 × 152.4 mm), 221 kW/297 bhp (DIN) at 2100 rpm. Dry plate clutch. 9F1R overdrive gearbox. 2-speed transfer box with front axle disconnect. 6.105:1 axle gear ratio. Diff. locks. Air brakes. Semi-elliptic leaf springs, inverted at rear. 16.00-20 tyres. 24-Volt electrics. 409-litre fuel tank.

Dimensions and Weights: Wheelbase 4728 mm. Track, front/rear 2029/2032 mm. Overall length and width 9045 × 2489 mm. Height 3607 mm (cab). Ground clearance 335 mm (axles). Angles of approach and departure 40° and 29°. Weight (loaded) 25830 kg, GVW 29464 kg.

above: tractor for FH70; *below left:* FH70 limber; *below right:* cargo truck with crane and powered-axle trailer

Truck, 10-ton, 6 × 4, Cargo/Prime Mover   **CH**
(Saurer D290FK)

6-cyl. 11.95-litre turbocharged diesel engine (D3KT) with 4F1R gearbox and 2-speed transfer box. Wheelbase 3660 mm. Overall length and width 6840 × 2300 mm. Weight 8250 kg (approx). GVW 26000 kg. Basically a commercial tipper chassis/cab which was available also with higher-output D2KT engine. 1978.

Truck, 10-ton, 6 × 6, Cargo   **GB**
(AEC Militant Mk 3 FV11047)

6-cyl. diesel engine (AV760) with 6F1R gearbox and 2-speed transfer box. Wheelbase 4877 mm. Overall length and width 8798 × 2500 mm. Used by British RCT for transport of cargo, including containers and NATO palletized loads. Chassis was used also for recovery vehicle (FV11044).

Truck, 10-ton, 6 × 6, Dump   **I**
(Astra BM20MT)

6-cyl. 13.8-litre diesel engine (Fiat 8210) with 6F1R gearbox and 2-speed transfer box with lockable differential. Hub reduction axles. Wheelbase 4135 mm. Overall length and width 7292 × 2500 mm. Weight 9400 kg. GVW 27000 kg. Also BM20MC2 prime mover, BM20MB1 with loading crane. Mid-1970s.

Truck, 10-ton, 6 × 6, Dump   **USA**
(Mack DMM6116S)

Introduced in the mid-1960s and continued in production for about 10 years, the Mack DM range was designed for the construction industry, DM standing for Dump and Mixer applications. The USAF acquired a number of the DMM 6 × 6 derivative, some fitted with dump body, others with fifth wheel coupling.

Truck, 10-ton, 6 × 6, Aircraft Fueller   **D**
(Magirus-Deutz 320D20FAT 6 × 6)

V-10-cyl. 15.9-litre aircooled diesel (Deutz F10L 413F) with 9F1R gearbox and 2-speed transfer box. Wheelbase 4190 mm. Overall dimensions 7700 × 2500 × 2930 mm. Weight 12200 kg. GVW 19500 kg. Produced for West German *Bundeswehr* as 'Flugfeld-tankwagen 8000'. Actual tank capacity was 8500 litres. 1978.

Truck, 10-ton, 6 × 6, Cargo   **D**
(MAN 20.280DFAEG)

6-cyl. 11.1-litre diesel engine (D2566MTFG) with torque converter, 6F1R gearbox and transfer box with lockable differential. Rigid axles with coil spring suspension. Wheelbase 4700 mm. Overall dimensions 8950 × 2500 × 3010 (cab) mm. Weight 10300 kg. GVW 20300 kg. 1976.

193

TRUCK, 10-TON, 6×6 (ÖAF 20.320)   A

General Data: When in the early 1970s the Austrian Army began to contemplate a replacement for its heavy 6 × 6 vehicles, tests were conducted with a German 'new generation' 6 × 6 MAN truck. The Austrian firm ÖAF-Gräf & Stift being closely linked with MAN, it was decided to produce a new Austrian truck, patterned on the German model. This was developed and tested from 1974 until 1976, when an order was placed for 350 units.

Technical Details: MAN D2538MT V-8-cyl. turbocharged diesel engine, 12763 cc (125 × 130 mm), 239 kW/320 bhp (DIN) at 2500 rpm. Fluid coupling with torque converter. 6F1R gearbox (ZF S6-90). Single-speed transfer box with lockable differential.

Hub reduction axles with 6.743:1 overall axle gear ratio. Air/hydraulic brakes. Rigid axles with coil springs. 14.00-20 tyres. 24-Volt electrics. 2 × 250-litre fuel tanks.

Dimensions and Weights: Wheelbase 4500 mm. Track 2070 mm. Overall length and width 8700 × 2500 mm. Height 3340 mm (crane). Ground clearance 410 mm (axles). Angles of approach and departure not specified. Weight 11800 kg, GVW 21800 kg.

above: early cargo truck; *below left:* 1977 cargo truck; *below right:* emergency vehicle (*Katastrophenschutzfahrzeug*)

TRUCK, 10-TON, 6×6 (SAMIL 100)

General Data: Heaviest in the range of South African military trucks produced by Armscor under IVECO/Magirus-Deutz licence and offered for export through the Nimrod marketing organization, the Samil 100 was available with numerous body styles, including cargo (with 'elephant trunk-type' crane), dump (7.5-m³, rear-tipping), 9100-litre water tanker/sprinkler (with stainless steel tank), recovery vehicle (twin-jib wrecker), artillery tractor (with crew compartment for 8 men and hydraulic loading crane). Certain models were available with armoured front end and cab.

Technical Details: Deutz V-10-cyl. aircooled diesel engine, 184 kW/247 bhp (net) at 2650 rpm. Dry plate clutch. 6F1R gearbox with front axle disconnect. Rear axles with hub reduction gearing. Air brakes. Semi-elliptic leaf springs, inverted at rear. 14.00-20 tyres. 24-Volt electrics. 2 fuel tanks, capacity not specified.

Dimensions and Weights: Wheelbase 5940 mm. Track, front/rear 2002/2048 mm. Overall length and width 9350 × 2500 mm. Height 3350 mm (cab protector). Ground clearance 359 mm (axles). Angles of approach and departure not specified. Weight 9135 kg, GVW 21000 kg.

above: dump truck; *below left:* artillery tractor; *below right:* cargo truck with mine-resistant cab

Truck, 10-ton, 6 × 6, Cargo   **J**
(Mitsubishi, Type 74)

V-8-cyl. 13.27-litre diesel engine with 6F1R gearbox and 2-speed transfer box. Overall dimensions 9220 × 2490 × 3000 mm. Weight 9850 kg. GVW 19850 kg. Max. speed 100 km/h. Heavy-duty militarized commercial 6 × 6 chassis, also with bridge-laying equipment (Type 81) and treadway bridge erector.

Truck, 10-ton, 6 × 6, Cargo/Prime Mover   **F**
(Renault TRM10000)

6-cyl. 9.8-litre turbocharged diesel engine (MIDS 06.20.45) with 9F1R gearbox and single-speed transfer box with lockable differential. Hub reduction axles. Wheelbase 4800 mm. Chassis/cab weight 9520 kg. GVW 22000 kg. Winch optional. Heavier, uprated version of the Renault TRM6000 6 × 6. 1981.

Truck, 10-ton, 6 × 6, Cargo   **CH**
(Saurer 10DM)

6-cyl. 11.95-litre turbocharged diesel engine (D4KT) with torque converter, 6F1R gearbox (10-speed semi-auto. optional) and transfer box with lockable differential. Hub reduction axles with lockable diffs. Air brakes. Wheelbase 4700 mm. Length and width 8905 × 2500 mm. GVW 22000 kg. From 1981.

Truck, 10-ton, 6 × 6, Cargo   **A**
(Steyr 1491M/6 × 6)

V-8-cyl. 11.97-litre turbocharged diesel engine (WD815.71) with 9F1R gearbox and 2-speed transfer box. Hub reduction axles. Tandem bogie suspension with 4 interconnected leaf springs. Wheelbase 4700 mm. Overall dimensions 9109 × 2500 × 3050 (cab) mm. Weight 11400 kg. GVW 22000 kg. Early 1980s.

Truck, 10-ton, 6 × 6, Cargo   **S**
(Volvo F88 6 × 6)

6-cyl. 9.6-litre diesel engine (TD100A) with 8F1R gearbox with torque converter (MR61) and single-speed transfer box. 4 differential locks. 14.00-20 tyres. Air brakes. Wheelbase 4285 mm. Chassis/cab dimensions 7800 × 2480 × 3000 mm. Weight 10500 kg. GVW 20700 kg. Commercially available, from 1973/74.

Truck, 11-ton, 6 × 6, Tipper   **CH**
(Saurer 5DM 6 × 6)

6-cyl. 11.95-litre diesel engine (D2KT) with 5F1R gearbox and 2-speed transfer box with lockable differential. Hub reduction axles with diff. locks at rear. Single rear tyres, size 18-22.5. Wheelbase 4050 mm. Overall dimensions 6360 × 2300 × 2850 mm. GVW 24000 kg. Right-hand drive. Prototype shown (1975).

Truck, 12-ton, 6 × 4, Dump   **CH**
(Saurer D330N)

6-cyl. 11.95-litre diesel engine (D2KT) with automatic transmission. GVW 25000 kg. 7-m³ capacity dump body by Rochat. 10-ton winch with 100 m cable. Suitable for towing low-bed trailers of up to 40 ton. 70 units delivered to the Swiss Army Engineers in 1979/80. Basically this was a militarized commercial truck.

Truck, 12-ton, 6 × 6, Cargo   **F**
(Berliet GBH12)

6-cyl. 12-litre diesel engine (MD 06.35.40) with 12F2R gearbox (ZF AK6-80) and 2-speed transfer box with lockable differential. Dual-ratio rear axles with hub reduction. Wheelbase 4650 mm. Military version of civilian tipper chassis, offered with several body types, including artillery tractor. 1979.

Truck, 12-ton, 6 × 6, Cargo/Prime Mover   **RA**
(Fiat Concord 697BN)

6-cyl. 13.8-litre diesel engine with 8F2R transmission. Hub reduction axles. 20-in. wheels. Wheelbase 3910 mm. Developed by Fiat Concord of Argentina and quantity-produced since September 1971 in their Cordoba plant. Used by Argentine Army for artillery towing. Also built as tractor truck for semi-trailers.

Truck, 12-ton, 6 × 6, Fueller   **CS**
(Tatra 148PP/T148CAPL15)

V-8-cyl. 12.6-litre aircooled diesel engine (T2-928-1) with 5F1R gearbox and 2-speed transfer box. Wheelbase 4920 mm. 15000-litre tank body and equipment by VSS of Kosice, Czechoslovakia, on 26000-kg GVW chassis. Tubular chassis with 2 cross members. Pump drive PTO on transfer box. Late 1970s.

Truck, 14-ton, 6 × 4, Tractor   **USA**
(AMG/CCC M915)

6-cyl. 14-litre turbocharged diesel engine (Cummins NTC400) with 16F2R semi-auto. trans. (CAT D7155). Hendrickson rear suspension. Air brakes. Wheelbase 4900 mm. Overall dimensions 6490 × 2440 × 2930 mm. Weight 8446 kg. GVW 22680 kg. 1978. M915A1 (1981) had Allison 5F1R auto. trans. and Eaton axles.

Truck, 14-ton, 6 × 4, Dump   **GB**
(Aveling Barford AB690)

6-cyl. diesel engine (Leyland) with 5F1R gearbox. Hub reduction axles. Tyres 11.00-22 front, 15.00-20 rear. Wheelbase 3860 mm. GVW 25650 kg. Quarry body, capacity 9 m³ (heaped). AEC design, later produced by Leyland's Scammell division as Model LD55, with Leyland AV760 diesel engine, for British Army Engineers.

197

SIX-WHEELED TRUCKS

Truck, 15-ton, 6 × 4, Dump   **USA**
(GMC MH9670)

This example from GMC's diesel-powered 9500 Series was equipped with a Perfection rear dump body. Delivered to the US Navy in 1972, the olive-drab painted vehicle was officially designated 'Truck, Dump, DED, 51000 GVW, 6 × 4', indicating a GVW rating of just over 23000 kg. Full air brakes were standard.

Truck, 15-ton, 6 × 4, Dump   **GB**
(Haulamatic Mil. 615)

V-8-cyl. 8.8-litre diesel engine (Perkins 540) with Allison 5F1R automatic transmission. Kirkstall front axle, Eaton rear bogie. Tyres, front 12.00-20, rear 16.00-20. Air brakes. Overall length and width 6500 × 2440 mm. 24-Volt electrics. 9.4-m³ exhaust-heated body with twin hydraulic rams. British Army, 1979/80.

Truck, 15-ton, 6 × 4, Tractor   **D**
(Magirus-Deutz 310D26FKS 6 × 4)

V-10-cyl. 14.7-litre aircooled diesel engine (Deutz F10L 413L) with 8F2R gearbox. Overall dimensions 6860 × 2500 × 2910 mm. Coupled to Van Hool 20-ton semi-trailer, measuring 10220 × 2490 × 4000 mm. Combination length 13500 mm. Used by Belgian Army, 1982. 68 bulk fuel tanker semi-trailers were also acquired.

Truck, 15-ton, 6 × 4, Tractor   **D**
(Magirus-Deutz 320D22FS 6 × 4)

V-10-cyl. 15.9-litre aircooled diesel engine (Deutz F10L 413F) with 9F1R gearbox. Wheelbase 3510 mm. Overall dimensions 6440 × 2500 × 2740 mm. Weight 8675 kg. GVW 22000 kg. Coupled to 24000-litre aircraft fueller semi-trailer (by Luther Werke) and known as 'Flugfeldtankwagen 24000'. *Bundeswehr* 1978.

Truck, 15-ton, 6 × 4, Tractor   **D**
(Magirus-Deutz 320D22FS 6 × 4)

V-10-cyl. 15.9-litre aircooled diesel engine (Deutz F10L 413F) with 9F1R gearbox. Wheelbase 3510 mm. Overall dimensions 6440 × 2500 × 2740 mm. Weight 8675 kg. GVW 22000 kg. Coupled to 30000-litre road tanker semi-trailer (by Stadler). Transport capacity 28500 litres. Produced from 1980 for *Bundeswehr*.

Truck, 15-ton, 6 × 4, Fuel Tanker   **D**
(Magirus-Deutz 320D26FT 6 × 4)

V-10-cyl. 15.9-litre aircooled diesel engine (Deutz F10L 413F) with 9F1R gearbox (ZF 5S-110GP), driving both rear axles. Wheelbase 5260 mm. Overall dimensions 9900 × 2500 × 2930 mm. Weight 11470 kg. GVW 26000 kg. Road transport capacity 17500 litres. Tank and equipment by Stadler, 1980.

Truck, 15-ton, 6 × 4, Aircraft Fueller   D
(Magirus-Deutz 320D26FT 6 × 4)

V-10-cyl. 15.9-litre aircooled diesel engine (Deutz F10L 413F) with 9F1R gearbox. Wheelbase 5260 mm (4600 + 1320 mm). Overall dimensions 9850 × 2500 × 2950 mm. Weight 12460 kg. GVW 26000 kg. 15800-litre tank with 1200-litre/min. pump for aircraft fuelling. Produced for West German Air Force, from 1979.

Truck, 15-ton, 6 × 4, Articulated, Dump   S
(Volvo BM860)

6-cyl. 5.48-litre diesel engine (TD60A) with torque converter and 4F4R Powershift transmission, driving the front and second axles, both with diff. locks. Hydraulically-actuated steering by articulation. Tyres 23.5-25 front, 20.5-25 rear. Wheelbase 4820 mm. Overall length and width 9290 × 2480 mm. Swedish Army.

Truck, 15-ton, 6 × 4, Cargo   S
(Volvo N1027)

6-cyl. 9.6-litre diesel engine (TD100B) with 4F1R gearbox and 3-speed transfer box. Trilex wheels with 11.00-20 tyres. Air brakes. Steel cab with tilting glassfibre front shell. Used by Peruvian Army since 1976. Peruvian Navy and Air Force employed Volvo N-Series 4 × 2 trucks and tractors, e.g. N720 and N1020.

Truck, 15-ton, 6 × 6, Articulated, Carrier   USA
(Caterpillar Goer Flatbed)

6-cyl. 8.6-litre multifuel diesel engine (D333) with 6F1R Powershift transmission. Walking-beam rear suspension. Steering by articulation. Designed for transport of larger, bulkier loads than the 4 × 4 Goer type of vehicle (of which Caterpillar had supplied various models) could accommodate. Prototype only, early 1970s.

Truck, 15-ton, 6 × 6, Aircraft Fueller   D
(Mercedes-Benz 2632A/41)

V-10-cyl. 15.9-litre diesel engine (OM403) with 5F1R gearbox and single-speed transfer box with lockable differential (axle diff. locks optional). Fitted with aircraft refuelling equipment (9200-litre tank, 2 × 400-litre/min. pumps and ancillaries) by Luther Werke of Braunschweig in the late 1970s.

Truck, 15-ton, 6 × 6, Tractor/Aircraft Fueller   D
(Mercedes-Benz LAS2624/6 × 6)

6-cyl. 11.6-litre diesel engine (OM355V) with 6F1R gearbox and 2-speed transfer box. 7.35:1 axles with 20-in. wheels. Wheelbase 4670 mm. GVW 24000 kg. GCW 38000 kg. Shown with Strüver aircraft refuelling equipment and 25000-litre tank semi-trailer of frameless construction for Chilean Air Force, early 1970s.

Truck, 16-ton, 6 × 4, Aircraft Fueller   **GB**
(Leyland Bison)

6-cyl. diesel engine (L12) with 6F1R overdrive-top gearbox and hub reduction rear axles. GVW 24390 kg. Bodied and equipped by Gloster Saro, this vehicle succeeded the similarly bodied AEC Mammoth Major in production (1978). Largest air-transportable refueller to fit into Hercules C130 aircraft. Royal Air Force.

Truck, 17-ton, 6 × 2, Aircraft Fueller   **NL**
(DAF FMT2300DHT)

One of a series of refuellers for the Belgian Ministry of Defence, produced in 1983. Chassis was modified 4 × 2 type with additional steering axle. Reinforced polyester 16500-litre tank and equipment, for over- and underwing fuelling, produced and installed by Didak of Grommendonk, Belgium. Prototype shown.

Truck, 18-ton, 6 × 4, Dump   **D**
(Magirus-Deutz 6 × 4)

V-8-cyl. 12.7-litre aircooled diesel engine (Deutz F8L 413F). Overall length and width 7740 × 2500 mm. 6 supplied to Belgian Army in 1977, fitted with Belgian ATF tipping body. Load capacity on roads 18000 kg, off roads 14000 kg. Belgian armed forces have for many years used various types of Magirus-Deutz trucks.

Truck, 20-ton, 6 × 4, Tractor   **GB**
(Leyland/Scammell Crusader)

6-cyl. 12.17-litre turbocharged diesel engine (RR Eagle 305) with 9F2R gearbox. Hub reduction rear axles. Wheelbase 3962 mm. Overall dimensions 6580 × 2500 × 3140 mm. Prime mover for British Army's FV3242 cargo semi-trailer. Fitted with 'day cab'. (For 'night cab' version see 'Heavy Equipment Transporters'.)

Truck, 20-ton, 6 × 4, Aircraft Fueller   **USA**
(Mack U-Series/Ramta)

Based on a US Mack 6 × 4 6020-mm wheelbase chassis/cab this refueller, with a capacity of 17000 litres, was a product of the Ramta Division of Israel Aircraft Industries in the late 1970s. The complete vehicle measured 9300 × 2500 × 3200 mm. Pump was of self-priming centrifugal type with flow rate of 1135 litres/min.

Truck, 25-ton, 6 × 4, Tractor   **GB**
(Foden 06A085G2504)

8-cyl. diesel engine (Gardner 8LXB) with 12F1R gearbox. Bendix-Westinghouse air brakes. 12.00-20 tyres. Wheelbase 3899 mm. Overall dimensions 5715 × 2500 × 2845 mm. Weight 9500 kg. GCW 85 tons. 2 of these heavy tractor units were produced for the British Ministry of Defence in 1974/75.

TRUCK, 20-TON, 6×6 (AMG/CCC M916)

USA

General Data: Designed by Crane Carrier Co. and licence-produced by AM General Corp., the M916 was a militarized CCC Centaur truck with all-wheel drive. It was one of a range of 6 vehicle types with common major componentry, the others being a 15-ton 6 × 4 line haul tractor (M915, M915A1), a 6 × 6 bituminous distributor (M918), a 20-ton 8 × 6 tractor truck (M920), a 20-ton 8 × 6 dump truck (M917) and an 8-cu-yd mobile concrete mixer (M919).

Technical Details: Cummins NTC400 6-cyl. turbocharged diesel engine, 14010 cc (140 × 152 mm), 298 kW/400 bhp (net) at 2100 rpm. Caterpillar D7155 16F2R semi-automatic transmission.

Oshkosh 18000 Series F-U29 single-speed transfer box with front axle lock-up. 5.29:1 axle gear ratio. Air brakes. Leaf springs at front, Hendrickson walking beams at rear. 11.00-24 tyres. 12/24-Volt electrics. 416-litre fuel tank.

Dimensions and Weights: Wheelbase 5131 mm. Track, front/rear 1980/1850 mm. Overall length and width 7480 × 2440 mm. Height 3250 mm (over horns). Ground clearance 290 mm (beam brackets). Angle of approach 42°. Weight 11327 kg, GVW 29937 kg.

above and *below left:* M916; *below right:* M918

Eight-Wheeled Trucks

Of all military wheeled vehicles, the eight-wheelers have traditionally been the most fascinating. The high-mobility 8 × 8 trucks in particular are often impressive, both in design and appearance as well as in off-road mobility.

In Britain and some other countries, the eight-wheeler was and is usually a road-going vehicle, driven by one or both of the rear tandem axles. The US armed forces, the Germans, the Czechs and the Soviets, however, have generally used eight-wheel drive for what is now often called 'enhanced mobility'. Especially in the 1930s and 1940s, some eyecatching designs were launched, albeit usually of an experimental nature. France, Sweden, Australia and a few others have also produced 8 × 8 trucks at some time or other.

Because of their inherent complexity, weight, and sheer cost, eight-by-eight trucks were in the main intended for specialized roles such as prime movers for tank transport semi-trailers, heavy artillery towing and as the basis for armoured vehicles. Of today's 8 × 8 trucks, the Tatra 815 'Kolos' is possibly the most numerous. It first appeared in the mid-1960s and is in service chiefly with the armed forces of Czechoslovakia and East Germany. Featuring a central tube backbone chassis with all-independent suspension by means of swinging half-axles, it is built in accordance with long-established Tatra design traditions. Its design also allows for the relatively easy production of 6 × 6 and 4 × 4 derivatives. In addition, this chassis is employed as the basis for several armoured vehicles.

The US Army has long experience with 8 × 8 trucks and has several types in service, viz. the late-1960s Ford-built 5-ton M656 (with M757 tractor truck and M791 expandable van derivatives) and the Chrysler-designed M746 22.5-ton HET tractor truck which was produced by Ward LaFrance in the mid-1970s on a lowest-bid contract and which appears elsewhere in this book (see chapter on 'Heavy Equipment Transporters').

In 1978 the US Army's Tank-Automotive Research and Development Command (TARADCOM) started design studies for a High-Mobility Tactical Truck (HMTT) in two payload classes: 4- to 6-ton and 8- to 10-ton. Prototypes were produced both by TARADCOM and by Pacific Car and Foundry. The former was a 5-ton truck based on the M656 chassis mentioned earlier but with a V6 Detroit Diesel engine and five-speed Allison automatic transmission (instead of six-in-line Continental with six-speed Allison), providing about 40 per cent more power than the standard-mobility M809 5-ton 6 × 6 series it was intended to replace. The new vehicle had a Kenworth cab and a side-mounted winch, Swedish style, providing front and rear winching without increase in vehicle length and thus affecting the angle of approach.

The 10-ton 8 × 8 HMTT, designated XM977 and again propelled by a team of General Motors Detroit Diesel and Allison (V8 and four-speed respectively), was intended as a replacement for the ill-fated 8-ton 4 × 4 'Goer' vehicles. The 'Goers' had proved another mixed blessing. Satisfactory if operated only at low speeds on the roughest of terrain, these vehicles, which relied on their big tyres for springing and were steered by articulation, caused such harmonic vibrations on smooth surfaces that operation of the controls became a real problem. The straight-frame 8 × 8, with double-bogie suspension, was thought to be a satisfactory substitute for the 'Goer' (with the exception of the 9500-litre fueller version, the M559, which was the first and only vehicle capable of quick refuelling of tanks right in the front line). At the time when the HMTTs were in the development stage, the Lockheed Missile and Space Co., which had developed a high-mobility articulated eight-wheeler known as the 'Dragon Wagon', joined forces with Oshkosh to prepare this vehicle to the point of acceptance by the Army. Eventually, the 'Dragon Wagon' became the Oshkosh DA-Series and went into production for the US Marine Corps, together with a similar but rigid-frame variant, the DS-Series, which was accepted by the US Army.

Meanwhile, throughout the early 1970s, the West German motor industry and armed forces had worked on the evolution of their own new generation eight-by-eights (together with 6 × 6 and 4 × 4 derivatives) and these trucks went into quantity production in 1976. Having been designed by a consortium, these MAN-built trucks were fitted with Deutz air-cooled diesel engines. In due course, MAN introduced their own versions, differing chiefly in being powered by liquid-cooled MAN diesels (and hence a radiator with a characteristic MAN grille). Some of these were also adapted to meet the US Army HMTT specifications, particularly for the tractor truck role in the GSRS missile system.

Truck, 2.5-ton, 8 × 8, Cargo/Personnel   **S**
(Volvo C300 Series-8 × 8)

6-cyl. 2.98-litre twin-carburettor petrol engine (B30) with 5F1R gearbox and 2-speed transfer box. 4 rigid portal-type axles with step-down gears. Produced experimentally in the early 1970s, derived from the makers' C306. Fitted with fully-enclosed bodywork with side and rear doors. Side-mounted recovery winch.

Truck, 5-ton, 8 × 8, Cargo   **USA**
(TARADCOM HMTT)

In 1977/78 the US Army's Tank-Automotive Research and Development Command prototyped a new medium-capacity (4- to 6-ton category) high-mobility tactical truck. Extensive use was made of commercial components, including 300-bhp diesel engine, Kenworth tilt cab, HIAB crane. etc. Experimental only.

Truck, 8-ton, 8 × 8, Cargo/Prime Mover   **CS**
(Tatra 2-815-12VN)

This Czech high-mobility truck was developed and produced in the early 1970s as a modernized version of Tatra's T813 'Kolos' (T813-12). It was later redesignated Tatra 2-815-12VN, as part of the makers' T815 Series, which also comprised 4 × 4 and 6 × 6 models. The engine was a V-12-cyl. multifuel diesel of 320 bhp.

Truck, 10-ton, 8 × 8, Tractor   **D**
(MAN-USA version)

Derived from the West German *Bundeswehr*'s Class 1 10-ton 8 × 8 truck, this version was developed for the US Army for production during 1981–84 (465 units). It differed from the *Bundeswehr* type in having a watercooled 365-bhp V-10-cyl. MAN engine with 8-speed gearbox, larger tyres, crane etc.

Truck, 10-ton, 8 × 8, Cargo   **USA**
(Pacific Car & Foundry Co. HMTT)

To supplement the 8-ton 4 × 4 'Goer' vehicles the US Army called for a new 8 × 8 truck. This prototype was produced by Paccar in conjunction with the US Army (TARADCOM) in 1977/78, using a Detroit Diesel 8V92TA engine with Allison HT740 auto. trans. Dimensions 8230 × 2440 × 3251 mm. GVW 20430 kg.

Truck, 10-ton, 8 × 8, Cargo/Prime Mover   **CS**
(Tatra 815VT 'Kolos')

V-12-cyl. 19-litre aircooled diesel engine. Backbone chassis with swinging axles. 15.00-20 tyres. Wheelbase 4520 mm (1650 + 2970 + 1450). Overall dimensions 9400 × 2500 × 2980 mm. Weight 15400 kg. GVW 25400 kg. GCW (on roads) 70000 kg. Tiltable 4-door cab. Introduced in the early 1980s.

TRUCK, 8-TON, 8 × 8 (TATRA 813 'KOLOS')   CS

General Data: Launched in 1965/66, employing the established Tatra design principles of backbone chassis, swinging axles and aircooled engine the T813 also appeared in 6 × 6 and 4 × 4 configuration and with a variety of body types, including dump, bridging, crane, rocket launcher, etc. There were also fully armoured vehicles, including APC (OT-64/SKOT) and a self-propelled 152-mm howitzer (DANA). A number of options were offered, e.g. a more powerful engine, 18.00-22.5 'Super Single' or 14.00-20 tyres, etc.

Technical Details: Own T930-3 V-12-cyl. aircooled diesel engine, 17640 cc (120 × 130 mm), 185 kW/250 bhp (net) at 2000 rpm. Triple plate clutch. 5F1R dual-range gearbox. 2-speed

transfer gear with lockable differential. Hub reduction gearing. 5.75:1 axle gear ratio (overall). Air brakes. Inverted semi-elliptic leaf springs. 15.00-21 tyres with central pressure regulation. 24-Volt electrics. 2 × 250-litre fuel tanks.

Dimensions and Weights: Wheelbase 3750 mm (1650 + 2200 + 1450). Track, front/rear 2050/2000 mm. Overall length and width 8800 × 2500 mm. Height 2780 mm (cab). Ground clearance 380 mm (axles). Angles of approach and departure 35° and 37°. Weight 14700 kg, GVW 22200 kg.

above: cargo/prime mover; *below left:* 'Vosovky' roadway layer (DDR); *below right:* rocket launcher M1972 (DDR).

TRUCK, 9-TON, 8 × 8 (LOCKHEED 'DRAGON WAGON' 901M)   USA

General Data: Lockheed Missiles and Space Co. of Sunnyvale, California, during the 1960s developed several advanced high-mobility vehicles, including the 8 × 8 articulated armoured car 'Twister' and truck 'Dragon Wagon'. The latter consisted of a power module and a driven trailer, with coordinated Ackerman and articulated steering. The trailer or rear body could be easily detached from the front power unit and exchanged for another.

Technical Details: Detroit Diesel 6V53T V-6-cyl. turbocharged diesel engine, 5220 cc (98 × 114 mm), 208 kW/280 bhp (net) at 2800 rpm. Allison MT650D 5F1R automatic transmission. 2-speed transfer box with front axle disconnect. Rockwell SHHD (M) axles

with 6.90:1 gear ratio. Air brakes. Semi-elliptic leaf springs. 16.00-20XS tyres. 12-Volt electrics. 325-litre fuel tank. *Note:* earlier Model 901 had CAT 3208 engine.

Dimensions and Weights: Wheelbase 5131 mm. Track 2006 mm. Overall length and width 9271 × 2438 mm. Height 2743 mm (cab). Ground clearance 343 mm (axles). Angles of approach and departure 54° and 45°. Weight (including crane) 12500 kg, GVW 20840 kg.

above: 901M (1978; 1979 902 similar); *below left:* 901 (1972); *below right:* 901M with air defence equipment (Raytheon)

TRUCK, 10-TON, 8 × 8 (MAN N4540)   D

General Data: Heaviest in the range of new-generation Class 1 tactical trucks of the West German armed forces, the 10-ton 8 × 8 was produced from 1976 (1924 units). Most of these trucks (1868 units) were equipped with an Atlas 1-ton loading crane with hydraulic outriggers; these were designated N4640. Final assembly of the trucks took place in MAN's Salzgitter-Watenstedt plant. All vehicles had a winch, supplied by Rotzler.

Technical Details: Deutz BF8L 413F V-8-cyl. turbocharged aircooled diesel engine, 12763 cc (125 × 130 mm), 253 kW/ 320 bhp (net) at 2650 rpm. Torque converter and dry plate clutch. ZF S6-90 6F1R gearbox. Single-speed transfer box with lockable differential. Differential locks in rear axles. 6.734:1 axle gear ratio (including hub reduction). Air/hydraulic brakes. Rigid axles with coil spring suspension. 14.00R20M tyres. 24-Volt electrics. 270-litre fuel tank.

Dimensions and Weights: Wheelbase 5335 mm. Track 2066 mm. Overall length and width 10120 × 2500 mm. Height 2860 mm (cab). Ground clearance 415 mm (axles). Angles of approach and departure 45° and 45°. Weight 15040 kg, GVW 25040 kg.

above and *below left:* N4540; *below right:* N4640 (early model)

TRUCK, 10-TON, 8 × 8 (OSHKOSH DS3838/M977 SERIES)   **USA**

General Data: This Heavy Expanded-Mobility Tactical Truck (HEMTT) was designed by Oshkosh Truck Corp. during 1979–81. It looked like the Lockheed design (902 'Dragon Wagon') but had a rigid frame. Oshkosh were awarded a US Army contract for 2140 units, to be delivered during 1982–87. The following types were ordered: M977 cargo truck; M978 fuel-servicing truck; M983 tractor truck; M984 recovery vehicle; M985 cargo truck.

Technical Details: Detroit Diesel 8V92TA V-8-cyl. turbocharged diesel engine, 12060 cc (123 × 127 mm), 332 kW/445 bhp (SAE) at 2100 rpm. Allison HT740D 4F1R torque converter transmission. 2-speed transfer box with front tandem disconnect. Manual inter-axle differentials. Oshkosh front, Eaton rear axles. 5.57:1 axle gear ratio. Air brakes. Hendrickson suspension with equalizing beams, front and rear. 16.00R20 tyres. 24-Volt electrics. 587-litre tank.

Dimensions and Weights: Wheelbase 5334 mm. Track 2007 mm. Overall length and width 10173 × 2500 mm. Height 2565 mm (cab). Ground clearance 350 mm (axles). Angles of approach and departure 43° and 45°. Weight 16284 kg, GVW 28123 kg.

above and *below left:* M977 cargo truck; *below right:* M978 fuel-servicing truck

TRUCK, 10-TON, 8 × 8 (ZIL-135L4)   SU

General Data: This vehicle was produced by the Bryansk Automobile Factory, hence it was sometimes referred to as BAZ-135L4. However, it was more frequently designated ZIL-135L4, ZIL being the factory where this high-mobility truck was designed and developed. In military service the chassis was employed mainly as a transporter and launching unit for missiles. In civil use the vehicle was used for transport of pipeline equipment.

Technical Details: 2 ZIL-375 V-8-cyl. petrol engines, 7000 cc each (108 × 95 mm), 134 kW/180 bhp (each) at 3200 rpm. Hydro-mechanical transmissions, with each engine driving the 4 wheels on one side. Air/hydraulic brakes. Torsion bar suspension on 1st

and 4th axles, both of which were steering axles. Fixed centre tandem axles. 16.00-20 tyres with central pressure regulation. 24-Volt electrics. 770-litre fuel capacity.

Dimensions and Weights: Wheelbase 6300 mm (overall). Track 2300 mm. Overall length and width 9275 × 2800 mm. Height 2535 mm (cab). Ground clearance 580 mm (axles). Angles of approach and departure not specified. Weight 9000 kg, GVW 19000 kg.

above: cargo truck; *below:* missile transporter/launcher and resupply vehicle (FROG-7 SSM)

TRUCK, 12.5-TON, 8 × 8 (OSHKOSH DA-SERIES)

USA

General Data: Designed and first built by Lockheed Missile and Space Co., the 'Dragon Wagon' (a name that was later dropped) was further developed by Oshkosh in 1979. The Oshkosh vehicle appeared in 1981 and was ordered by the US Marine Corps. Variants were: DA3838 cargo truck, DA3858-1 dropside cargo truck, DA3858-2 tractor truck, DA3858-3 logistics truck and DA3858-4 recovery vehicle.

Technical Details: Detroit Diesel 8V92TA V-8-cyl. turbocharged diesel engine, 12060 cc (123 × 127 mm), 332 kW/445 bhp (SAE) at 2100 rpm. Allison HT740D torque converter with 4F1R automatic gearbox. 2-speed transfer box with lockable differential.

Oshkosh front, Eaton No. 2 and rear axles. 5.57:1 front and 5.43:1 rear axle gear ratio. Air brakes. Semi-elliptic taper leaf springs. 16.00R21 tyres. 24-Volt electrics. 2 × 283-litre fuel tanks.

Dimensions and Weights (DA3838): Wheelbase 5613 mm. Track 2007 mm. Overall length and width 10442 × 2438 mm. Height 2591 mm (cab). Ground clearance 350 mm (axles). Angles of approach and departure 45° and 45°. Weight 19068 kg, GVW 28030 kg. *Note:* rear tandem capacities of DA3838 and DA3858 models were 14515 and 24676 kg respectively.

above: early DA3838; *below:* DA3858-3 logistics

EIGHT-WHEELED TRUCKS

**Truck, 14-ton, 8 × 8, Water-Drilling   AUS
(RFW CA3)**

V-8-cyl. 12-litre diesel engine (Detroit Diesel 8V92TA) with auto. trans. (Allison HT750DRD) and RFW transfer box with power divider, permanently driving all wheels. Air brakes. Spider hub wheels with 'Super Single' tyres. Atlas Copco water drilling rig. One supplied to Australian Army in 1981.

**Truck, 15-ton, 8 × 8, Missile Transporter/Erector   F
(Berliet)**

First appearing in 1969, this limited-production low-slung 8-wheeled tractor unit towed a tri-axle semi-trailer with Marrel hydraulic gear to erect a strategic 2-stage surface-to-surface ballistic missile (by SEREB) prior to launching. The missile was 14.8 m long, 1.5 m in diameter and weighed 31900 kg.

**Truck, 15-ton, 8 × 8, Cargo/Prime Mover   SU
(MAZ-537A)**

V-12-cyl. diesel engine with hydromechanical transmission. 15.00-23.5 tyres. Wheelbase 2200+3300+2200 mm. High-mobility chassis used for missile/launcher (MAZ-543; 2 types), cargo/prime mover (MAZ-7310), dump truck (MAZ-7510) and pipe carrier (MAZ-7910). The last 3 were modernized versions. 1975.

**Truck, 16-ton, 8 × 4, Cargo   GB
(Foden 48K030R2208)**

6-cyl. diesel engine (Rolls-Royce 220 Mk 3) with 9F1R gearbox. 11.00-20 tyres. Wheelbase 5058 mm. GVW 30 tons. Prototype for trials shown. Quantity production comprised 120 units for British Ministry of Defence, late 1974 to mid-1975. 20 trucks had extended cab for driver-training purposes.

**Truck, 16-ton, 8 × 4, Ampliroll   GB
(Foden 58T030R2209)**

Standard Foden low-mobility chassis/cab, equipped with hydraulic loading gear (Ampliroll 160) for platforms, tipper bodies, containers, etc. Originated in France, the system was introduced to Britain by the Boughton Group. It could be fitted to chassis with payload ratings of up to 40 tons.

**Truck, 19-ton, 8 × 8, Dump   SU
(MAZ-7510)**

V-12-cyl. 38.8-litre diesel engine (D12A-525A) with torque converter transmission (3 speeds and overdrive). Independent suspension on first 2 axles. 1500 × 600-635 tyres. Wheelbase 2200+2470+1700 mm. Track 2375 mm. Overall dimensions 10240 × 2980 × 2930 mm. 11.5-m³ rear tipping body. From 1975.

TRUCK, 16-TON, 8 × 4 (FODEN 58T030R2209)

GB

General Data: A militarized commercial-type truck, using the same 'off-the-shelf' components as several other Foden-built low-mobility vehicles of the British Army. The tipper (FV11703) had an 11-m³ body (by Edbro) of fabricated steel construction with hardwood timber sandwiched between the floor plates to provide improved impact resistance. The tipping gear comprised a single telescopic power-operated hydraulic ram, providing a maximum tip angle of 54°. The following data apply to the tipper.

Technical Details: Rolls-Royce 220 Mk 3 6-cyl. diesel engine, 12170 cc (130.2 × 152.4 mm), 163 kW/218 bhp (DIN) at 2100 rpm. Dry plate clutch. 9F1R gearbox, constant-mesh, incor-

porating epicyclic range change with overdrive. 7.0:1 axle gear ratio. Air brakes. Semi-elliptic leaf springs, inverted at rear. 24-Volt electrics. 227-litre fuel tank.

Dimensions and Weights: Wheelbase 4652 mm. Track, front/rear 2076/1778 mm. Overall length and width 8344 × 2497 mm. Height 3353 mm (cab protector). Ground clearance not specified. Angles of approach and departure 23° and 25°. Weight 9616 kg, GVW 24280 kg.

above: tipper; *below left:* 22500-litre fuel tanker (Clarke Chapman); *below right:* load carrier with ISO container

TRUCK, 20-TON, 8 × 6 (AMG/CCC M917)

USA

General Data: This dump truck was one of a range of CCC-designed militarized commercial trucks produced under licence by AM General Corp. for the US Army. It had 3 Rockwell rear axles, namely a tandem bogie with Hendrickson suspension and, ahead of it, a so-called 'pusher' axle with trailing-arm suspension, which could be raised pneumatically. The chassis was also used for a heavy tractor truck, the M920, and for a concrete mixer, M919.

Technical Details: Cummins NTC400 6-cyl. turbocharged diesel engine, 14010 cc (140 × 152 mm), 298 kW/400 bhp (net) at 2100 rpm. Caterpillar D7155 16F2R semi-automatic transmission and Oshkosh 18000 Series F-U29 single-speed transfer box with front axle lock-up. 5.29:1 axle gear ratio. Air brakes. Semi-elliptic leaf springs at front, walking-beam suspension for tandem bogie and trailing arms for pusher axle. 11.00-24 tyres. 12/24-Volt electrics. 416-litre fuel tank.

Dimensions and Weights: Wheelbase 5360 mm. Track, front/rear 1980/1850 mm. Overall length and width 8900 × 2440 mm. Height 3581 mm (cab protector). Ground clearance 300 mm (beam brackets). Angle of approach 42°. Weight 14768 kg, GVW 34019 kg.

above and *below left:* M917; *below right:* M919

Heavy Equipment Transporters

Although in recent years some six- and eight-wheeled AFV transporter trucks have appeared which use the Amplicar or Ampliroll hydraulic loading system (i.e. self-loading and -unloading of a platform on which a tank or other vehicle can be placed), by far the majority of heavy-equipment and tank transporters (HETs) still comprise semi-trailers coupled to suitable tractor trucks.

As in other classes of military vehicles, the HET tractor trucks are nowadays of military or commercial design, the latter usually militarized, i.e. modified in detail for optimum military suitability. The purely military designs have in a number of instances proved too expensive. This became very evident again in the case of what was known as the 'HET-70': the Heavy Equipment Transporter for the 1970s. It was required for the Main Battle Tank for the 1970s (MBT-70) which the US Army and the West German *Bundeswehr* were jointly developing in the 1960s. The development work on the HET-70 was done by Chrysler Corporation in the USA and by Faun in West Germany, where it was known as the SLT-70 (*Schwerlast Transporter*). In due course, however, it was decided for a variety of reasons to terminate the joint venture and carry on individually, with both the new 50-ton main battle tank and its transporter. The German development (Faun tractor unit, Krupp semi-trailer) then became known as the SLT50-2 'Elefant' and during 1977–79 324 of these combinations were supplied to the *Bundeswehr*, the Krupp-designed trailers being produced by Kässbohrer. The SLT-70 was a highly sophisticated, i.e. high-technology, design capable of impressive performance when loaded to its designed payload rating of 50 tons. However, it had two major drawbacks. First, the production costs were exceedingly high, and secondly the latest *Bundeswehr* main battle tank – the Leopard 2 – weighs around 56 tons. For these two reasons, Faun designed a simplified version of the 'Elefant', utilizing a maximum of commercial off-the-shelf components (Deutz diesel engine, ZF gearbox, own axles, etc.) with a twelve-wheeled Kässbohrer semi-trailer. Known as the Faun FS42.75/42, this combination had a 56-ton payload capacity and the *Bundeswehr* ordered 70 units for delivery from 1981.

In the US, industry was invited to tender for the manufacture of the Chrysler-designed HET-70 and Ward LaFrance, being the lowest bidder, received a production contract. The tractor unit was designated M746, the semi-trailer M747. Most of these combinations were shipped to Europe for use by the US Army, chiefly in West Germany. Production was restricted to 125 units (with a smaller follow-up order for Morocco) when, again for financial and technical reasons (including transmission problems), the US Army looked at and purchased militarized commercial tractor units, in this instance the Oshkosh M911 which was derived from this manufacturer's J2065 heavy tractor. This was also in line with the US Government's policy of buying off-the-shelf commercial vehicles wherever possible, the expected savings in total HET costs amounting to approximately $40 million. Nearly 1200 M911 tractors were built and they were used in conjunction with the already standardized M747 semi-trailer.

In the British Army, tank-hauling was for many years executed by means of 50- and 60-ton trailers towed by several variants of the famed Thornycroft Mighty Antar, the Mk 1 version of which dated back to the early 1950s. In 1978 the prototype for its successor, the Scammell Commander, was launched. With a 466-kW (625-bhp) Rolls-Royce V12 engine and two-axle (i.e. two rows of wheels) semi-trailer by Fruehauf, it had a GCW of well over 100 tons. Scammell also offered HET tractor versions of their S24 and S26 commercial trucks.

Of course, not all HETs are intended to carry heavy tanks and other tracked AFVs in the 50- to 60-ton class. (Indeed, many if not most tracked AFVs, including armoured personnel carriers, are considerably lighter and are road-hauled on smaller transporters, of which there are a great number.) Similar transporters are also employed for the carrying of engineers' material such as bulldozers and other low-speed earthmoving equipment.

In Sweden a new HET concept was launched in 1982 by Hafo Maskin and Volvo. It comprised a Volvo N12 6 × 4 Mk 2 tractor truck coupled to a Hafo 50- to 60-ton low-bed semi-trailer with four-wheel drive: of the trailer's three axles, the outer ones were hydraulically driven. Nicolas in France, well-known for their ultra-heavy trailers, started assembling tailor-made six- and eight-wheeled tractor units in 1979, enabling them to offer complete combinations.

In this chapter the entries are presented in alphabetical order, by make, with the six-wheelers (6 × 4 and 6 × 6) first, followed by the eight-wheelers (8 × 6 and 8 × 8).

Truck, 13-ton, 6 × 6, HET   I
(Astra BM20NF1)

6-cyl. 13.8-litre diesel engine (Fiat 8210) with 6F1R gearbox and 2-speed transfer box. Double-reduction axles with hub reduction. Air brakes. Wheelbase 4135 mm. Overall dimensions 8300 × 2500 × 3215 mm. Weight 13100 kg. Amplicar T25 hydraulic loading platform for hauling M113 and similar tracked vehicles.

Truck, 40-ton, 8 × 6, HET   F
(PRP/Creusot Loire T40A)

Ultra-heavy chassis with 320-kW diesel engine (DB OM404) and 8-speed transmission. 18.00-25 tyres. Overall dimensions 11600 × 3620 × 3350 mm. Weight 34500 kg. Ampliroll hydraulic system (by Bennes Marrel) with 6000 × 3100 mm platform that could be lowered at the rear to ground level.

Truck, Tractor, 6 × 6, HET   F
(Berliet TBD)

6-cyl. 8.8-litre turbocharged diesel engine with 6F1R gearbox and 2-speed transfer box with lockable differential for full-time all-wheel drive. Hub reduction axles. 37.5 tons GCW derivative from GBD 6 × 6 truck, used with various semi-trailers for transporting AFVs and Engineers' plant and equipment.

Truck, Tractor, 6 × 6, HET   F
(Berliet TBH280)

6-cyl. 12-litre diesel engine (MDS 06.35.40) with 9F1R gearbox and 2-speed transfer box. 28.8-ton tandem with inter-axle diff. lock. 20-in. wheels. Wheelbase 4650 mm. Twin hydraulic winches behind cab, capacity 15000 kg each. Militarized commercial tractor, as relatively low-cost tank-transporter tractor. 1975.

Truck, Tractor, 6 × 4, HET   F
(Berliet TRH350 6 × 4 TS)

V-8-cyl. 14.9-litre diesel engine (MIVS 08.35.30) with Fuller RTO-12513 13F2R gearbox and dual-ratio tandem axles with hub reduction. Wheelbase 3625 mm. Weight 10300 kg. GCW 70500 kg. Shown with 55-ton semi-trailer. Strategic tank transporter, adopted by the French Army in the late 1970s.

Truck, Tractor, 6 × 4, HET   NL
(DAF FTT3500DDTR450)

V-12-cyl. 13.9-litre diesel engine (Detroit Diesel 12V71N65) with Allison semi-automatic 6F1R transmission. Kirkstall axles. Trilex wheels with 14.00-24 tyres. Wheelbase 4500 mm. 2600-type tiltable cab. 2 produced experimentally in the early 1970s. Only the semi-trailer (DAF YTS10050) was produced in quantity.

Truck, Tractor, 6 × 4, HET   E
(Dodge C3464)

6-cyl. 11.9-litre turbocharged diesel engine (BS36) with 8F2R (BS26) or 9F2R (Fuller RTO-9509A) transmission. Spanish Dodge 300-Series truck (previously Barreiros). Military version (R3464) used for towing medium and heavy semi-trailers, carrying Engineers' equipment and tanks respectively. 1981 chassis/cab shown.

Truck, Tractor, 6 × 4, HET   D
(Faun HZ32.25/40 6 × 4)

V-10-cyl. 14.7-litre aircooled diesel engine (Deutz F10L 413F) with 15F3R transmission (Fuller RT-12515). Other power plants available. Wheelbase 4100 mm. GVW 34000 kg. GCW 90000 kg. Tropicalized and militarized commercial tractor unit, 250 of which were supplied to Egypt from 1978 with 50-ton semi-trailers.

Truck, Tractor, 6 × 6, HET   D
(Faun HZ32.25/40 6 × 6)

V-10-cyl. 14.7-litre aircooled diesel engine (Deutz F10L 413F) with 15F3R transmission (Fuller RT-12515) and single-speed transfer box. Wheelbase 4100 mm. Overall width and height 2500 × 2900 mm. Chassis/cab weight 10600 kg. GCW 100 000 kg. Militarized commercial truck for Middle East.

Truck, Tractor, 6 × 6, HET
(Fiat 330PTM35)

V-8-cyl. 17.2-litre diesel engine (8280.02) with torque converter. Separately-mounted 8F1R gearbox-cum-transfer box with lockable differential. Hub reduction axles. 3 diff. locks in tandem. Wheelbase 4540 mm. Weight 12200 kg. Fifth wheel load 20000 kg. Suitable for hauling tanks of up to 50 tons. 1982.

Truck, Tractor, 6 × 6, HET   I
(Fiat 320PTM45 – Sand Version)

V-8-cyl. 17.2-litre turbocharged diesel engine (8280.22) with torque converter, 8F1R gearbox and transfer box with lockable differential. Hub reduction axles with 14.00-24 tyres front, 24-20.5 rear (standard version: 14.00-20 all round). Wheelbase 4290 mm. Weight 14500 kg. GVW 34500 kg. 1982.

Truck, Tractor, 6 × 6, HET   RA
(Fiat Concord 697BT)

6-cyl. 13.8-litre diesel engine with 8F2R gearbox. Hub reduction axles. Air brakes. Wheelbase 3910 mm. Tractor variant of 697BN artillery prime mover. Developed in Argentina from commercial 697N-T 6 × 4 truck, for Argentine Army. Used with various types of semi-trailers for transport of tanks and heavy equipment. 1970s.

Truck, Tractor, 6 × 4, HET   **GB**
(Foden Super Haulmaster)

Cummins NTC400 diesel engine with torque converter and Foden 8-speed gearbox. Air brakes. 12.00-20 tyres. 32.5-ton tandem bogie with rubber suspension. Coupled to 60-ton tri-axle semi-trailer with rocker beam suspension and dual 12.00R20XZY tyres. Sleeper cab was steel tilting type, seating 4. 1970s.

Truck, Tractor, 6 × 4, HET   **NL**
(FTF MS4050/F-8-28D)

Detroit Diesel 12V71N diesel engine with Allison torque converter and 6F1R semi-auto. gearbox with torquematic retarder. Trilex wheels with 14.00-24 tyres. Wheelbase 4200 mm. Overall length and width 7480 × 2800 mm. Weight 16265 kg. 2 winches. 39 produced for the Netherlands Army, early 1970s.

Truck, Tractor, 6 × 4, HET   **GB**
(Leyland Contractor)

Cummins NTK335 6-cyl. turbocharged diesel engine with RV30 8-speed air-operated semi auto. transmission. 30-ton rear bogie. Supplied to Australian Army and shown here (in 1974) with tri-axle low-bed semi-trailer with collapsible gooseneck for front loading. Manufactured by Leyland's Scammell division.

Truck, Tractor, 6 × 4, HET   **GB**
(Leyland Crusader)

Rolls-Royce Eagle 12.17-litre diesel engine with 15F3R gearbox. Hub reduction tandem axles. Wheelbase 3962 mm. Length and width 6200 × 2500 mm. 130 ordered by British Army in 1978 for towing Crane Fruehauf 35-ton RE plant semi-trailer. Commercial Scammell-built tractor with 'night cab' and 8-ton Plumett winch.

Truck, Tractor, 6 × 6, HET   **USA**
(Mack RM600 Series)

RM-Series Macks had set-back front axle and full-time all-wheel drive with lockable differential in transfer box (1/3-2/3 torque proportioning). Basically a commercial tractor truck, some were employed for tank hauling, the example shown, with 5-axle semi-trailer, being in service with the South African armed forces. 1981.

Truck, Tractor, 6 × 6, HET   **D**
(Magirus-Deutz 310D34AS 6 × 6)

Deutz F10L 413L V-10-cyl. 14.7-litre aircooled diesel engine with torque converter, 8-speed gearbox and 2-speed transfer box. Tyres 14.00R20 front, 24-20.5XS rear. Wheelbase 4725 mm. Overall dimensions 7715 × 2500 × 2970 mm. Weight 13020 kg. Late 1970s.

Truck, Tractor, 6 × 6, HET D
(Magirus-Deutz 400M34AS 6 × 6)

V-10-cyl. 15.9-litre aircooled diesel engine (Deutz BF10L 413F) with torque converter, 8F1R gearbox and 2-speed transfer box. Tyres 14.00R20 front, 24-20.5 rear (sand tyres). Wheelbase 4725 mm. Overall dimensions 7715 × 2500 × 2970 mm. Weight 13150 kg. GVW 34150 kg. GCW 87150 kg. Late 1970s.

Truck, Tractor, 6 × 6, HET D
(MAN 22.304DFSA)

V-8-cyl. 15.4-litre diesel engine (D2858M1) with 9F1R gearbox and 2-speed transfer box. Wheelbase 2950 mm. Overall dimensions 7470 × 2520 × 2930 mm. Weight 16700 kg. 29 used by Belgian Army, with DAF YTS10050 55-ton semi-trailer. Combination length 16730 mm. Weight 31840 kg. 1972.

Truck, Tractor, 6 × 6, HET J
(Mitsubishi W120 Series)

V-8-cyl. 13.27-litre diesel engine (8DC20W) with 5F1R gearbox and 2-speed transfer box. Wheelbase 4000 mm. Overall dimensions 6680 × 2400 × 2760 mm. GVW 20250 kg. GCW 40000 kg. Fifth wheel load 11000 kg. Militarized commercial tractor unit, used by Japanese Army with open and closed cab. From 1970.

Truck, Tractor, 6 × 6, HET B
(MOL T5266-05)

6-cyl. 18.8-litre turbocharged diesel engine (Cummins KT450) with 8F4R auto. trans. (Clark). Hub reduction axles with 29.5-25 sand-rib tyres. Wheelbase 5000 mm. Overall dimensions 8800 × 3340 × 3800 mm. Weight 21300 kg. 6-seat cab. Coupled to MOL 60-ton semi-trailer. 1983.

Truck, Tractor, 6 × 6, HET F
(Nicolas Tractomas)

V-12-cyl. turbocharged diesel engine (Daimler-Benz OM404A) with ZF Transmatic 8F1R transmission. Hub reduction axles. Wheelbase 4475 mm. One of a wide range of tank-transporter tractors (including 8 × 8 models) with matching semi-trailers offered by Nicolas of Champs/Yonne, France, in the early 1980s.

Truck, Tractor, 6 × 4, HET GB
(Scammell Commander)

V-12-cyl. turbocharged diesel engine (Rolls-Royce CV12TCE) with Allison 6-speed automatic gearbox. Hub reduction tandem axles. 24-in. wheels. Wheelbase 5030 mm. Overall dimensions 9010 × 3150 × 3500 mm. Weight 19920 kg. British Army's HET for the 1980s, with suitable semi-trailer for tanks of up to 65 tons.

TRUCK, 22.5-TON, TRACTOR, 8 × 6 (OSHKOSH F2365/M911)　　　USA

General Data: Officially known as 'Truck Tractor, Commercial, Heavy Equipment Transporter (C-HET), 85000 GVWR, 8 × 6, M911' this was basically a commercial 6 × 6 tractor with pusher axle, derived from the Oshkosh J2065 (XM911). In the mid-1970s, the US Army ordered 1000 units for use with M747 4-axle semi-trailers. This happened after the Army had bought 125 M746 8 × 8 tractors, the Oshkosh product being considerably less costly. The first units were completed in late 1977.

Technical Details: Detroit Diesel 8V92TA-90 V-8-cyl. turbo-charged diesel engine, 12060 cc (123 × 127 mm), 325 kW/ 435 bhp (SAE) at 2100 rpm. Allison TC499 torque converter and 5F1R auto. trans. (CLBT-750) with Fuller 2-speed auxiliary gearbox and Oshkosh single-speed transfer box with lockable differential. Eaton tandem axles. Axle gear ratios 6.143:1 front, 6.21:1 rear. Air brakes. Leaf springs front, Hendrickson spring-type suspension rear. 14.00-24 tyres. 24-Volt electrics. 570-litre fuel capacity.

Dimensions and Weights: Wheelbase 5969 mm (to centre of tandem). Overall dimensions 9373 × 2896 × 3280 mm. Ground clearance 360 mm (axles). Angle of approach 28°. Weight 18138 kg, GVW 39022 kg. GCW rating 87146 kg.

above: pusher axle raised; *below:* with M747 semi-trailer

Truck, Tractor, 6 × 4, HET   **S**
(Scania LT110S42A)

6-cyl. 11-litre diesel engine (DS11R01B) with 5F1R gearbox and 2-speed transfer box. Air brakes. Wheelbase 4860 mm. Weight 13560 kg. 2 hydraulic 20-ton winches. Known as 'Dragbil 851MT'. Coupled to Kalmar/DAF YTS10050S 48-ton semi-trailer (791MT). Combination length and width 16968 × 3400 mm. Late 1960s.

Truck, Tractor, 8 × 6, HET   **USA**
(AMG/CCC M920)

6-cyl. 14-litre turbocharged diesel engine (Cummins NTC400) with 16F2R semi-auto. trans. Rockwell tandem and pusher axle with raising system. Wheelbase 5359 mm. Overall dimensions 8110 × 2440 × 3250 mm. Weight 12414 kg. GVW 34019 kg. GCW 61235 kg. Used by US Army from 1978.

Truck, Tractor, 8 × 6, HET   **D**
(Faun FS42.75/42 8 × 6)

V-12-cyl. 19.1-litre aircooled diesel engine (Deutz BF12L 413FC) with torque-converter and 8-speed gearbox, permanently driving axles 1, 3 and 4. (Optional: 8 × 8 and MTU V8 with Allison auto. trans.) Wheelbase 4200 mm (8 × 8 4700 mm). Introduced in 1981, with 6-axle semi-trailer as 'austere' version of the SLT50-2 'Elefant'.

Truck, Tractor, 8 × 6, HET   **D**
(Magirus-Deutz 310D34FAS 8 × 6 × 4)

V-12-cyl. 16.9-litre aircooled diesel engine (Deutz F12L 413) with torque converter, 5F1R gearbox and 2-speed transfer box with lockable differential. 14.00-20 tyres. Wheelbase 2650 + 1380 + 1380 mm. Overall length and width 7700 × 2500 mm. Weight 14900 kg. Supplied in the early 1970s to an African country.

Truck, Tractor, 8 × 8, HET   **SU**
(MAZ-537)

V-12-cyl. 38.3-litre diesel engine (D-12-A-375) with torque converter and 3F1R planetary transmission with 2-speed transfer box. Hub reduction axles. Air/hydraulic brakes. 18.00-24 tyres. Wheelbase (overall) 6050 mm. Overall dimensions 8960 × 2885 × 3100 mm. Weight 21600 kg. Coupled to 50-ton semi-trailer.

Truck, Tractor, 8 × 8, HET   **USA**
(Oshkosh DA3858-2)

V-8-cyl. 12-litre diesel engine (Detroit Diesel 8V92TA) with 4F1R auto. trans. (Allison) and 2-speed transfer box with lockable differential. Steering No. 1 axle. Wheelbase 5615 mm. Overall dimensions 9830 × 2438 × 2591 mm. Weight 18144 kg. GCW 85277 kg. 27-ton winch. Articulated frame. 1982.

TRUCK, 19-TON, 8 × 8, TRACTOR (FAUN SLT50-2 'ELEFANT')   D

General Data: In the late 1960s, when Germany and the USA were collaborating in the design of a new 'Main Battle Tank for the 1970s' (MBT 70), a common design was also drawn up for a transporter, the HET 70 (or SLT 70). This comprised an 8 × 8 tractor truck and an 8-wheel all-wheel-steer semi-trailer. Faun-Werke developed it in Germany, Chrysler Corp. in the USA. Faun-Werke were contracted for 324 tractors (SLT50-2).

Technical Details: MTU/MB837Ea-500 V-8-cyl. diesel engine, 29920 cc (165 × 175 mm), 537 kW/730 bhp (DIN) at 2100 rpm. ZF W500-10 torque converter with Hydromedia 4PW200H2 automatic 4F2R transmission. 2-speed transfer box with lockable differential. 10.24:1 axle gear ratio. Differential locks in and between axles. Air brakes. Semi-elliptic leaf springs and equalizing beams. 18-22.5XS tyres. 24-Volt electrics. 800-litre fuel tank. Twin 17-ton hydraulic winches.

Dimensions and Weights: Wheelbase 4200 mm. Track, front/rear 2535/2593 mm. Overall length and width 8830 × 3070 mm. Height 2795 mm (cab roof). Ground clearance 303 mm (axles). Angles of approach and departure 30° and 50°. Weight 23200 kg, GVW 43000 kg. GCW 92000 kg.

above: tractor; *below:* with semi-trailer

TRUCK, 22.5-TON, 8 × 8, TRACTOR (WARD LAFRANCE M746)   USA

General Data: The sophisticated 8 × 8 tractor truck, M746, and 4-axle 60-ton semi-trailer, M747, were designed in the late 1960s in conjunction with West Germany to transport the projected MBT 70. Dubbed HET 70, the US M746/M747 combination was developed by Chrysler Corporation. The MBT 70 did not materialize but Ward LaFrance was awarded a contract for the production of 125 units of the tractor truck. These were built during 1973–76. During 1977–78 another 68 units were built for Morocco.

Technical Details: Detroit Diesel 12V71T V-12-cyl. turbocharged diesel engine, 13962 cc (107.95 × 127 mm), 448 kW/600 bhp (SAE) at 2500 rpm. Twin Disc TAD-51-2012 powershift 5F1R transmission. Single-speed transfer box with locking differential. Rockwell double-reduction axles (no-spin differential in rear axles). Air brakes. Taper leaf bogie suspension. 18.00-22.5 tyres. 24-Volt electrics. 532-litre fuel tank.

Dimensions and Weights: Wheelbase 4200 mm. Track 2576 mm. Overall length and width 8230 × 3048 mm. Height 3048 mm (cab roof). Ground clearance 329 mm (axles). Angle of approach 30°. Weight 20430 kg. GVW 39044 kg. GCW 68950 kg. Max. length with M747 semi-trailer 18440 mm.

above: M746; *below:* M746/M747 HET

Tractors and Wreckers

Tractors and wreckers are vehicles used principally for towing other vehicles and equipment. The armed forces employ a multitude of different types, ranging from mundane agricultural-type tractors to sophisticated purpose-built machines for recovering and evacuating damaged or otherwise defective material.

The tractors shown in this chapter are presented in alphabetical order, by make. Some are common enough, whilst others are seldom seen away from their place of work, e.g. those which are designed and used specifically for the towing of aircraft on airfields (or on aircraft carriers). Others, exemplified by the large British Douglas Tugmaster 111/TT, are employed for the shunting of immobilized heavy tracked vehicles like tanks at workshops where these vehicles are repaired and overhauled and cannot move under their own power. Also shown is a typical 'terminal tractor', used for the manoeuvring of semi-trailers, especially on and off RoRo (roll-on, roll off) ships after they have been taken there by normal road-going tractor trucks, and vice versa. As a military vehicle, this is a relatively new phenomenon. In the early days, these tractors were specially constructed (in the US 4 × 4 units by FWD and Walter, for the handling of 30-ton container trailers) but later, when containerization and RoRo became more common, several companies started producing them in quantity. Most of these commercial terminal tractors have a short wheelbase, one-man cab with facilities for driving in either direction and a hydraulically-operated power-lift/fifth-wheel coupling. The latter feature enables the manoeuvring of loaded semi-trailers with the front end at a height where it is not necessary to adjust the landing gear, thus saving a great deal of time and effort.

Wreckers or recovery vehicles (in Britain also known as 'recovery tractors') are usually based on existing commercial- or military-pattern chassis/cabs, as just another body style variant. Sometimes a wrecker comprises a simple recovery crane on the back of a standard truck, but usually it is a specially-constructed vehicle, incorporating multipurpose lifting equipment, winches, recovery and repair tools, etc. There are three main types, all differing considerably but all with their own typical characteristics. First there is the twin-boom type which became so popular during the Second World War when the Ernest Holmes company built many thousands of them, chiefly on the ubiquitous Diamond T 4-ton 6 × 6 chassis. This design was introduced by Holmes at the time of the First World War and is still supplied today, by Holmes as well as other manufacturers in several countries. It features two hinged cable-suspended booms which can be used individually on the sides of the truck or, combined, at the rear. In recent years, the heavier types have also been made with extendible and power-operated booms. The second type is the hydraulic design. Essentially a modern and sophisticated edition of the swinging-boom type of the 1930s and 1940s, it was first made in great numbers in the 1950s on US military M-Series 6 × 6 chassis. Fully revolving, these cranes had hydraulic operation of all movements, controlled from a cabin mounted on the side and turning with the crane. Principal suppliers were Austin-Western and Garwood but they were also made, under licence, in other countries. These two, the twin-boom and the hydraulic revolving type, are by far the most numerous. Another, totally different type made its appearance in the 1960s and has been gaining in popularity ever since. Developed by Bärgningsbilar EKA of Sweden, it was a complete departure from all the established systems in that the lifting force was applied from beneath the casualty vehicle rather than from above it. Several versions, for light and heavy lifts, are available but all have a single lifting arm, raised by a hydraulic ram located towards the rear. Various attachments can be fitted to this arm, ranging from a rack to slide beneath the wheels of a disabled vehicle and lifting forks for heavier jobs to crane jib extensions for high-level work. Among the advantages of these EKA wreckers are a very low silhouette, clean uncluttered bodywork with neat lockers and full hydraulic actuation with the possibility of radio-control of all operations, enabling one man to single-handedly deal with extensive recovery problems. Several armies, including the British, have taken this equipment into service.

The development of the hydraulic articulated swinging-arm loading crane as made by HIAB and others, also had great influence on recovery work. The heavier types, as normally fitted to cargo trucks for self-loading/unloading, can easily cope with numerous recovery operations up to their rated lifting capacity. It is interesting to note that two of the latest US military wreckers, the Oshkosh-built 8 × 8 M984 and DA3858-4, both feature a midship-mounted cargo box with a 20-ton recovery winch and a hydraulic articulated crane (with lifting capacities of 16.6 and 18.7 ton/metre resp.) behind it. When not in use, these cranes can be neatly folded out of the way.

Tractor, 4 × 4, General Purpose   **F**
(Agrip ARD60)

4-cyl. 5.9-litre diesel engine (Berliet M420.30) with 5F1R gearbox and 2-speed transfer box. Optional 4-wheel steering (rear wheels could be locked). Wheelbase 2650 mm. Basically a multipurpose commercial model, made in Lignières, France. French Air Force used a more powerful version, with larger wheels and tyres.

Tractor, 4 × 4, Aircraft-Towing   **USA**
(American Coleman G-40-H)

4-cyl. 3.3-litre turbocharged diesel engine (Allis-Chalmers 433I) with 4-speed auto. trans. driving all wheels through a lockable differential. Independently controlled front- and rear-wheel steering. Wheelbase 2285 mm. Overall dimensions 4211 × 1990 × 2413 mm. Weight 4989 kg. USAF 1980 MB-4 type shown.

Tractor, 4 × 2, Aircraft-Towing   **I**
(ATA)

Powered by a Renault/Saviem engine, this aircraft tractor had a towing capacity of 2480 kg. Made in Modena, Italy, it was in service with the Belgian Air Force. Wheelbase 1590 mm. Overall length (without towing hooks) 2750 mm, width 1500 mm, height (with cab removed) 1480 mm. Max. speed 22 km/h. 1970s.

Tractor, 4 × 4, Multipurpose   **F**
(Brimont ETR206S)

6-cyl. diesel engine (Saviem 797) with 6F1R gearbox (ZF) and 2-speed transfer box. Portal axles. All-wheel steering. Articulating chassis. 500-litre loader bucket at the front (shown removed), hydraulic digger at the rear. Launched in 1979. Many variants available. French Air Force acquired 14 units.

Tractor, 4 × 4, Aircraft-Towing   **GB**
(Dennis Mercury Mk 1A and 1B)

V-8-cyl. diesel engine (Perkins) with powershift transmission. 2 steering axles with hub reduction. 14.00-25 tyres. Weight 22 tons. Towing capacity 300 tons. Some 80 units supplied to Royal Air Force. Mk 1A and 1B differed only in engine details. Dennis' Mercury branch was sold to Reliance, now Reliance-Mercury.

Tractor, 4 × 2, Aircraft-Towing   **GB**
(Douglas Taskmaster)

4-cyl. diesel engine (David Brown) with 6F2R dual-range transmission and hub reduction rear axle, all integral with engine. Tyres 6.00-16 front, 10.00-20 rear. Wheelbase 1828 mm. Overall length and width 3353 × 1778 mm. Weight 3150 kg. Maximum drawbar pull 2250 kg. Originally a David Brown design. Early 1970s.

TRACTORS AND WRECKERS

Tractor, 4 × 2, Aircraft-Towing   **GB**
(Douglas Super Taskmaster Mk II)

4-cyl. diesel engine (Perkins) with 3F3R powershift transmission. Wheelbase 2057 mm. Overall dimensions 3372 × 1829 × 2525 mm. Weight 5790 kg. Tyres 6.00-16 front, 10.00-20 rear. Used by the Netherlands Air Force, from 1978. Alternative roles included snow-clearing and runway-sweeping.

Tractor, 4 × 2, Terminal   **GB**
(Douglas Tugmaster NS8/180)

V-8-cyl. 8.8-litre diesel engine (Perkins 540) with Allison 2F2R powershift transmission. Double-reduction rear axle. Wheelbase 2743 mm. Weight 8650 kg. Hydraulically-elevated 25-ton capacity 5th wheel coupling. Used by British Army for handling semi-trailers on and off RoRo vessels at military ports.

Tractor, 4 × 4, Shunting   **GB**
(Douglas Tugmaster P111/TT)

V-8-cyl. 8.8-litre diesel engine (Perkins 540) with 4F4R powershift transmission. Single-speed transfer box. 14.00-24 tyres. Wheelbase 2286 mm. Weight 28448 kg. RB hydraulic winch at rear. Several were bought by the British Army, primarily for towing and shunting tanks and other heavy equipment at workshops.

Tractor, 4 × 4, Aircraft-Towing and -Starting   **DDR**
(IFA W50LA/A)

4-cyl. 6.56-litre diesel engine with 5F1R gearbox and 2-speed transfer box. Used by the Air Force of the East German NVA (National People's Army) this vehicle was equipped with a small gas turbine and two DC generators for starting jet aircraft engines. It was a straight modification of the makers' 3-ton 4 × 4 truck.

Tractor, 4 × 2, General Purpose   **USA**
(International 523)

3-cyl. 2.9-litre diesel engine (DD179) with 4F4R gearbox. Basically an agricultural model with safety cab, this tractor was taken into service by the Danish armed forces in the early 1970s, following examples of Model 276 (4-cyl.). Danish Air Force employed 12-ton IHC T180FB Paymover aircraft tractors with V8 petrol engine.

Tractor, 4 × 2, Aircraft-Towing   **D**
(Magirus-Deutz Orion)

V-12-cyl. 19-litre aircooled diesel engine (Deutz F12L 714A) with semi-automatic transmission (Voith Diwa), driving the rear wheels. Wheelbase 2570 mm. Overall dimensions 4760 × 2500 × 1850 mm. Weight 15050 kg. Used by the West German Air Force as *Radschlepper, schwer*. Max. speed 36 km/h.

Tractor, 4 × 2, Aircraft-Towing   **GB**
Massey-Ferguson MF50)

4-cyl. diesel engine (Perkins A4.212) with 'instant reverse' 4F4R torque converter transmission. Overall dimensions 3810 × 2133 × 2640 mm. Weight 4900 kg. Tyres 9.00-16 front, 16.9/14.28 rear. This aircraft tug, with 5-seat crew cab, was used by the British RAF for towing aircraft of up to 45360 kg.

Tractor, 4 × 2, Shunting   **GB**
(Massey-Ferguson MF50 'Shunter Tug')

4-cyl. diesel engine (Perkins A4.212) with 'instant reverse' 4F4R torque converter transmission. Overall dimensions 3835 × 2007 × 2381 mm. Weight 4900 kg. Maximum sustained drawbar pull 4082 kg. Pushing blade 2007 × 762 mm. Power-assisted steering. Radio suppressed. Maximum speed 30 km/h, forward and reverse.

Tractor, 4 × 4, Aircraft-Towing   **D**
(Mercedes-Benz MB Trac 65/70)

4-cyl. 3.78-litre diesel engine (OM314) with 4F1R gearbox and 4-speed auxiliary box, Portal axles with diff. locks. Wheelbase 2400 mm. Overall length and width 4170 × 2400 mm. Used by the Netherlands Air Force from 1976/77. Shown with 10.50-20 tyres for trials (normally 14.9-24) and Werner 6.2-ton winch.

Tractor, 4 × 4, Multipurpose   **D**
(Unimog 406)

6-cyl. 5.67-litre diesel engine (OM352) with 8F4R gearbox/transfer box. Portal axles with diff. locks. Wheelbase 2380 mm. Overall length and width 4100 × 2140 mm. GVW 5800 kg. Used by Belgian Air Force for aircraft- and trailer-towing (up to 27 tons) and for snow-clearing, sprinkling, etc.

Tractor/Carrier, 4 × 4   **SF**
(Valmet 865BM)

4-cyl. 4.18-litre diesel engine (411A) with 4F1R gearbox and 2-speed transfer box. Rigid axles with 18.4-26 tyres. Hydrostatic steering by articulation. Air-actuated disc brakes. Wheelbase 3270 mm. Overall length and width 7060 × 2370 mm. Weight 6250 kg. Hydraulic winch. Used by the Finnish Army from 1969.

Tractor, 4 × 4, Aircraft-Towing   **S**
(Volvo F85 4 × 4)

6-cyl. 5.1-litre diesel engine (TD50B) with powershift transmission with torque converter (Clark). Single-reduction axles with diff. locks. Air brakes. Wheelbase 2640 mm. Overall dimensions 5250 × 2340 × 2650 mm. Weight 6070 kg. Speed range 3–70 km/h. In service with the Swedish Air Force from the mid-1970s.

225

Truck, 4 × 2, Wrecker   **USA**
(Dodge D600)

V-8-cyl. 5.2-litre petrol engine with 5F1R gearbox. Wheelbase 4445 mm. Standard commercial Dodge 2.5-ton 4 × 2 chassis/cab of 1975 with No-Mar Retriever 5D10 twin boom wrecker equipment supplied by E.R. Buske of Pocahontas, Iowa, for the US Army. Photo was taken in Vicenza, Italy, in 1976.

Truck, 4 × 2, Wrecker   **USA**
(GMC 6000 Series)

V-8-cyl. petrol engine with 5F1R gearbox (other engines and gearboxes available). Equipped with No-Mar Model 5D10 twin-boom equipment this vehicle was supplied in 1976 to the US Army. Official nomenclature was 'Truck, Wrecker, 16000 GVW, 4 × 2'. Chassis serial was TCE616V590328.

Truck, 4 × 2, Wrecker   **USA**
(GMC 6500 Series)

V-8-cyl. petrol engine with 5F1R gearbox (other power train combinations were available). Supplied to the US Marine Corps in 1973 and 1974 (shown) with twin-boom wrecker equipment by Weld-Built Body Co. Official nomenclature was 'Truck, Wrecker, 24000 GVW, 4 × 2', indicating a GVW of 10896 kg.

Truck, 4 × 2, Wrecker   **USA**
(Mack R-Series)

Conventional chassis/cab with Holmes 600 twin-boom wrecker gear of 16-ton rating (this rating was based on structural factors only and did not indicate load, cable strength or vehicle capability). Body was of the 'Continental' style, also by Dover Corporation's Holmes Division. Supplied in 1977 to an African military customer.

Truck, 4 × 4, Wrecker   **E**
(Ebro E70/1)

4-cyl. 3.86-litre diesel engine (Perkins 4.236) with 4F1R gearbox and 2-speed transfer box. Wheelbase 2935 mm. Overall length and width 5130 × 1988 mm. Weight 4400 kg. GVW 7000 kg. 3-seat tilt cab. Light recovery crane with manual control. Power winch at front. Supplied to Government of Madagascar in 1978.

Truck, 4 × 4, Wrecker   **BR**
(Engesa EE-25)

6-cyl. 5.67-litre diesel engine (Mercedes-Benz OM 352A) with 5F1R gearbox and 2-speed transfer box. Wheelbase 4200 mm. Air/hydraulic brakes. Brazilian truck with unusual lifting equipment, comprising manually-operated telescopic boom and vertical lift for suspended tows. Horizontal drum winch.

Truck, 4 × 4, Wrecker   **GB**
(Foden 4 × 4)
6-cyl. diesel engine (Rolls-Royce) with 9F1R gearbox and 2-speed transfer box. Kirkstall axles. Air brakes. Wheelbase 4250 mm. GVW 16260 kg. 24-Volt electrics. Holmes 750 wrecker equipment (supplied by Crane Fruehauf) with twin extension booms (rated at 11350 kg each), heavy-duty tow hitch, snatch blocks, etc.

Truck, 4 × 4, Wrecker   **DDR**
(IFA W50/LA/AB)
4-cyl. 6.5-litre diesel engine with 5F1R gearbox and 2-speed transfer box. Wheelbase 3200 mm. 9.00-20 tyres, dual rear. Hydraulic crane and recovery equipment by VEB Specialfahrzeug-bau Löbau, 1976. Maximum lifting capacity (using outriggers) 6300 kg. Maximum hook height 4000 mm.

Truck, 4 × 4, Wrecker   **USA**
(International Loadstar 1600 4 × 4)
No-Mar Model 5D10 Retriever twin-boom wrecker equipment on commercial International swb chassis/cab for the US Marine Corps. The USMC also used the somewhat heavier 1700 4 × 4 chassis with the same wheelbase, fitted with dump body. Engine was the IHC V-345 petrol unit, with 4- or 5-speed gearbox.

Truck, 4 × 4, Wrecker   **USA**
(Oshkosh P-Series)
Holmes Model 750 twin-boom wrecker on a comparatively unusual chassis in the form of a 4-wheel drive Oshkosh with large sand tyres. It was produced in 1977 for the armed forces of an undisclosed country in the Middle East. The Holmes 750 was rated at 25 tons (based on structural factors only).

Truck, 4 × 4, Wrecker   **F**
(Saviem SM8)
6-cyl. diesel engine with 5F1R gearbox and 2-speed transfer box. Wheelbase 3500 mm. GVW 9100 kg. Holmes twin-boom recovery equipment. Limited-scale military application, also with Model 812 all-steel cab, 1979. The Saviem SM8 was also available with Model 815 Torpedo softtop military-pattern cab.

Truck, 4 × 4, Wrecker   **S**
(Volvo F88 4 × 4)
6-cyl. 9.6-litre diesel engine (TD100A) with 8F1R gearbox and 2-speed transfer box. Hub reduction axles with diff. locks. 14.00-20 tyres. Wheelbase 4200 mm. Overall dimensions 7100 × 2490 × 3050 mm. Weight 12480 kg. EKA C/D10-15 recovery equipment with 7- and 20-ton winch plus HIAB 550 crane. 1973/74.

Truck, 6 × 4, Wrecker   **USA**
(Dodge CT700)

V-8-cyl. 5.9-litre petrol engine with 10F1R gearbox. Commercial Dodge 'Low Cab Forward' (LCF) truck as produced for many years, starting in 1960 and continuing until the mid-1970s. Shown is a Weld-Built twin-boom wrecker on this chassis, operated by the US Marine Corps in Japan in the early 1970s.

Truck, 6 × 4, Wrecker   **USA**
(International F1850)

The 6 × 4 IHC Loadstar chassis was used for several wreckers. Shown is a diesel-engined example, equipped by Weld-Built and officially known as 'Truck, Wrecker, 34500 GVW, 6 × 4'. It was delivered to the US Army in 1973. Similar wreckers were supplied by Holmes (Model 750M) and E.R. Buske (No-Mar Model 12D24).

Truck, 6 × 4, Wrecker   **GB**
(Leyland/Scammell Crusader)

6-cyl. turbocharged diesel engine (Rolls-Royce Eagle 305 Mk 3) with 15F3R gearbox (range-change). Hub reduction tandem axles. Air brakes. Wheelbase 4590 mm. Overall dimensions 8370 × 2980 × 3280 mm. Swedish EKA D2030B single lift boom with 7.5-ton capacity. 7-ton front winch, 20-ton main winch.

Truck, 6 × 4, Wrecker   **USA**
(Mack R685ST)

Based on a Mack R-Series 6 × 4 conventional chassis (with centre-mounted cab as opposed to the DM- and U-Series' off-set type) this unit belonged to a large fleet of Holmes wreckers supplied to the armed forces of an African country in 1977. The wrecker gear was of the 25-ton rating type (Model 750).

Truck, 6 × 6, Wrecker   **GB**
(AEC Militant Mk 3/FV11044)

6-cyl. diesel engine (AV760) with 6F1R gearbox and 2-speed transfer box. Wheelbase 3924 mm. Overall length and width 8230 × 2500 mm. Weight 21000 kg. Hydraulic crane by Coles. Officially known as 'Recovery Vehicle, Wheeled, Medium'. Slewing angle 240°. Maximum hook height 6706 mm. British Army.

Truck, 6 × 6, Wrecker   **F**
(ALM/ACMAT VLRA TPK6.40WRT)

6-cyl. 5.8-litre diesel engine (Perkins 6.354.4) with 5F1R gearbox and 2-speed transfer box. Wheelbase 4100 mm. Overall dimensions 7910 × 2460 × 2650 mm. Weight 10500 kg. HAP 2860T7 5-ton hydraulic wrecker equipment with hydraulic outriggers. Maximum hook height 6600 mm. Produced in the early 1980s.

Truck, 6 × 6, Wrecker USA
(AMG M816)

6-cyl. 14-litre diesel engine (Cummins NHC250) with 5F1R gearbox and 2-speed transfer box. Wheelbase 4547 mm. Overall dimensions 9049 × 2500 × 2896 mm. Weight 16385 kg. Revolving hydraulic crane with extendible boom. Cross-country load of 3178 kg on boom hook, 5448 kg during highway operation. 1970s.

Truck, 6 × 6, Wrecker GB
(Bedford MK)

Modified commercial Bedford M-type 4 × 4 chassis/cab, converted to 6 × 6 by Reynolds Boughton and equipped by the same firm with 3- to 6-ton capacity twin-boom wrecker gear, front winch and ancillary equipment. Supplied for export to Uganda, through the British Crown Agents, in the mid-1970s.

Truck, 6 × 6, Wrecker F
(Berliet TBD)

6-cyl. 8.8-litre turbocharged diesel engine (MIDS 06.20.30) with 6F1R gearbox and 2-speed transfer box. 14.00-20XL tyres. Overall dimensions 8810 × 2400 × 2974 mm. Weight 19375 kg. 12-ton Pinguely hydraulic crane. 4.5-ton front winch, 15- to 18-ton rear winch. Later redesignated Renault TRM9000.

Truck, 6 × 6, Wrecker H
(Csepel D-566)

6-cyl. diesel engine (Rába-MAN 2156HM6/01) with 6F1R gearbox and 2-speed transfer box. 20-in. wheels, all independently suspended with torsion bars. Wheelbase 3600 mm. Hinged land anchor for heavy winching and recovery operations. Short lifting jib at the rear. Mid-mounted revolving jib with block and tackle.

Truck, 6 × 6, Wrecker I
(Fiat 6605AG)

6-cyl. 13.8-litre diesel engine (8212.02) with 8F2R gearbox and 2-speed transfer box with lockable differential. Hub reduction axles. Wheelbase 3900 mm. Overall length and width 7350 × 2500 mm. 14-ton crane by ISOLI, Model M140. Hydraulically-operated fully-revolving crane with telescopic boom. Produced in 1982.

Truck, 6 × 6, Wrecker I
(Fiat 6605DM)

6-cyl. 13.8-litre diesel engine (8212.02) with 8F2R gearbox and 2-speed transfer box with lockable differential. Hub reduction axles. Wheelbase 3900 mm. Overall length and width 8627 × 2500 mm. Weight 17100 kg. 9200-kg front winch. 20000-kg rear winch. Hydraulic telescopic boom crane, 360° rotation. 1974.

Truck, 6 × 6, Wrecker   **GB**
(Foden 6 × 6)

6-cyl. diesel engine (Rolls-Royce Eagle) with 9F1R overdrive-top gearbox. Chassis as Foden medium-mobility truck (FH70 tractor, etc.), fitted with Swedish EKA recovery equipment with hydraulically-operated jib, lifting bar, 40-ton winch, hydraulic stiff legs, etc. Only a few were built, c.1980.

Truck, 6 × 6, Wrecker   **CDN**
(Foremost HDW)

6-cyl. diesel engine (Detroit Diesel 6-71-T; Cummins NT270 optional) with 6F1R powershift transmission (Allison) and 2-speed transfer/auxiliary box (Dana). Wheelbase 4826 mm. Overall dimensions 8737 × 2667 × 3429 mm. Weight 21300 kg. 10-ton swinging boom crane. 20-ton recovery winch. Prototype, 1979.

Truck, 6 × 6, Wrecker   **USA**
(GMC 7500 Series)

Typical example of commercial-type heavy wrecker as supplied to the US forces for service in various countries. This 1972 USAF model had Weld-Built equipment, including Model 6BHD bodywork but similar twin-boom wreckers were produced by Holmes and E.R. Buske (No-Mar) throughout the 1970s.

Truck, 6 × 6, Wrecker   **USA**
(International M6123-50)

Commercial IHC M-Series 6 × 6 chassis/cab with front winch, carrying twin-boom wrecker equipment by Weld-Built Body Co., for the USMC in 1972 ('Truck, Wrecker, 44000 GVW, 6 × 6'). The US Air Force used diesel-engined 6 × 4 tractor trucks from IHC's M-Series with 20-ton low-bed semi-trailers.

Truck, 6 × 6, Wrecker   **AUS**
(International Mk V)

6-cyl. twin-carburettor petrol engine with 5F1R gearbox and 2-speed transfer box. Air/hydraulic brakes. Wheelbase 3772 mm. Australian-designed and -built truck which appeared with various body types (as well as 4 × 4 version). Wrecker had Holmes twin-boom outfit. Photo was taken at Colo River, NSW, in 1975.

Truck, 6 × 6, Wrecker   **USA**
(Kenworth 6 × 6)

This exceptionally large vehicle was built in the mid-1970s for a military customer in the Middle East. It carried Holmes Model 850 wrecker equipment. Each boom could be raised by power under full load. Due to the height above ground it had a special operator's platform behind the cab for controlling movements.

Truck, 6 × 6, Wrecker USA
(Mack RM600 Series)

Introduced in 1972 the Mack RM range comprised all-wheel-drive trucks (RM400 4 × 4 and RM600 6 × 6). Both had full-time all-wheel drive with a central differential in the transfer box. Shown is a late-1970s chassis with Holmes Model 750 wrecker equipment, delivered to an undisclosed African military customer.

Truck, 6 × 6, Wrecker D
(Mercedes-Benz 2626A/41)

V-8-cyl. 12.76-litre diesel engine (OM402) with 5F1R gearbox (ZF) and 2-speed transfer box. Wheelbase 4100 mm. Fitted with Holmes 750X7H wrecker equipment with twin hydraulic booms and French Titan bodywork. Supplied to Iraq in 1978. Similar chassis (2626 and 2632) fitted with other wrecker gear.

Truck, 6 × 6, Wrecker D
(Mercedes-Benz LA2624)

6-cyl. 11.6-litre diesel engine (OM355V) with 6F1R gearbox and 2-speed transfer box. Wheelbase 4270 mm. GVW 24000 kg. Fitted with MFL hydraulic crane with telescopic boom, fully-revolving. One of 2 supplied to NATO Northag HQ forces in Germany in the early 1970s. Same chassis/cab also with Kirsten crane.

Truck, 6 × 6, Wrecker E
(Pegaso 3050)

6-cyl. 10.17-litre diesel engine (9100/40) with 6F1R gearbox and 2-speed transfer box. Wheelbase 3987 mm. Hydraulic telescopic crane by Bazan-Onara for Spanish Army, 1970s. Recovery winch located behind cab. 6-ton winch below front bumper. A similar but heavier model was the GT10/10 by Luna Gruas Hidraulicas, 1982.

Truck, 6 × 6, Wrecker F
(Renault GBH280 6 × 6 TS)

6-cyl. diesel engine (MDS 06.35.40) with 8F1R gearbox (ZF) and 2-speed transfer box. Wheelbase 4725 mm. Weight 21565 kg. Pinguely GIC136 hydraulic revolving crane, capacity 15000 kg. 2-section telescoping boom, maximum length 6630 mm, slewing over 360°. 20/27-ton hydraulic winch at rear. 1981.

Truck, 6 × 6, Wrecker GB
(Scammell Super Constructor)

6-cyl. turbocharged diesel engine (Rolls-Royce C6TFL) with fluid coupling, 8F2R semi-automatic overdrive gearbox and single-speed transfer box. Suspension with coil springs front, walking beams rear. Unit shown, with Boughton recovery equipment, delivered to Dubai Government in 1974.

231

TRACTORS AND WRECKERS

Truck, 6 × 6, Wrecker   **ZA**
(Samil 100)

V-10-cyl. aircooled diesel engine (Deutz) with 6F1R gearbox and 2-speed transfer box. Hub reduction axles. Wheelbase 5940 mm. Overall dimensions 9350 × 2500 × 4100 mm. Twin-boom wrecker. Large recovery winch on rear deck. Similar equipment on Samil 50 4 × 4, both made in South Africa in the early 1980s.

Truck, 6 × 6, Wrecker   **S**
(Scania SBAT111)

6-cyl. 11-litre turbocharged diesel engine (D11LB28) with automatic 6F1R gearbox and 2-speed transfer box. Air brakes. Wheelbase 4290 mm. Horizontal-spindle self-recovery winch on right-hand side of chassis. Multipurpose recovery equipment, hydraulic lift and bodywork by EKA. Lifting capacity 16 tons.

Truck, 6 × 6, Wrecker   **A**
(Steyr 1490.320/K33)

V-8-cyl. 12-litre turbocharged diesel engine (WD815.70) with 5F1R gearbox and 2-speed transfer box. Wheelbase 4025 mm. Introduced in the late 1970s. Wrecker equipment by Rau of Germany, 1978. Designated R6002TS, it had a maximum lifting capacity of 12 tons (9.5 tons when travelling). Swing area 270°.

Truck, 6 × 6, Wrecker   **S**
(Volvo N1233)

Swedish EKA System D wrecker with hydraulic lift and winch, as well as hydraulic crane (behind cab) on normal-control Volvo N12 6 × 6 chassis with 6-cyl. 12-litre turbocharged engine. This vehicle was a prototype, tested by the Belgian Army in 1982/83 as possible replacement for M543 and Berliet TBU15CLD.

Truck, 8 × 8, Wrecker   **H**
(Csepel D-588)

6-cyl. 10.3-litre diesel engine (Rába-MAN) with 5F1R gearbox and 2-speed transfer box. Hub reduction gearing. Independently suspended wheels with 14.00-20 tyres. Central tyre-pressure regulating system. Heavy hydraulic telescopic crane on turntable. Hungarian production on extended Csepel D-566 chassis. 1970s.

Truck, 8 × 8, Wrecker   **USA**
(Oshkosh DS3838/M984)

In the early 1980s, Oshkosh launched two ranges of 8-wheelers, the articulated DA-Series and the rigid-frame DS, both including a recovery vehicle. The M984 featured a hydraulic crane and a rear-mounted recovery winch. When operating in the wrecker mode the lifting capacity was 11340 kg.

Fire, Crash and Snow-Fighting Vehicles

One of the few things which fire- and snow-fighters have in common is that the majority of them are operated on airfields. Ranging from simple appliances to high-tech purpose-built apparatus, there is a huge diversity of models in use by the world's air forces. Additional types, often very similar to the military ones, are used at civilian airfields, ranging from local strips to international airports.

Numerically, most fire tenders are intended to combat structural and brush fires. The armed forces use them at barracks, shooting ranges, camps, and other facilities. The more spectacular fire appliances are those designed to deal with aircraft accidents, usually crashes on or near airport runways. Although some of these vehicles are equipped only to provide first aid and rescue service, the larger ones are comprehensively-equipped for all aspects of saving lives and combating fire in the event of a crash. One of the most important requirements of a Crash/Fire/Rescue (CFR) truck is the speed at which it can reach the crashed plane. Both the travelling speed and the acceleration performance are stipulated in the order specification for the vehicle and some manufacturers manage to surpass them. In 1978 the USAF took delivery of their first 59 P15 units, their largest CFR vehicles so far. These huge vehicles, which fully loaded with nearly 25000 litres of water, 1960 litres of foam compound (AFFF), crew and standard equipment, each weigh 59410 kg, yet accelerate from 0 to 80 km/h in 48 seconds and travel at 80 km/h. Two turbocharged Detroit Diesel 8V92T engines, one at each end, each with automatic transmission and separate transfer box, provide the propulsion and power the two water and two foam pumps. The P15, built by Oshkosh, has a gradability and a side-slope stability of 50 per cent grade, can negotiate a 457-mm vertical obstacle and maintains a tractive effort with a simultaneous diagonally-opposite wheel motion of 508 mm. It measures 14275 × 3099 mm.

The Soviets, not to be outdone, constructed an 8 × 8 CFR truck in the early 1980s which measured 14285 × 3160 mm. Its normal service weight was less, at 42490 kg, but it carried only (!) 12000 litres of water and 900 litres of foam compound. Based on the MAZ-7310 chassis (a development from the old MAZ-537A, see chapter on eight-wheeled trucks), its 525-bhp V12 engine provided a maximum speed of 60 km/h.

The most widely-used crash tender chassis in Britain is the Nubian Major, the origins of which can be traced back to the Second World War and the Thornycroft-built Nubian 4 × 4 truck. After the war, this chassis was continued in production, mainly for fire and crash tender applications and a 6 × 6 variant was added in the early 1950s. Most of these chassis were Rolls-Royce-powered and they were sold all over the world. In 1964 the Cummins-powered larger-capacity Nubian Major was launched. When Thornycroft's new owners, Leyland, eventually sold the company's Basingstoke plant, Nubian production was transferred to the Scammell Motors plant in Watford, where in the late 1970s a new generation of CFR chassis was developed. These new chassis were of the modern rear-engine design and comprised five basic models: 4 × 4 Nubian 2 (300 bhp), Super Nubian (400 bhp) and Nubian RIV (Rapid Intervention Vehicle, 500 bhp) all with a GVW rating of up to 18290 kg, and 6 × 6 Nubian Major 2 (400 bhp) and Super Major (500 bhp) with GVW ratings of 26410 and 28450 kg respectively. All models were powered by developed versions of the Cummins V903-Series diesel engines, coupled to a five-speed Allison HT750DRD transmission. Transfer boxes and axles were of Kirkstall manufacture and the standard cab was a Motor Panels Mk IV pressed-steel unit. As with earlier Nubians, the bodywork and equipment was produced and fitted by outside specialist suppliers, e.g. Carmichael, Chubb, Gloster Saro and HCB-Angus.

In West Germany, Faun-Werke is a major supplier of CFR vehicle chassis. 4 × 4, 6 × 6 and 8 × 8 configurations are available and several specialist builders, e.g. Bachert-Ziegler in West Germany and Saval-Kronenburg in the Netherlands, use them as bases for their appliances. Many countries now have manufacturers of fire-truck chassis and bodywork/equipment and several companies produce complete vehicles.

Snow-fighting vehicles range from trucks and tractors on the front of which a snow-plough blade can be temporarily fitted to purpose-built machines of incredible performance. American machines with triple-auger (or 'rotary plow') equipment are particularly effective in clearing runways at high speed. The German Unimog, a family of multipurpose vehicles with numerous possibilities, is also frequently used with various types of snow-clearing equipment.

FIRE, CRASH AND SNOW-FIGHTING VEHICLES

Truck, 6-ton, 4 × 2, Fire Tender   GB/NZ
(Bedford TK/KLC EFN3B)

6-cyl. 4.9-litre petrol engine with 5F1R gearbox. Commercial chassis/cab with bodywork by Wormalds for the New Zealand Army. Rear-mounted Coventry-Climax high- and low-pressure pump, 1125-litre tank. NZ Army also used fire tenders based on normal-control Bedford TJ-Series (J6) chassis.

Truck, 5-ton, 4 × 2, Fire Tender   USA
(Ford C-Series)

The Ford C-Series Tilt Cab chassis with set-back front axle was produced from 1957 until the early 1980s, with only detail modifications. This USAF pumper truck was bodied and equipped by Ward LaFrance in 1974. The cab could tilt 45°. Variants available include 4 × 4, 6 × 4 and diesel models.

Truck, 5-ton, 4 × 2, Fire Tender   USA
(Ward LaFrance Patriot)

V-6-cyl. diesel engine (Detroit Diesel 6V53N) with auto. trans. (Allison MT64), driving 5.83:1 Rockwell rear axle. Top speed 88 km/h, acceleration 0–40 km/h in 30 sec. Supplied to USAF in 1979/80. Fitted with PTO-driven 2850-litre/min. 2-step turbine pump, 2280-litre first-aid water tank and 210-litre foam tank.

Truck, 1.25-ton, 4 × 4, Fire Tender   USA
(Dodge W200/M880)

V-8-cyl. 5.2-litre petrol engine with 3F1R auto. trans. and 2-speed transfer box with lockable differential. Wheelbase 3327 mm. Overall length and width 5563 × 2019 mm. Standard US military '5/4-ton' pickup truck (militarized 1977 Dodge W200) with first-aid fire-fighting equipment module, used by the USAF.

Truck, 5-ton, 4 × 4, Fire Tender   NL
(DAF V1600DD)

6-cyl. 4.77-litre diesel engine with 5F1R gearbox and 2-speed transfer box. Wheelbase 3580 mm. Crew cab, body and equipment by Motorkracht of Hoogeveen for Netherlands Army. Used for heath and brush fires. Carried VW-powered pump, large water tank, suction hoses, 3 roof-mounted monitors. 1970s.

Truck, 5-ton, 4 × 4, Fire Tender   NL
(DAF FFV1800DT)

6-cyl. 6.15-litre diesel engine (DT615) with 5F1R overdrive-top gearbox and 2-speed transfer box. Self-locking rear differential. Air brakes. 11R22.5 tubeless tyres. Wheelbase 3600 mm (3200 optional). Weight (chassis) 4890 kg. GVW 14500 kg. Pumper and equipment carrier of Netherlands Ministry of Defence, 1979.

Truck, 2.5-ton, 4 × 4, Fire Tender   **AUS**
(International C1610)

Used by the Australian Army in the early 1970s, this general purpose fire truck was very similar to the later-type Bushfire Brigade truck. It also appeared on the IHC 4 × 4 Mk 3 chassis. It featured a 1500-litre water tank, a detachable pumping set at the rear and a front winch. Colour scheme red.

Truck, 0.75-ton, 4 × 4, Fire Tender   **AUS**
(Land-Rover 109 Series IIA)

Australian Army long-wheelbase Land-Rover chassis/cab with purpose-built domestic-type fire truck bodywork. Painted red with silver-colour number on doors. AFS sign was red on white. Photo was taken at School of Military Engineering, Casula, in 1974. Equipment included a 200-litre water tank.

Truck, 0.75-ton, 4 × 4, Fire Tender   **AUS**
(Land-Rover 109 Series IIA)

Standard Australian Army lwb Land-Rover truck with 'drop-in' fire-fighting unit, used as Early Rescue Fire Truck. Generally similar to RAAF 'Truck, Fire, Crash, Tactical'. Straight front mudguard cut-outs, brush guard and tail light unit protectors were typical Australian Land-Rover features.

Truck, 1-ton, 4 × 4, Fire Tender   **GB**
(Land-Rover FC110)

4-cyl. (6-cyl. optional) petrol engine with 4F1R gearbox and 2-speed transfer box. Wheelbase 2790 mm. 9.00-16 tyres. Commercially-available chassis/cab, used for a variety of fire-fighting vehicles. This unit, by HCB-Angus for the British Army, carried a 520-litre water tank and a pump with hose reel at rear.

Truck, 1.2-ton, 4 × 4, Fire Tender   **F**
(Saviem TP3M39)

4-cyl. diesel engine with 4F1R gearbox and 2-speed transfer box. Wheelbase 2640 mm. 2-seat closed cab. Fire-fighting equipment by SAIREP of Voiron for the French Navy. 500-litre water tank with 3-stage centrifugal pump, driven by 1-cyl. ILO 197 2-stroke petrol engine; capacity 250 litre/min.

Truck, 1.5-ton, 4 × 4, Fire Tender   **D**
(Unimog 404.0)

Equipped by Somati (Model P750) this was one of several Unimog-based fire-fighting appliances used by the Belgian armed forces from about 1974. It measured 4840 × 2120 × 2600 mm and weighed 4353 kg. The double cab seated 5 persons. The 840-litre tank carried 750 kg of powder.

Truck, 0.75-ton, 4 × 4, Rescue   **GB**
(Land-Rover 109 Series III)

4-cyl. petrol engine with 4F1R gearbox and 2-speed transfer box. 16-in. wheels with oversize tyres. Wheelbase 2768 mm. Bodied and equipped by HCB-Angus for dealing with crashes at RAF airfields especially with Harrier squadrons, from 1974. Note unusual observation hatch in cab roof.

Truck, 6 × 4, Rescue   **GB**
(Range Rover/Gloster Saro Mk 2)

V-8-cyl. petrol engine with 4F1R gearbox and 2-speed transfer box. Full-time 4-wheel drive; trailing rearmost axle. Overall dimensions 5480 × 1780 × 2440 mm. Weight, laden, 4100 kg (approx). Rapid intervention fire/rescue vehicle with 4-door crew cab, Godiva pump, 900-litre tank, for RAF 1978.

Truck, 4 × 4, Rescue   **D**
(Unimog 404.0)

6-cyl. 2.7-litre petrol engine (M130) with 6F2R gearbox/transfer box. Rigid portal axles. Coil spring suspension. Wheelbase 2900 mm. GVW 5000 kg. 4-door extended cab. In service with the Netherlands Air Force from 1973. Dutch-made body and equipment. Known as 'Rescue Vehicle P500/BFC50'.

Truck, 4 × 4, Aircraft CFR   **F**
(Berliet GBD)

6-cyl. diesel engine with 6F1R gearbox and 2-speed transfer box with central differential for full-time 4-wheel drive. Extended crew cab, bodywork and fire-fighting equipment by BIRO for the French Air Force, c. 1979. Chassis was same as French Army's GBD 6-ton 4 × 4 truck. From 1981 they were renamed Renault.

Truck, 4 × 4, Aircraft CFR   **D/DK**
(Faun LF15.12/38V)

V-12-cyl. 16.96-litre aircooled diesel engine (Deutz) with automatic transmission. Wheelbase 3800 mm. Overall dimensions 7800 × 2500 × 3380 mm. Weight 13100 kg. GVW 18000 kg Water tank capacity 4100 litres. Bodied and equipped by Ginge of Copenhagen, Denmark, for Swiss Air Force in 1970/71.

Truck, 4 × 4, Aircraft CFR   **D**
(Faun LF16.30/45V)

V-8-cyl. 12.7-litre aircooled diesel engine (Deutz BF8L 413F) with auto. trans. (ZF). Wheelbase 4500 mm. Overall dimensions 8360 × 2750 × 3230 mm. Weight 13950 kg. GVW 17200 kg. Bodied and equipped by Bachert/Ziegler, this *Bundeswehr Feuerlösch-Kfz. 3000* carried 3000 kg of extinguishing powder. 1980.

Truck, 4 × 4, Aircraft CFR USA
(Oshkosh T6)

In addition to the smaller MB1 and MB5 CFR vehicles, Oshkosh produced the high-performance T6 which could accelerate from 0–80 km/h in 30 sec. It had a water tank capacity of 6000 litres and a 367-kW (492-bhp) diesel engine, rear-mounted, with 5-speed automatic transmission. Produced in 1980.

Truck, 4 × 4, Aircraft CFR NL
(Saval-Kronenburg SK/MAC-06-S)

V-8-cyl. diesel engine (Detroit Diesel 8V92TA), rear-mounted, with Allison 5F1R auto. trans. Transfer box and axles with lockable differentials. Air brakes. Wheelbase 4000 mm. Overall dimensions 8660 × 2500 × 3540 mm. Max. speed 110 km/h. 4000-litre water tank, 300-litre foam tank. 1981.

Truck, 4 × 4, Aircraft CFR GB
(Scammell Nubian 2)

V-8-cyl. diesel engine (Cummins V903), rear-mounted, with Allison HT750DRD 5-speed auto. trans. Kirkstall 2-speed transfer box. Wheelbase 3990 mm. GVW 18000 kg. 300- and 400-bhp versions offered. Motor Panels cab. 1978 chassis/cab shown, prior to bodywork and equipment being fitted by outside manufacturer.

Truck, 4 × 4, Aircraft CFR USA
(Walter B-Series)

V-8-cyl. petrol engine (Ford), rear-mounted, with automatic transmission and 'positive' 4-wheel drive. Air brakes. 25-in. wheels. Acceleration 0–80 km/h in 35 sec. Water capacity 3875 litres. Foam compound capacity 425 litres. Pump driven by separate Chrysler V-8-cyl. petrol engine. Belgian Air Force, from 1975.

Truck, 6 × 6, Aircraft CFR D
(Faun LF22.30/45V)

V-8-cyl. 12.7-litre aircooled diesel engine (Deutz BF8L 413F) with auto.trans. (ZF). 16.00R20XL tyres. Wheelbase 4500 mm (1500 + 3750). Overall dimensions 8860 × 2750 × 3300 mm. Weight 16950 kg. Reservoirs for 3500 litres of water, 400 litres of foam compound. Bodied and equipped by Bachert/Ziegler.

Truck, 6 × 6, Aircraft CFR GB
(Leyland/Scammell Nubian Major)

Dennis of Guildford was one of the UK specialist firms to fit the bodywork and fire-fighting equipment to this high-speed crash tender chassis (originally a Thornycroft product). Water capacity of over 8000 litres, with 1140 litres of foam compound. Pumping rate up to 24843 litres/min. Used by Royal Air Force, from 1976.

FIRE, CRASH AND SNOW-FIGHTING VEHICLES

Truck, 6 × 6, Aircraft CFR   **GB**
(Leyland/Scammell Nubian Major)

V-8-cyl. 14.8-litre diesel engine (Cummins) with 5F1R semi-automatic transmission and 2-speed transfer box. Wheelbase 4570 mm. GVW 20830 kg. Bodywork and fire-fighting equipment were supplied by several British specialist firms, example shown being by Gloster Saro of Hawker-Siddeley.

Truck, 6 × 6, Aircraft CFR   **A**
(ÖAF 20.320 Cobra)

V-8-cyl. 12.8-litre turbocharged diesel engine (MAN D2538MT) with 6F1R transmission. Hub reduction axles. Wheelbase 4500 mm. This 22-ton 80-km/h crash tender was used by the South African Air Force from 1982. Based on a cargo/platform truck, it had a 4000-litre water tank. Note ground-level nozzles.

Truck, 6 × 6, Aircraft CFR   **USA**
(Oshkosh P4)

Rear-engined crash truck, more than 200 of which were ordered from Oshkosh in the mid-1970s, for use by the USAF in the US and abroad. 1977 example in Britain shown. They carried 5700 litres of water and could be airlifted. Similar units were acquired by the Royal Australian Air Force.

Truck, 6 × 6, Aircraft CFR   **S**
(Scania SBAT 111S)

6-cyl. 11-litre turbocharged diesel engine (D11LB28) with 6F1R automatic transmission and 2-speed transfer box. Rigid axles with epicyclic hub reduction gearing. Fire-fighting equipment and bodywork by Fjeldhus Bruk of Oslo, on crew cab version of Swedish Army TGB411A2MT chassis. Swedish Air Force, 1979.

Truck, 8 × 8, Aircraft CFR   **D/NL**
(Faun LF40.30X2/48V)

Twin V-8-cyl. 12.7-litre aircooled diesel engines (Deutz BF8L 413F) with automatic gearboxes (ZF). Wheelbase 4800 mm. Overall dimensions 10800 × 2750 × 3160 mm. Weight 23510 kg. GVW 32800 kg. Used by West German *Bundeswehr* as *Feuerlösch-Kfz. 8000*. Equipped by Saval-Kronenburg. From late 1970s.

Truck, 8 × 8, Aircraft CFR   **USA**
(Oshkosh P15)

Twin V-8-cyl. 12-litre turbocharged diesel engines (Detroit Diesel DDA8V92T) with 7F1R powershift trans. Front and rear tandems with diff. locks and 26.5-25 tyres. Wheelbase 7722 mm. Overall dimensions 14275 × 3099 × 4191 mm. Weight 32390 (fully operational 59410) kg. US Air Force, 1977.

Truck, 4 × 4, Snow-Fighting   **USA**
(FWD/Klauer Snogo TU-3)

One of a range of rotary-type snow-clearing machines produced by Klauer Manufacturing Co. of Dubuque, Iowa, and mounted on a heavy-duty 4-wheel drive and steer FWD chassis. The triple augers were driven by a separate engine on the rear of the chassis. Supplied chiefly for use at civil and military airfields.

Truck, 4 × 4, Snow-Fighting   **USA**
(Oshkosh H2218)

V-8-cyl. 8.2-litre diesel engine (Detroit Diesel) with 5F1R auto. trans. (Allison) and single-speed transfer box (with rear axle disconnect). Rotary head driven by separate V-8-cyl. 12-litre engine (Detroit Diesel). Wheelbase 3429 mm. Overall length and width 8754 × 2591 mm. Weight 14528 kg. 1981.

Truck, 4 × 4, Snow-Fighting   **USA**
(Oshkosh P-Series)

Oshkosh Truck Corp. of Oshkosh, Wisc., have long been manufacturers of snow-removal truck chassis. In the 1970s they offered 4 × 4 and 6 × 6 models with diesel engine, 5- to 10-speed manual and 4- or 5-speed automatic transmission options and 2- or 3-speed auxiliary transmissions.

Truck, 4 × 4, Snow-Fighting   **CH**
(Rolba R400)

6-cyl. aircooled diesel engine (Deutz) driving both axles and snow-blower. Capacity 500 ton/h. Throw 25 m. Used for clearing airfield runways, etc. 1970/71. Rolba, a Swiss company founded in 1949, supplied wheeled and tracked snow-fighters and other equipment, including Ratrac oversnow vehicles (Thiokol/USA licence).

Truck, 4 × 4, Snow-Fighting   **S**
(Scania SBA111)

6-cyl. 11-litre diesel engine (D11LB28) with 6F1R automatic transmission. Snow-blower with rear-mounted Scania DS14 V-8 engine. Capacity 30–35 ton of snow per min. Snow-clearing was effected with vehicle reversing, controlled from second cab. 45 units were ordered by the Swedish Air Force in 1976.

Truck, 4 × 4, Snow-Fighting   **D**
(Unimog 406.121)

The Daimler-Benz Unimog (*Universal Motor Gerät*) has over the years been used for snow-clearing work with various types of equipment, exemplified by this Schmidt VF3-Z *Schneefräse*, which was delivered to the Danish Air Force in 1974. It cleared a path 2450 mm wide. 2000 kg of ballast carried on truck body floor.

Amphibious and Tracked Vehicles

Vehicles which can be used both on land and in water have always attracted attention from the military, for obvious reasons. From time to time, the armed forces have used swimming vehicles and among the most successful were the German Volkswagen 'Schwimmer' and the American GMC 'Duck', both developed during the Second World War. The latter remained in service in several countries for many years after the war and was copied by the Soviet Union (BAV and BAV-A, by ZIL, from the early 1950s) and Brazil (Biselli Camanf, c. 1970).

The US Army acquired some developed versions of the wartime amphibian, viz. the 'Superduck' and the 'Drake', and in the 1950s and 1960s several other types appeared, notably the LARC (Lighter, Amphibious, Resupply, Cargo) range which comprised 5-, 15- and 60-ton versions. Of these, the first two – LARC-V and -XV – were produced in quantity and the LARC-V was also supplied to some friendly nations, including Australia, Britain and West Germany. These vehicles are better described as land-going boats than water-going trucks. Many tactical trucks on the other hand and particularly in the US, have been swimmable types, i.e. the ability to swim was a military requirement. The following pages show some types which had swimmability as one of their primary functions. Many experimental amphibious vehicles have appeared over the years but they will probably always remain compromises, performing well in the water and poorly on the road or vice versa. The LARC-V, for example, was a good swimmer but when used on the roads tended to pitch rather badly. In the 1970s Fiat of Italy brought out a 2-ton amphibious truck which was further developed to become a reliable proposition for both civil and military service. ENASA in Spain produced a somewhat larger model (which in Italy was marketed by Astra) which had originally been designed and developed for the Spanish Marines. Both are four-wheeled, as is the West German EWK Bison, which is bigger still and appeared in the early 1980s.

Also presented in this chapter are the various European 0.5-ton 4 × 4 amphibious multipurpose trucks, once referred to as 'Europa-Jeeps'. These were conceived in the 1960s when NATO partners France, West Germany and Italy studied the possibility of replacing their contemporary 0.25-tonners (Hotchkiss Jeep M201, Auto Union/DKW Munga and Fiat Campagnola respectively) by one new 0.5-ton vehicle, to be developed trilaterally and to incorporate countless desirable features, including the ability to swim. No fewer than three groups of three manufacturers each became engaged in this project. At the time it was expected that orders for some 50000 of these vehicles would be forthcoming, so the interest on the part of the manufacturers was quite understandable. However, for a variety of reasons, chiefly the investment in relation to actual sales potential, several of the manufacturers involved decided to pull out. The admission by the Italian High Command that they did not really need a swimming off-road car anyway, did not help either. By the mid-1970s, Fiat and MAN were the only companies still involved, but not for long: excessive unit cost and diminishing demand eventually killed the project and hopefully another lesson was learned.

Few non-armoured vehicles today use tracks for propulsion and among the exceptions are the rather unique Swedish 'Bandvagns', as made by Volvo's Bolinder-Munktell Division (BV202 Series, from 1963) and Hägglunds (BV206 Series, from 1976). The former version was widely used by the Swedish and Norwegian armed forces as well as by the British and Dutch (for combined NATO operations in Norway). Both are truly all-terrain vehicles, which can be operated on roads, over snow, through deep mud and in water. They comprise two tracked modules which are connected in such a way that they work as a fully-articulated unit, steering being accomplished by hydraulically controlling the position of one module in relation to the other. The four tracks, all driven by the front-mounted engine, maintain their contact with the ground under all prevailing terrain conditions. The Hägglunds product in particular is a very sophisticated vehicle, capable of transporting seventeen fully-equipped soldiers or 2000 kg of cargo, plus towing a trailed load of 2500 kg. In mid-1979 the Swedish Army ordered more than 3500 units in three versions: carrier, radio/command post and open-topped weapon mount.

Half-track vehicles, common as they were in the 1930s and 1940s, have not been made in any large numbers since 1945 although the availability of huge quantities of war surplus must have been one of the main reasons (1940–45 US types are still widely used by the Israeli Army). The only modern half-track vehicle of any importance is the British Centaur, made by Laird (Anglesey) but their numbers are restricted.

Truck, 0.4-ton, 4 × 4, Amphibious   SU
(LUAZ 967M)

V-4-cyl. aircooled petrol engine (MeMZ-967A) with 5F1R gearbox. Independent suspension. Rear diff. lock. Overall dimensions 3682 × 1712 × 1550 mm. Weight 930 kg. Max. speed on roads 75 km/h, in water 5–6 km/h. Fitted with winch. Intended for evacuation of casualties, it carried 2 stretchers. 1976.

Truck, 0.4-ton, 6 × 4, Amphibious   PL
(LPT)

Twin-cyl. aircooled petrol engine (Polski Fiat 126P) with 4F1R gearbox, driving the 2nd and 3rd axle. Front-wheel steering. Hinged, engine-driven propeller at rear. Overall dimensions 3250 × 1650 × 1000 mm. Weight 650 kg. Prototyped by Polish Institute for AFV and motor vehicle engineering in 1977.

Truck, 0.4-ton, 8 × 8, Amphibious   CDN
(Argocat 8)

Twin-cyl. aircooled petrol engine (Chapperal) with torque converter and 2F1R planetary gear system. Lever-steering with disc brakes on differential. 12-20 low-pressure tubeless tyres. Overall length and width 3023 × 1460 mm. Weight 368 kg. Speed on land 40 km/h, in water 4.8 km/h. Royal Navy, 1970s.

Truck, 0.5-ton, 4 × 4, Amphibious   D
(BMW)

4-cyl. 2-litre petrol engine with 5F1R gearbox (also tested with 4-cyl. 2.4-litre MAN multifuel aircooled diesel engine). Wheelbase 1995 mm. Overall dimensions 3782 × 1780 × 1835 mm. Weight 1900 kg. GVW 2400 kg. Max. speed on roads 105 km/h, in water 8 km/h. Prototype of the early 1970s.

Truck, 0.5-ton, 4 × 4, Amphibious   I/D/F
(Fiat/MAN/Saviem VCL)

4-cyl. 2-litre petrol engine (Fiat), mounted at rear, with 5F1R gearbox, hub reduction units and limited-slip differentials. Wheelbase 2150 mm. Dimensions 4050 × 1600 × 1935 mm. Weight 2145 kg. PTO-driven jet drive for water propulsion (max. speed 7.6 km/h). 1970s trilateral design with limited production by Fiat.

Truck, 0.5-ton, 4 × 4, Amphibious   F/I/D
(Hotchkiss/Lancia/Büssing)

Flat-4-cyl. 2-litre petrol engine (Lancia) with 5F1R gearbox (also tested with torque converter and 4F1R gearbox), driving either front or all wheels. Wheelbase 2100 mm. Overall dimensions 4140 × 1600 × 1965 mm. Weight 1750 kg. 4-blade screw for water propulsion (max. speed 10.5 km/h). Prototypes only.

AMPHIBIOUS AND TRACKED VEHICLES

Truck, 0.75-ton, 4 × 4/8 × 8, Amphibious   **USA**
(Lockheed TerraStar)

This 'marginal terrain vehicle' was developed in the 1960s and early 1970s by Messrs Forsyth of the Lockheed Aircraft Corp. Its outstanding feature was the 4 'major-wheel' assemblies, each of which comprised 3 'minor-wheels', enabling the unit to run on 4 or 8 low-pressure tyres. Paddle-wheel action in water.

Truck, 0.9-ton, 8 × 8, Amphibious   **GB**
(Saboteur Mk IIC)

4-cyl. 1.8-litre petrol engine (VW) with automatic gearbox. Chain drive to all wheels. Lever steering on transmission disc brakes. 20 × 12 × 8 low-pressure tyres. Overall dimensions 3670 × 1700 × 900 mm. Weight 500 kg. Max. speed, road/water 80/15 km/h. One of several prototypes. Some acquired by British Army.

Truck, 0.9-ton, 8 × 8, Amphibious   **GB**
(Saboteur Mk VI 'Trooper')

4-cyl. aircooled petrol engine (VW127; 6-cyl. diesel optional) with hydraulic drive to one master axle, from which all wheels were driven by chains. A further development of the makers' earlier models, available for military and commercial use. The tyres, which also provided the springing, were Goodyear 21X1100-8NHS.

Truck, 2-ton, 4 × 4, Amphibious
(Fiat 6640/A)

6-cyl. 5.18-litre diesel engine (8060.02) with 5F1R gearbox and 2-speed transfer box. Hub reduction axles with 20-in. wheels. Wheelbase 2700 mm. Overall dimensions 7300 × 2500 × 2715 mm. Weight 4810 kg, GVW 6950 kg. Max. speed road/water 90/11 km/h. 3-ton winch. PTO-driven 4-blade screw. Early 1970s.

Truck, 2-ton, 4 × 4, Amphibious
(Fiat 6640/G)

6-cyl. 5.5-litre turbocharged diesel engine (8062.24) with auto. trans. (TX100) and 2-speed transfer box. Hub reduction axles with diff. locks. Wheelbase 3100 mm. Overall dimensions 8200 × 2500 × 3050 mm. Weight 6500 kg. GVW 8500 kg. Water propulsion up to 11 km/h by rotating pump-jet. Early 1980s.

Truck, 2.5-ton, 6 × 6, Amphibious   **BR**
(Biselli Camanf)

4-cyl. diesel engine (Detroit Diesel 4-53N) with 5F1R gearbox (Clark) and 2-speed transfer box. Overall dimensions 9500 × 2500 × 2650 mm. GVW 13500 kg. ZF power-assisted steering. Brazilian replica of wartime GMC DUKW-353 ('Duck'), delivered to Brazilian Navy in 1979. 'Camanf' derived from *caminhao anfibio*.

242

Truck, 3-ton, 4 × 4, Amphibious   E
(Pegaso 3550VAP)

6-cyl. 10.17-litre diesel engine (9135/5) with 6F1R gearbox and 2-speed transfer box. Hub reduction axles with 13.00-20 tyres. Wheelbase 3450 mm. Overall dimensions 9058 × 2500 × 2830 mm. Weight 9500 kg. Loading crane and 5-ton winch. Produced by ENASA, late 1970s. Max. speed in water 6 knots.

Truck, 5/7-ton, 4 × 4, Amphibious   D
(EWK Bison)

Launched in 1982 by Eisenwerke Kaiserslautern Göppner, this amphibian was powered by a 235-kW V-8-cyl. aircooled diesel engine (Deutz). It featured central tyre pressure regulation. 2 screws, rotatable through 360°, provided a max. speed in water of 12 km/h. Road speed was 80 km/h.

Vehicle, Amphibious, 4 × 4, Bridging/Ferrying   D
(EWK M2B)

Twin aircooled diesel engines (Deutz F8 413F) driving all wheels and 3 propellers (one central, two lateral; Schottel system). 16.00-20 tyres. Hydraulically-adjustable suspension. Wheelbase 5350 mm. Overall dimensions (travelling mode) 11315 × 2995 × 3579 mm. Weight 22 tons. Used by several NATO forces.

Vehicle, Amphibious, 4 × 4, Bridging/Ferrying   J
(Hitachi Type 70)

V-8-cyl. 2-stroke diesel engine, developing 246 kW (330 bhp) driving all wheels or propellers for water propulsion. Overall dimensions (travelling mode) 11400 × 2800 × 3500 mm. Weight 24 tons. Part of self-propelled floating bridge/ferry system, similar to NATO's M2(B) design, used by Japanese Army Engineers.

Truck, Half-Track, Crane   NL
(DAF V1600DD)

6-cyl. diesel engine (DD575) with 5F1R gearbox and 2-speed transfer box. This 1964 winch-equipped truck was converted to half-track configuration in 1977 by Terberg-Techniek. The ex-IHC track bogie had previously been used on a similarly-converted Hanomag ALO28 4 × 4. Netherlands Air Force.

Truck, Half-Track, Multirole   GB
(Laird Centaur)

Launched in 1978, the Centaur combined components of the Land-Rover V8 truck with (shortened) track bogie of the British MoD's Scorpion CVRT. Soft-skin and armoured variants were developed and tested by the British and other military forces. Overall length and width 5620 × 2000 mm.

Carrier, 1-ton, 4-Track, Articulated   **S**
(Volvo/BM BV202)

4-cyl. 1.78-litre petrol engine (Volvo) with 4F1R gearbox and 2-speed transfer box driving sprockets at forward end of both tracked units which steered by articulation. Overall dimensions 6180 × 1760 × 2210 mm. Weight 2900 kg. Max. payload on/off roads 1000/800 kg. Max. speed in water 1.25 knots.

Carrier, 2-ton, 4-Track, Articulated   **S**
(Hägglunds BV206A MT)

V-6-cyl. 2.8-litre petrol engine (Ford 2658E) with 4F1R auto. trans. (Mercedes) and 2-speed transfer box, driving front sprockets of all 4 rubber tracks. Hydrostatic steering by articulation. Glassfibre reinforced plastic bodywork. Overall dimensions 6890 × 1850 × 2400 mm. Weight 4200 kg. 1980.

Carrier 2-ton, 4-Track, Articulated, AT Gun   **S**
(Hägglunds PVPJBV2062A MT)

Basically as Swedish Army's BV206A MT (qv) but open body with roll-bar and anti-tank weapon (recoilless rifle or TOW) on vertically-adjustable mount. Ammunition and equipment stowage in rear unit. Overall dimensions 7390 × 1850 × 2200 mm. Weight 4600 kg. Max. speed 55 km/h on roads, 3–4 km/h in water.

Carrier, Full-Track, Cargo/Personnel   **S**
(Aktiv Snow-Trac ST4)

Flat-4-cyl. aircooled 1.6-litre engine (VW126A) with 4F1R gearbox, driving the front sprockets. Controlled-differential steering. Overall dimensions 3640 × 1900 × 1850 mm. Weight 1350 kg (excl. radio equipment). GVW 1850 kg. Oversnow vehicle. Users incl. British Royal Navy (shown), France. Early 1970s.

Carrier, Full-Track, Cargo   **USA**
(FMC M584)

V-6-cyl. 5.1-litre diesel engine (Detroit Diesel 6V53) with auto. trans. (Allison TX100-1). Overall dimensions 5900 × 2690 × 3300 mm. Weight 7500 kg. GVW 12500 kg. Cargo area dimensions 3300 × 2450 × 1560 mm. Crew 4. 9-ton winch at front. In service with many armed forces (New Zealand shown). 1970s.

Carrier, Full-Track, Cargo/Personnel   **CH**
(Ratrac S/GRD)

6-cyl. 3.27-litre petrol engine (Ford 170CID), driving the rear sprockets. Overall dimensions 4300 × 2550 × 2670 mm. Track width 920 mm (640 mm optional). Weight 2900 kg. GVW 3500 kg. Also with open dropside body with max. payload rating of 1000 kg. Produced under Thiokol/USA licence, for Swiss Army.

Handling and Construction Equipment

The term 'handling and construction equipment' covers a large variety of specialized machines ranging from small forklift trucks (usually commercial types in scores of models and sizes) and a variety of self-propelled cranes to sophisticated multipurpose earthmoving machines.

Presented first in this section is a selection of cranes, including rough-terrain and truck-mounted types. At one time a crane which was not intended to travel on roads (due to lack of speed and not being road-legal) was either a mobile yard crane or a rough-terrain type, i.e. a 4 × 4 or 6 × 6 model designed for off-road use only. Truck-mounted cranes are crane structures mounted on existing or specially-designed truck chassis, often with walking-beam rear tandem suspension replacing the conventional leaf springs. They have from two to five (or more) axles, depending on lifting capacity and vehicle weight, and either a so-called 'lattice-type' or a hydraulic telescoping-type jib or boom. The first of these is inherently stronger and is also known as the 'strut jib-type'. Hydraulic telescopic-type cranes are more compact, easier to erect and operate, more versatile, lighter, faster and less cumbersome. They have replaced the lattice-type to a great extent, both in commerce and for military applications. The telescopic crane is often equipped with a pinned boom tip extension, usually referred to as a 'fly jib'; in some instances it is hinged and stowed along the main boom when not in use, alternatively it is removed entirely and carried separately.

In recent years, several types of crane have appeared which combine the distinctive features of two. An example is the all-terrain crane which is a rough-terrain type suitable also for relatively fast road travel between job sites. These have a more comfortable cab and a transmission system which allows both crawling speeds with all-wheel drive and acceptable highway traffic speeds. Their significant advantage is that they do not need road transport by low-loader but, on the other hand, due to their added complexity they tend to be less able to stand up to rough use.

The same applies to some extent to forklift trucks. Some of these, with small wheels and low speeds, are suitable only for use in warehouses, workshops, stores and the like and many of them, especially when employed only indoors, have environment-friendly electric propulsion. At the other extreme there are large-wheeled diesel-engined high-speed types which can be used on roads, although this is not often done and certainly not with their lethal forks *in situ*. A relative newcomer is the forward-reach lift which has a more or less horizontal telescopic boom which can be raised and lowered hydraulically. The tip, with the forks – and thus the load – can be manoeuvred much further away, e.g. to the forward end of a cargo truck body when loading from the rear. The Liner Giraffe, first shown at the 1978 British Army Equipment Exhibition and subsequently supplied to the British Army and RAF in some numbers, is a good example of this modern and useful piece of state-of-the-art equipment.

Scoop-type loaders (also known as 'shovels' or 'bucket loaders') are generally rear-engined tractors with large wheels, sometimes with four-wheel steering or steering by articulation, and are used for several kinds of operation. In addition to handling materials (lifting, moving) especially in confined areas, they can perform all manner of earthmoving operations. Some are fitted with an excavator (narrow bucket on hydraulic articulated arm) at the rear, making them even more versatile. Really great progress has been made in recent years in this field and in several countries. If anything, it is getting increasingly hard now to come up with something entirely novel, but perfecting the existing machines is equally important, particularly in terms of reliability. Further sophistication at the cost of added complexity is undesirable.

Bulldozers are still being used all over the world and have hardly changed in concept from those of the Second World War, the main exception being the increased use of hydraulic systems. Their considerable drawbacks are their weight and low speed, two factors which necessitate their site-to-site movement by means of low-bed trailers or HETs. Therefore, many armies' engineers now use large-wheeled earthmoving tractors which can do most of the things crawler-type bulldozers used to do, at much higher speed and are also able to travel on roads in military convoys without tearing up the surface.

The US Army experimented for a long time with a Family of Military Engineer Construction Equipment (FAMECE) but it proved impossible for the prototypes to meet the exceedingly high and stringent requirements. These requirements were not relaxed until the tests had been terminated and the Army had to purchase commercial equipment again.

HANDLING AND CONSTRUCTION EQUIPMENT

Crane, 7.5-ton, 4 × 4   **USA**
(Grove RT48MC)

Hydraulic telescopic rough-terrain crane with 2-section boom (6.7–12.2 m). Detroit Diesel 4-53N engine. Fordability 1500 mm. 200 of these cranes were supplied to the USMC from 1979. Earlier military contracts were placed with Grove during 1967–72 when the USN ordered 5-ton RT38M and 8-ton RT48M cranes.

Crane, 12-ton, 4 × 4   **F**
(Haulotte HA12)

Aircooled diesel engine with 6-speed powershift transmission. 25-in. wheels with 16.00-25 tyres. Wheelbase 4100 mm. Overall length and width (carrier) 7665 × 2480 mm. 2-section boom, max. length 12.8 m. Full hydraulic control of all crane motions, from separate seat in cab. Used by French Army Engineers. Early 1980s.

Crane, 15-ton, 4 × 4   **GB**
(Coles Hydra-Husky 150T)

6-cyl. diesel engine (AEC AV505). 2 steering axles with 16.00-25 tyres. Overall length and width 9200 × 2500 mm. Weight 22400 kg. Boom length 7.6–18.3 m. Maximum lift 18000 kg (7000 kg mobile) at 3-m radius. Turning circle with all wheels steering 6860 mm. Supplied to British Army in the early 1970s.

Crane, 25-ton, 4 × 4   **CH**
(Hydrokran Saturn 25)

V-8-cyl. 11.3-litre aircooled diesel engine (Deutz F8L 413) with 5F1R powershift transmission and 2-speed transfer box with lockable differential. Steering axles with diff. locks. Air/hydraulic brakes. 16.00-25 tyres. Wheelbase 3650 mm. Weight 22300 kg. 2-section boom, max. length 20 m. Netherlands Army, mid-1970s.

Crane, 10-ton, Truck-Mounted, 4 × 4   **D**
(Faun LK 15.08/36/MFL AK912)

V-8-cyl. aircooled diesel engine (Deutz), mounted behind cab. Fully revolving hydraulic crane by MFL (formerly Wilhag) of Langenfeld, West Germany. Overall dimensions (travelling mode) 8200 × 2500 × 3450 mm. Wheelbase 3600 mm. GVW 18000 kg. 10-ton winch. Supplied to the Swiss armed forces in 1971.

Crane, 12.5-ton, Truck-Mounted, 4 × 4   **DDR**
(Takraf ADK-125)

6-cyl. diesel engine (6VD14,5/12-1SRW) with 5F1R gearbox. Overall dimensions (travelling mode) 8445 × 2500 × 3400 mm. Weight 19100 kg. Max. road speed 70 km/h. Hydraulic telescopic crane, fully revolving. Max. lift, with outriggers, 12500 kg, on rubber 5000 kg. Produced from the mid-1970s.

Crane, 15-ton, Truck-Mounted, 4 × 4   **GB**
(Coles 315M)

Cummins V555 diesel engine with 6-speed semi-automatic transmission. Weight 22540 kg. Max. road speed 75 km/h. 8–11.5-m 2-section telescopic boom. Lifting capacity 15000 kg at 3-m radius, using outriggers, 9000 kg mobile. 27 ordered in 1982 by the British MoD for use as medium field crane by RE and REME.

Crane, 15-ton, Truck-Mounted, 4 × 4   **GB**
(Jones 15/18RT)

Introduced in 1976 and sold to the British MoD this crane could travel at over 80 km/h and lift 15 tons. Lifting height (with fly jib installed) was 24.6 m. It was rather similar in appearance to the 10-ton Smith Model 5/10, of which the RAF ordered 53 units in the late 1970s. Both were suitable for operation on and off roads.

Crane, 10-ton, Truck-Mounted, 6 × 6   **D**
(Magirus-Deutz 232D16AL/Kirsten)

V-8-cyl. 11.3-litre aircooled diesel engine (Deutz F8L 413) with 6F1R gearbox and 2-speed transfer box. Wheelbase 4890 mm. Chassis/cab dimensions 8115 × 2450 × 3310 mm. Weight 8500 kg. Militarized commercial chassis, fitted with Kirsten hydraulic crane.

Crane, 15-ton, Truck-Mounted, 6 × 6   **D**
(Faun MKF33.35/485/MFL TW1531)

V-12-cyl. 19.1-litre aircooled diesel engine (Deutz F12L 413). MFL-built hydraulic revolving crane. Pump drive by PTO from carrier engine. Wheelbase 4850 mm. Overall dimensions 10500 × 2500 × 3320 mm. GVW 32500 kg. 10-ton winch. Carrier superseded Model LK1212/485A of the 1960s.

Crane, 16-ton, Truck-Mounted, 6 × 6   **CS**
(Tatra 148PP7/CKT AD160)

Hydraulic telescopic revolving crane with 16.1-m boom (20.8 m with fly jib), produced in Czechoslovakia from 1974 on specially-adapted Tatra 6 × 6 chassis with V-8-cyl. aircooled diesel engine. Overall dimensions 9850 × 2500 × 3400 mm. Weight 24600 kg. Similar in appearance was the CKD PRAHA AD20 (20-ton).

Crane, 20-ton, Truck-Mounted, 6 × 6   **E**
(Luna AT20/20)

6-cyl. diesel engine with 6F1R gearbox and 2-speed transfer box. Hub reduction axles. 16.00-25 tyres. Wheelbase 4450 mm. Overall dimensions (travelling mode) 10635 × 2500 × 2900 mm. Boom length 18.7 m (with fly jib 23.7 m). 2 hoist winches. Angles of approach and departure 45°. Made in Spain in the early 1980s.

Crane, 25-ton, Truck-Mounted, 6 × 6   **GB**
(Smith L2825)

Lattice-jib crane with 10.6-m boom, power load lowering and Perkins 6.354 diesel engine. Crane Traveller (Vickers) V515/37 carrier with hydraulic outriggers at the rear. Supplied to the British Army in the 1970s. Similar crane was mounted on Saviem EPG246 6 × 6 carrier for the Ministry of Defence of Oman.

Crane, 30-ton, Truck-Mounted, 6 × 6   **D**
(Krupp AS35M)

Developed by Fried. Krupp, this was the heaviest of a new generation of rear-engined military cranes, the others being the 4 × 4 10-ton AS15M and 20-ton AS25M. Overall dimensions 11460 × 2730 × 3150 mm. Lifting height 19.6 m. 2200 ordered by the *Bundeswehr* in 1979, 16 by Belgian Army in 1981.

Crane, 25-ton, Truck-Mounted, 8 × 4   **USA**
(Grove TMS300-5)

Hydraulic telescopic crane with 3-section boom (10–33.6 m, plus 9.6-m swingaway extension). Single Detroit Diesel 6-71N power unit. 11.00-20 tyres. Suitable for clamshell and pile-driving operations. 133 ordered in 1976. Deliveries from 1978. Equipment included 25-ton 4-sheave hook-block and 5-ton headache ball.

Crane, 25-ton, Truck-Mounted, 8 × 4   **USA**
(P&H T300)

Supplied to the US Army in the late 1970s this was basically a commercial 25- to 30-ton crane with single engine (Cummins V8) powering both crane and carrier. In 1968–70, P&H (Harnischfeger) had supplied the 15-ton M315T for the USMC and the 20-ton M320T for the USAF.

Truck, Aircraft Cargo-Loading/Unloading, 8 × 2   **USA**
(Oshkosh 40K/USAF Type A/S32H-6A)

Self-propelled hydraulically-operated elevated platform with tandem steering front axles and tandem rear axles, one of which was driven by a diesel engine with 1F1R transmission. Overall length and width 12624 × 3937 mm. Cargo deck loading height 1–4 m. Weight 20 tons. Load capacity 18 tons.

Tractor, Multipurpose, 4 × 2   **S**
(Volvo LM620 and LM640)

3-cyl. 3.78-litre diesel engine (BM1113A) with 2F2R transmission, driving the front wheels (all wheels on Model LM640). Tyres 14.00-30 front, 9.00-20 rear. Disc brakes. Overall dimensions 4600 × 2110 × 2520 mm. Weight 6420 kg. Used by Netherlands Army with various attachments, e.g. crane, forklift. 1970s.

Truck, Forklift, 4 × 2   **GB**
(Hyster Challenger 40)

Typical example of numerous kinds of industrial-type forklifts used by the military all over the world. This was a diesel-engined 1800-kg-capacity model, one of 800 supplied for service with the British armed forces at home and abroad, during the late 1970s and early 1980s, by Hyster Europe at Basingstoke, Hants., England.

Tractor, Forklift, 4 × 2   **GB**
(Massey-Ferguson/Cameron-Gardner)

Based on MF40 industrial tractor with 3-cyl. diesel engine (Perkins 3.152) and 'instant reverse' 6F2R transmission. Overall length and width 5181 × 1854 mm. Weight 3227 kg. Lifting capacity 1820 kg. One of over 250 cross-country forklifts supplied by Cameron-Gardner to the British Ministry of Defence. 1978.

Truck, Forklift, 4 × 2   **D**
(Steinbock DFG2SC)

4-cyl. 4.2-litre diesel engine (MWM) with 3F3R gearbox, driving the front wheels. ZF Loc-o-matic differential. Trilex wheels with 8.25-20 tyres, front and rear. Wheelbase 2000 mm. Overall dimensions (travelling mode) 3620 × 1670 × 2630 mm. Weight 6200 kg. Max. lift 2000 kg. Lift height max. 2960 mm. Made for Swiss Army.

Truck, Forklift, 4 × 4   **GB**
(Liner Giraffe 342)

Rough-terrain forklift truck with telescoping boom, enabling loading at difficult angles. Perkins 3-cyl. diesel engine. 4-wheel steering. Weight 5488 kg. Max. forward reach 3.7 m with load of 860 kg. 32 units supplied to British forces, 1978/79. Name changed to Markhandler when Liner became part of Mark (UK).

Truck, Forklift, 4 × 4   **F**
(SALEV/Manox TT15)

Rough-terrain forklift truck, developed for the French Army, produced by SALEV of Boulogne/Seine in the early 1970s. Lifting capacity 1500 kg. 4-wheel steering. SALEV supplied many forklifts to the French armed forces, including 350 5-ton Model C50s and 3-ton Model BR30s.

Tractor, Forklift, 4 × 4   **USA**
(Terex 72-31)

4-cyl. diesel engine (Detroit Diesel 4-71) with auto. trans. (Allison). 20.5-25 tyres. Weight 12750 kg. Basically a 1.9-m³ loader but fitted with fork attachment. In service with the USAF and USMC, Argentine, Belgian and Israeli air forces and Nigerian and South African armies. Could be wadeproofed to 1.5 m.

HANDLING AND CONSTRUCTION EQUIPMENT

Loader, Scoop-Type, 4 × 4
(Case W24C)
USA

Articulated loader, produced by J. I. Case for the USAF in 1980 SAE rating 1.9–2.3 m³. Previous military orders with Case had included 4 × 2 industrial tractors (e.g. Models 440 and 540) for the US Army, USAF and USN, for general towing purposes, as well as wheeled and tracked scoop-type loaders for the USMC.

Loader, Scoop-Type, 4 × 4
(Caterpillar 966B)
USA

Rear-mounted diesel engine with planetary-type single-lever powershift transmission. 25-in. wheels. Wheelbase 3100 mm. Overall length 6900 mm. Bucket width 2920 mm. Max. forward speed 34 km/h. One of a wide range of Caterpillar wheeled loaders (commercial type) this unit served with the Australian Army.

Loader, Scoop-Type, 4 × 4
(Genemat 125A Series 2)
F

Rear-mounted diesel engine (Unic MZ42C) with semi-auto. trans. (Clark). 25-in. wheels with 20.5-25XL tyres. Basically a French commercial machine, produced in 1971 by Genemat of Charleville-Mézières, with Ulrich 4-in-1 bucket of 2560-litre capacity. When used for recovery work, the hydraulic system could lift 10 tons.

Loader, Scoop-Type, 4 × 4
(Huta Stalowa Wola SL-34)
PL

6-cyl. turbocharged diesel engine (SW680/59/1) with torque converter and 4F4R transmission. Steering by articulation. Air/hydraulic disc brakes. 23.5-25 tyres. Overall dimensions 8110 × 3000 × 3665 mm. Weight 19560 kg. Bucket capacity 3.4 m³. Lifting capacity 6000 kg. 10-ton winch. Polish Army.

Loader, Scoop-Type, 4 × 4
(IHC/Hough H65C)
USA

6-cyl. 5.8-litre turbocharged diesel engine (DT358) with torque converter and 3F3R semi-auto. trans. Wheelbase 2745 mm. Overall dimensions 7300 × 2616 × 3350 mm (including cab, shown removed). Weight 13020 kg. Capacity 2 m³. 11.4-ton winch at rear. Netherlands Army, from early 1970s.

Loader, Scoop-Type, 4 × 4
(K701)
SU

V-12-cyl. diesel engine, driving all wheels through a hydro-mechanical transmission system. Steering by articulation, with hydraulic actuation. 21-ton loading capacity. Produced by Kirov tractor works, succeeding K700. This machine was exported under the BelAZ marque name from the mid-1970s.

Loader, Scoop-Type, 4 × 4   **GB**
(Muir-Hill A5000)

6-cyl. diesel engine (Perkins 6.354) with auto. trans. High-speed air-transportable multipurpose loading shovel with attachments for digging, loading, winching, lifting and snow-clearing. Over 200 were supplied to the British forces in the early 1970s. Bucket capacity 1.27 m³. Forward reach 1.32 m.

Loader, Scoop-Type, 4 × 4   **BR/CDN/L**
(Terex 72-51)

V-6-cyl. diesel engine (Detroit Diesel 6-71N) with auto. trans. (Allison). 23.5-25 tyres. Wheelbase 2740 mm. MWT (Military Wheeled Tractor), made in Brazil, Canada and Luxembourg. Specimen shown delivered to the British Army (153 units, 1977–83) with 2.7-m³ multipurpose bucket, front-mounted winch.

Tractor, Wheeled, Earthmoving   **CS**
(DOK-M)

This machine was made in Czechoslovakia from the early 1970s to replace the less satisfactory DOK-L in Pioneer units of the Czech and DDR forces. Like its predecessor it featured diesel-electric drive (Tatra T930-42 V12 engine), articulated steering and complex system of electric/hydraulic/pneumatic controls.

Tractor, Wheeled, Earthmoving   **D**
(Hanomag D18C)

6-cyl. 10.8-litre turbocharged diesel engine (D963A1) with torque converter and 4F4R transmission. Final drive reduction gearing in wheel hubs. 26.5-25XRB tyres. Wheelbase 3000 mm. Overall dimensions 6860 × 3550 × 3240 mm. Track width 2020 mm front, 2000 mm rear. Weight 19200 kg. 16-ton hydraulic winch.

Tractor, Wheeled, Earthmoving   **SU**
(PKT)

V-12-cyl. 38.8-litre engine (D-12-A-375) with 3F1R gearbox and 4-speed hydromechanical transmission (torque converter with planetary gearbox and transfer box) driving all 4 wheels. 21.00-28 tyres. Weight 19400 kg. Multipurpose dozer blade at rear of vehicle. Employed by Soviet and DDR forces from the early 1970s.

Tractor, Wheeled, Earthmoving   **D**
(Zettelmeyer ZD3000)

V-10-cyl. diesel engine with torque converter, 4F4R powershift transmission. Diff. locks in both axles. Hydropneumatic suspension. Disc brakes. 30/65-25EM tyres. Max. road travel speed 62 km/h. Hydraulically-actuated dozer blade, measuring 3500 × 1350 mm. In service with the West German *Bundeswehr* from the late 1970s.

Excavator, Wheeled, 4 × 4   USA
(International 3965)

6-cyl. 5.8-litre diesel engine (D358) with 5F1R gearbox and single-speed transfer box. Wheelbase 2950 mm. Overall dimensions (travelling mode) 7930 × 2490 × 4100 mm. Weight 14320 kg. Bucket capacity 610 litres. Could be used with auger, demolition hammer or crane hook. Netherlands Army, late 1970s.

Loader, Scoop-Type/Excavator, Tracked   USA
(Caterpillar 955K)

Front-mounted diesel engine with single-lever 3F3R powershift transmission. 6-roller non-oscillating track frame. Bucket width 2250 mm. Excavator at rear was additional bolt-on equipment. Max. speed, forward/reverse 9.3/11.3 km/h. Employed by the Australian Army. Operating weight nearly 14 tons.

Excavator, Tracked   GB
(Hy-Mac HM580BT)

One of more than 60 all-hydraulic excavators supplied to the British Army in the early 1970s by Hy-Mac (a Powell Duffryn company). Each machine could be equipped with crane, face shovel, grab and ripper tooth attachments. Capacity of bucket shown 0.48 m³. Operating weight 10.5 tons.

Excavator, Tracked   D
(Liebherr R911B)

Powered by an aircooled 4-cyl. diesel engine (Deutz F4L 912), driving the various oil pumps, this 14-ton machine had hydraulic operation of all main functions. It could be used with a wide range of implements, e.g. bucket, grab, shovel and 8-ton crane hook. Machine shown was in service with Belgian Army in the 1970s.

Tractor, Tracked, Bulldozer   D
(Hanomag K 12DE)

6-cyl. 9.5-litre diesel engine (D962K) with torque converter and 3F3R transmission. Planetary reduction gearing in drive sprocket hubs. Length and width, including dozer blade and rear-mounted winch 5680 × 3985 mm. Height 3220 mm. Weight 16650 kg. Users included the Belgian and Netherlands armies.

Tractor, Tracked, Bulldozer   USA/GB
(Terex 82-30B)

V-8-cyl. diesel engine (Detroit Diesel 8V-71T) with 3F3R power-shift transmission (Allison CRT6031). Speed range, forward, 3.7–11.2 km/h. Overall dimensions 4673 × 2603 × 2623 (cab) mm. Shipping weight 22900 kg. 43 were taken into service by British Army Royal Engineers, from 1978, as Heavy Crawler Tractors.

252

Scraper, Motor, Twin-Engined   **GB**
(Terex TS-8)

Twin Bedford 330 diesel engines with Allison MT650 automatic transmissions. Capacity 6.1 m³. Developed for the British Army. Air-transportable in Hercules C130 aircraft. 23.5-25 tyres. Overall dimensions 10645 × 2745 × 2616 mm. Weight 15095 kg. Max. payload 10450 kg. Road speed 50 km/h. 35 supplied from 1978.

Scraper, Motor, Twin-Engined   **USA/GB/BR**
(Terex TS-14B)

Twin Detroit Diesel 4-71N engines with Allison CLT3461 power-shift transmissions. 10.7-m³ capacity. Suited to medium-length hauls in military construction tasks, e.g. airstrips, bridge approaches, etc. 29.5-25 tyres. Wheelbase 7061 mm. Weight 23950 kg. Shown is one of the British Army's 10 units.

Grader, Motor, 6 × 4   **USA**
(Caterpillar 120G)

Cat. 3304T diesel engine with 6F6R powershift transmission, driving the 4 wheels of the tandem rear bogie. 25-in. wheels. Overall dimensions 8950 × 1800 × 3380 mm. Length with snowplough, as shown, 10500 mm. Weight 14200 kg. Danish Army, 1979. Caterpillar also made special air-transportable Model 130G.

Grader, Motor, 6 × 4   **D**
(Frisch F115P)

6-cyl. 8.5-litre aircooled diesel engine (Deutz F6L 413) with 4F4R preselective transmission (Frisch G95/4PW). Chain-drive tandem bogie. 15.50-25XRB tyres. Wheelbase 5510 mm. Overall dimensions 9075 × 2525 × 3250 mm. Weight 11640 kg. Ripper at rear. Used by Netherlands Army for dozing, grading, profiling, etc.

Engineer Construction Equipment   **USA**
(Clark FAMECE)

Clark Equipment Co. were one of two contractors in 1972/73 to design, for the US Army, a Family of Military Engineer Construction Equipment, comprising a power module and quickly-interchangeable work modules. Clark used a Cummins engine with 4F4R transmission. Prototype delivered in 1973.

Engineer Construction Equipment   **USA**
(Lockheed FAMECE)

Lockheed Missile and Space Co. were the other suppliers of a prototype FAMECE machine in 1973. It had a Ford turbine engine and walking-beam suspension for the power module. Working modules comprised scraper (shown), loader, compactor, water distributor, dozer, dumper and grader.

Index

INDEX